McGraw-Hill
networks™
A Social Studies Learning System

Discovering Our Past:
A History of the United States
Early Years

READING
ESSENTIALS
& STUDY GUIDE

Student Workbook

Mc Graw Hill **Education**

Bothell, WA • Chicago, IL • Columbus, OH • New York, NY

Discovering Our Past: United States 2013 National Early Years
Cover Credits:
Sacagawea, William Ahrendt Inc./Cover painting from the
collection of Mr. and Mrs. Frank Wylie

Send all inquiries to:
McGraw-Hill Education
8787 Orion Place
Columbus, OH 43240

ISBN: 978-0-07-659690-4
MHID: 0-07-659690-7

Printed in the United States of America.

7 8 9 RHR 15 14

The **McGraw·Hill** Companies

Table of Contents

Growth and Expansion

The Jackson Era

Manifest Destiny

North and South

The Spirit of Reform

Toward Civil War

The Civil War

The Reconstruction Era

To the Student

Dear Student,

We know that taking notes, using graphic organizers, and developing critical thinking skills are vital to achieve academic success. Organizing solid study materials can be an overwhelming task. McGraw-Hill has developed this workbook to help you master content and develop the skills necessary for success.

This workbook includes all core content found in the *Discovering Our Past: History of the United States* program. The note-taking, graphic organizer, and Foldables® activities will help you learn to organize content for improved comprehension and testing.

Note-Taking System

You will notice that the pages in the *Reading Essentials and Study Guide* are arranged in two columns. The large column on the page contains running text and graphics that summarize each lesson of the chapter. The smaller column will help you use information in various ways and develop note-taking skills.

Graphic Organizers

Many graphic organizers appear in this workbook. Graphic organizers allow you to see the lesson's important information in a visual format. In addition, they help you summarize information and remember the content.

Notebook FOLDABLES®

Notebook Foldables®, invented by Dinah Zike, M.Ed., show you how to make interactive graphic organizers based upon skills. Foldables® are easy to create. Every Notebook Foldable® is placed directly within the content pages to help you with your note-taking skills. Making a Foldable® gives you a fast way to organize and retain information. Each Notebook Foldable® is designed as a study guide for the main ideas and key points presented in lessons of the chapter.

The *Reading Essentials and Study Guide* is a thoroughly interactive workbook that will help you learn social studies content. You will master the content while learning important critical-thinking and note-taking skills that you will use throughout your life.

Notebook Foldable® Basics

Notebook Foldables® are an easy-to-use, unique way to enhance learning. Instructions are located where the Foldable® is used and every template is provided at the back of this workbook. You will cut out the appropriate Foldable® template and place it into the workbook as instructed. This quickly turns a workbook into a study guide.

Using Notebook Foldables®

You will write information such as titles, vocabulary words, concepts, questions, main ideas, summaries, definitions, and dates on the tabs of the Foldables®. This will help you easily recognize main ideas and important concepts as you read the content.

In the back of this workbook are several pages with four different Foldable® templates—one-tab, two-tab, three-tab, and Venn diagram styles. Each style has an instruction page followed by the templates. Cutting and using the different templates is very simple to master.

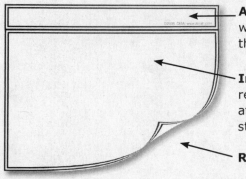

Anchor Tab—Glue the back of the Foldable® to the workbook with the anchor tab. A dotted line is provided on the workbook page to guide you to proper placement.

Information Tab—Write information on the front and reverse of the information tab. This tab may be cut again after gluing if it is a two-tab, three-tab, or Venn diagram style.

Reverse Tab

Folding Instructions

1. **Cut** out the appropriate Foldable® template.
2. **Fold** the anchor tab over the information tab.
3. **Glue** the anchor tab to the workbook page according to the instructions. *(Just a dab is needed!)*

Multiple Foldables® can be placed together by gluing anchor tabs on top of anchor tabs. This creates a small book on the page.

Supplies

The only supplies needed to utilize Notebook Foldables® are scissors and glue. All paper templates are in the back of the workbook. Consider using crayons and colored pencils, a stapler, clear tape, and anything else you like to make your Foldables® more interesting.

Who is Dinah Zike?

Dinah Zike, M.Ed., is an award-winning author, educator, and inventor known for designing three-dimensional hands-on manipulatives and graphic organizers known as Foldables®. Foldables® are used nationally and internationally by teachers, parents, and educational publishing companies. Dinah has developed more than 150 supplemental educational books and materials. Her two latest books, *Notebook Foldables®* and *Foldables®, Notebook Foldables®, & VKV®s for Spelling and Vocabulary 4th–12th* were both awarded *Learning®* magazine's Teachers' Choice℠ Award for 2011. In 2004, Dinah was honored with the Council for Elementary Science International (CESI) Science Advocacy Award. Dinah received her M.Ed. from Texas A&M, College Station, Texas. Dinah has been a valued contributing editor to the McGraw-Hill K–12 education programs for many years.

The First Americans

Lesson 1 Migration to the Americas

ESSENTIAL QUESTION

What are characteristics that make up a culture?

GUIDING QUESTIONS

1. **Who were the first Americans and how did they live?**
2. **How did agriculture change the way of life for early Americans?**

Terms to Know

archaeology the study of ancient peoples

artifact a tool, weapon, or object left behind by early peoples

strait narrow strip of water connecting two larger bodies of water

migration the movement of a large number of people into a new area

nomad a person who moves from place to place

maize a type of corn

carbon dating a scientific way to find out the age of an artifact

culture a people's shared values, beliefs, traditions, and behaviors

Where in the world?

When did it happen?

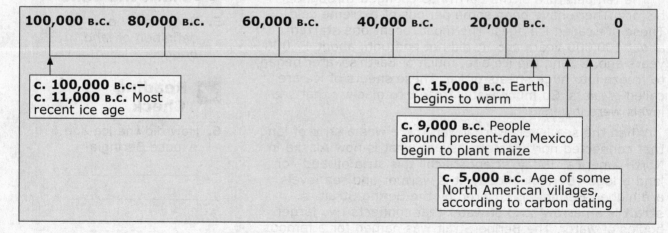

1

The First Americans

Lesson 1 Migration to the Americas, *Continued*

The Migration Begins

People lived in the Americas for thousands of years before Christopher Columbus arrived. Where did they come from? How did they get there? When did they arrive?

Scientists want to answer these questions. Some are experts in the study of ancient peoples, which is called **archaeology.** To discover clues, they study **artifacts,** or things that ancient peoples left behind. These things can be tools, weapons, or other objects. Artifacts are one of the tools archaeologists use to put together the pieces of the puzzle.

Some archaeologists think they understand how the first people arrived in North America. They believe that many thousands of years ago, a strip of land connected Asia and the Americas. This gave people a way to travel from one continent to the other. These scientists think that people used this strip of land to cross from Asia to the Americas 20,000 or more years ago.

Learning About Ancient Peoples	
archaeology	the study of ancient peoples
archaeologist	a scientist who studies ancient peoples
artifacts	objects left behind by ancient peoples, such as tools and weapons

The temperature of the Earth has changed throughout history. There have been some periods of extreme cold. These are called ice ages. The most recent one started about 100,000 years ago. It did not end until about 12,000 years ago. During the ice age, much of Earth's water began to freeze into huge sheets of ice. These sheets of ice are called *glaciers.* So much water froze into glaciers that sea levels were lower.

When the sea levels were lower, there was a strip of land that connected northeastern Asia to what is now Alaska in North America. Today, scientists call this strip of land—or land bridge—Beringia. Today, it is warmer and sea levels are higher. Beringia is covered by the Bering Strait. A **strait** is a narrow strip of water that connects two larger bodies of water. The Bering Strait was named for a famous explorer, Vitus Bering.

🖊 Identifying

1. What scientists study ancient peoples? What do they use for clues?

_____

_____

❓ Assessing

2. When do some scientists think people first arrived in North America?

🔤 Defining

3. What is an *ice age*?

_____

🖊 Calculating

4. How long did the last ice age last?

_____

🔤 Mark the Text

5. Underline the definition of *land bridge.*

✔ Reading Check

6. How did the ice age expose Beringia?

_____

_____

_____

networks

The First Americans

Lesson 1 Migration to the Americas, *Continued*

Identifying

7. What are two ways scientists think people may have traveled from Asia to the Americas?

_____

_____

Mark the Text

8. Underline the definition of *migration*.

Identifying

9. What did nomads eat?

_____

_____

Mark the Text

10. What did mammoths and mastodons look like? Circle the answer in the text.

? Understanding Cause and Effect

11. How did farming change the lives of early Americans?

_____

_____

_____

Many scientists think that people traveled from Asia to North America over this land bridge, but some scientists disagree. They think people may have come from Asia in boats. Coming by boat would have made it easier for people to spread throughout North and South America faster.

Ice age

↓

Ocean water freezes into glaciers and lowers sea levels

↓

Ancient peoples from Asia use land bridge to cross into North America

No matter how they came, people eventually spread east all the way to the Atlantic Ocean. They also spread south to the southern tip of South America.

When a lot of people move from one area to another like this, it is called **migration.** People probably traveled in search of food. Early peoples were **nomads.** Nomads are people who move from place to place, looking for good hunting grounds. Even though these people also ate wild grains and fruits, much of their food came from hunting.

When the first peoples arrived from Asia, they found many animals to hunt. For example, they hunted bison and two animals that looked like elephants—mammoths and mastodons. These people hunted with spears.

Around 15,000 years ago, Earth began to warm. As temperatures rose, glaciers began to melt. The oceans rose, and water covered the Beringia land bridge. This cut Asia off from North America once again. The large animals began to disappear, too. Early Americans had to find other sources of food, which included fish and small animals.

Settlement

Around 10,000 years ago, there was a major change in how people got food: farming. People in what is now Mexico began planting a type of corn called **maize.** They also grew pumpkins, beans, and squash. These crops gave them a good supply of food. Because they could grow their own food, they did not have to move around anymore. This meant they could spend more time doing other things. Their quality of life got better.

The First Americans

Lesson 1 Migration to the Americas, *Continued*

After the early people learned to farm, some remained nomads. Others lived in permanent settlements, or villages. They built houses from clay, stone, or wood. They made pottery, tools, and cloth. Today, we sometimes find such artifacts where their villages once stood.

Carbon dating is a scientific process that measures how much radioactive carbon an artifact contains. Scientists use this measurement to decide how old the artifact is. They have used this process on artifacts from North American villages and found that some villages existed about 5,000 years ago.

Scientists can tell that farming changed people's lives. As early Americans settled down, they began to share beliefs and ways of doing things. These shared traditions and behaviors are called **cultures.**

/ / / / / / / / / / / / Glue Foldable here / / / / / / / / / / /

Check for Understanding

List two ways that changes in the climate affected the migration of prehistoric peoples.

1. _____

2. _____

How did farming change the lives of early people?

_____

_____

☑ **Reading Check**

12. What changes affected the nomadic way of life?

_____

_____

_____

❓ **Analyzing**

13. How can scientists tell how old a village is?

_____

_____

_____

🔤 **Defining**

14. What is a *culture*?

_____

FOLDABLES

15. Place a two-tab Foldable along the dotted line to cover Check for Understanding. Label the tabs *Nomadic Culture* and *Farming Culture*. Use both sides of the tabs to list the characteristics that you remember about each kind of lifestyle.

4

net w⭑rks

The First Americans

Lesson 2 Cities and Empires

ESSENTIAL QUESTION

How do civilizations rise and fall?

GUIDING QUESTIONS

1. **What civilizations in Mexico, Central America, and South America predated the arrival of Europeans?**

2. **Why were the Inca considered a highly developed culture?**

Terms to Know

civilization highly developed society

theocracy a society ruled by religious leaders

hieroglyphic a form of writing that uses symbols or pictures to represent things, ideas, and sounds

terrace broad platform of land cut into a slope

Where in the world?

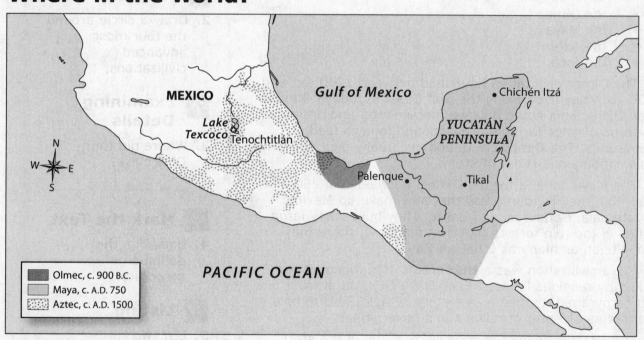

Olmec, c. 900 B.C.
Maya, c. A.D. 750
Aztec, c. A.D. 1500

When did it happen?

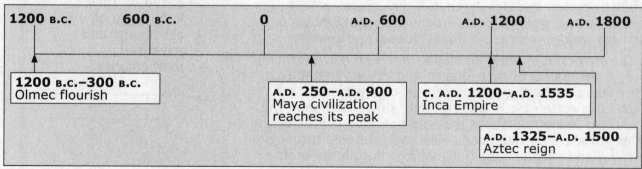

1200 B.C.   600 B.C.   0   A.D. 600   A.D. 1200   A.D. 1800

1200 B.C.–300 B.C. Olmec flourish

A.D. 250–A.D. 900 Maya civilization reaches its peak

C. A.D. 1200–A.D. 1535 Inca Empire

A.D. 1325–A.D. 1500 Aztec reign

networks

The First Americans

Lesson 2 Cities and Empires, *Continued*

Great Civilizations of Mexico, Central America, and South America

Hundreds of years before European explorers arrived, there were great **civilizations** in Mexico, Central America, and South America. Each civilization controlled large areas and had millions of people. They built cities in forests and on mountains. They created great art and advanced tools. This included complex, or very detailed, ways to track time, count, and write.

The largest and most advanced civilizations were:

- the Olmec
- the Maya
- the Aztec
- the Inca.

The Olmec civilization flourished between 1200 B.C. and 300 B.C. They lived along the Gulf Coast in today's Mexico. The Olmec built stone houses, monuments, and drainage systems. Olmec farmers grew enough food to feed thousands. The Olmec civilization eventually died out. Why this happened is still a mystery.

The Maya came after the Olmec. Between A.D. 250 and A.D. 900, they lived in areas that now make up Mexico, Guatemala, Honduras, and Belize. They built many large cities in the rain forests there. At one time, there may have been as many as 2 million Maya.

Maya civilization was a **theocracy.** This means it was ruled by religious leaders. Each Maya city had at least one stone pyramid, topped with a stone temple. This temple served as a center of religion and government.

The Maya believed the gods were visible in the stars, sun, and moon. Maya priests studied astronomy and advanced mathematics. They used their knowledge to predict eclipses and develop a 365-day calendar. To write, they used **hieroglyphics.** Hieroglyphics are symbols or pictures used to represent things, ideas, and sounds.

The Maya fed a large population with extensive farming. They grew maize, beans, squash, and other vegetables. They would trade their food crops at city markets for things like cotton cloth, pottery, deer meat, and salt. The Maya had many roads, but they did not have horses or the wheel. Traders carried goods—like jade statues, turquoise jewelry, and cacao beans (for making chocolate)—on their backs or by canoe up and down the east coast of Mexico.

Identifying

1. List two facts about the great civilizations before the Europeans arrived.

_____

_____

Mark the Text

2. Draw a circle around the four most advanced civilizations.

Examining Details

3. Where did the Olmec live?

_____

Mark the Text

4. Underline the definition of *theocracy*.

Listing

5. List two accomplishments of the Maya that were based on their knowledge of astronomy and advanced mathematics.

_____

_____

6

The First Americans

Lesson 2 Cities and Empires, *Continued*

Describing

6. How did the Aztec know where to settle down?

_____

_____

_____

Reading Check

7. Name the capital city of the Aztec Empire, and describe its location.

_____

_____

_____

Explaining

8. How did the Aztec treat the people they conquered?

_____

_____

_____

Making Connections

9. How were the Inca like the Aztec?

_____

_____

_____

Eventually the Maya civilization declined. No one knows why. One idea is that the soil grew weak and could not produce enough food for the population. Its once-great cities were nearly empty by 1200. The descendants of the Maya still live in Mexico and Central America.

Many centuries later, another great civilization arose in central Mexico—the Aztec. An Aztec legend said that a god would send them a sign to tell them where to build their permanent home. In 1325, a group of Aztec hunters saw that sign on an island in the middle of Lake Texcoco: an eagle with a snake in its beak sitting on a cactus.

The Aztec built their capital city on the island and called it Tenochtitlán. It was a wonder of construction. Workers dug soil from the bottom of the lake to build bridges between the city and the shore and to make fields for crops in the lake. Tenochtitlán became an important trade center. It was the largest city in the Americas and one of the largest in the world.

In the 1400s, the Aztec used their military to conquer many other groups. They forced conquered people to give them food and goods and to work as slaves. They also sacrificed prisoners of war to their gods to ensure rich harvests. Their empire was still strong when the Europeans came.

	Location	Accomplishments
Olmec	Gulf Coast of Mexico	Built stone houses, monuments, and drainage systems Grew crops to feed thousands
Maya	Mexico, Guatemala, Honduras, and Belize	Could predict eclipses Developed 365-day calendar Wrote with hieroglyphics Grew crops to feed millions
Aztec	Central Mexico	Built Tenochtitlán Conquered large empire

The Great Inca Civilization

The largest early American empire developed in western South America—the Inca. Like the Aztec, the Inca had a powerful military and conquered many neighboring groups.

The First Americans

Lesson 2 Cities and Empires, *Continued*

All Inca men between 25 and 50 might have to serve in the army. They were skilled warriors and used weapons like clubs, spears, and slings. At its peak, the Inca empire stretched from Columbia to northern Argentina and Chile.

The Inca founded their capital city of Cuzco around 1200. Another important city was Machu Picchu, which may have been a place for religious ceremonies. Religion was a central part of Inca life. The Inca believed their emperor was a descendant of the sun god. They made beautiful jewelry and tributes for this god.

Farming was important to Inca life. In order to farm in their mountainous land, the Inca cut broad platforms called **terraces** into the slopes. They grew:

- maize
- squash
- tomatoes
- peanuts
- chili peppers
- cotton
- potatoes

To connect the large empire, the Inca built more than 10,000 miles (16,093 km) of roads. These were built over mountains, across deserts, and through rain forests. The Inca, who spoke Quechua, used quipus for keeping records. Quipus were different colors of string knotted in special patterns.

/ / / / / / / / / / / / Glue Foldable here / / / / / / / / / / / / /

Check for Understanding

List four great early cultures of Mexico, Central America, and South America.

1. _____

2. _____

3. _____

4. _____

How were the Aztec and Inca civilizations similar? How were they different?

_____

_____

✓ Reading Check

10. How did the Inca Empire grow so large?

_____

_____

_____

👁 Visualize It

11. In the box, draw a diagram of the terraces the Inca built for their crops.

✍ Mark the Text

12. Circle the name of the Inca language.

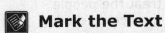

13. Place a three-tab Foldable along the dotted line to cover Check for Understanding. On the anchor tab write *Accomplishments*. Label the tabs *Olmec*, *Maya*, and *Aztec*. List two accomplishments for each group.

netwrks

The First Americans

Lesson 3 North American Peoples

ESSENTIAL QUESTION
What makes a culture unique?

GUIDING QUESTIONS

1. **What did the Adena, Hopewell, Mississippian, Hohokam, and Ancient Puebloan cultures have in common?**
2. **How did early Native Americans adapt to their environment?**

Terms to Know
irrigate to supply water to crops by artificial means
federation government that links different groups

Where in the world?

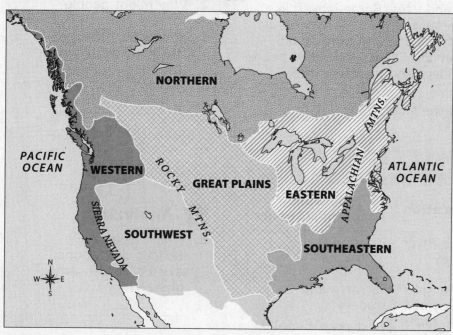

When did it happen?

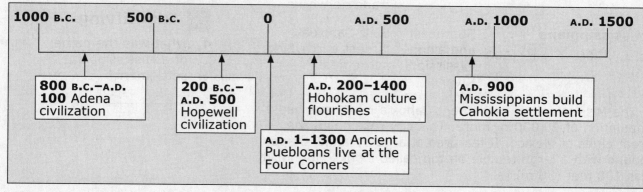

9

networks

The First Americans

Lesson 3 North American Peoples, Continued

Early North American Cultures

North America produced advanced cultures in the centuries before Europeans arrived. Among them were:

- the Adena
- the Hopewell
- the Mississippians
- the Hohokam
- the Ancient Puebloans.

In Central and Eastern North America lived the Mound Builders. Scientists call them the Mound Builders because they built thousands of mounds out of earth. These mounds had different shapes and uses. Some looked like animals, such as snakes. Others looked like Maya or Aztec pyramids. Some were burial chambers, and others had temples on top like Maya pyramids. Could there have been a link between the Mound Builders and the Maya and Aztec?

Archaeologists have divided the Mound Builders into three different groups.

Mound Builder Cultures		
Culture	**Location**	**Notable Accomplishments**
Adena c. 800 B.C.—A.D. 100	Ohio River valley	Hunters and gatherers
Hopewell c. 200 B.C.—A.D. 500	Ohio River valley and Mississippi River valley	Farmers and traders Built huge burial mounds Indications of wide trade networks
Mississippians c. A.D. 700—c. A.D. 1500	Southeast and along Mississippi River	Built Cahokia, largest earthworks settlement

The Mississippians settlement Cahokia may have had a population of 20,000 or more. This city resembled the great cities of Mexico. It featured a large pyramid-shaped mound with a large temple on top called Monks Mound. It was 100 feet (30 m) tall.

Listing

1. List two shapes the Mound Builders used in their earthworks.

_____

_____

Making Inferences

2. Why might people think there was a connection between the Mound Builders and the Maya and Aztec?

_____

_____

_____

_____

Analyzing

3. Which Mound Builder civilzations existed at the same time? When?

_____

_____

Identifying

4. What was the name of a Mississippian settlement?

_____

The First Americans

Lesson 3 North American Peoples, *Continued*

Mark the Text

5. Underline the definition of *irrigate*.

Describing

6. Describe the area called the Four Corners.

_____

_____

_____

Reading Check

7. Name two types of dwellings the Ancient Puebloans built.

_____

_____

Defining

8. What is an *igloo*?

_____

_____

Reading Check

9. Give two examples of how Western peoples adapted to their environment.

_____

_____

_____

_____

The Hohokam lived in the hot desert of what is now Arizona from about A.D. 200 to 1400. In order to farm in that climate, the Hohokam built hundreds of miles of channels to **irrigate,** or bring water to, their fields. They grew corn, cotton, and other crops. They also made pottery, carved stone, and used acid to make patterns in shells, which they got from coastal peoples.

From about A.D. 1 to 1300, the Ancient Puebloans lived in the Four Corners region. This is the area where the modern states of Utah, Colorado, Arizona, and New Mexico meet. The Ancient Puebloans are known for their huge stone dwellings, later called *pueblos* by Spanish explorers. One pueblo—Pueblo Bonito—has four stories and hundreds of rooms.

The Ancient Puebloans also built shelters into the walls of steep cliffs. These cliff dwellings were good protection from winter weather and enemy attacks. One of the largest was Mesa Verde in Colorado, where thousands lived.

The Native Americans Circa 1492

The Inuit settled the cold region of North America near the Arctic Ocean. Scientists think they originally came from Siberia, which is also very cold, and brought cold-weather survival skills with them. They built shelters called *igloos* out of snow blocks. They hunted whales, seals, and walruses from small boats and caribou on land. They used animal skins to make clothes and burned seal oil in lamps.

The western coast of North America provided a milder climate and dependable food sources. Western peoples included:

- The Tlingit, Haida, and Chinook of the northwestern coast (present-day Canada, Washington, and Oregon). These cultures relied on the woods and the waters. They built houses and canoes from wood. Their main food was salmon.

- The Nez Perce and Yakima of the plateau region between the Cascade Mountains and the Rocky Mountains. These groups lived in earthen houses. They fished, hunted deer, and gathered roots and berries.

- Today's California was home to many groups. Along the northern coast, people fished for food. In the central valley, the Pomo pounded acorns into flour. In the southern deserts, nomads gathered roots and seeds.

The First Americans

Lesson 3 North American Peoples, *Continued*

- In the Great Basin of the Southwest between the Sierra Nevada and the Rocky Mountains, the Ute and Shoshone hunted small game and gathered pine nuts, juniper berries, roots, and even some insects.

The Hopi, Acoma, and Zuni of the Southwest descended from the Ancient Puebloans. They built houses from bricks made of dried mud called *adobe*. They irrigated their fields and farmed maize, beans, squash, melons, pumpkins, and fruit. In the 1500s, the nomadic Apache and Navajo came to this region. The Navajo later formed villages, living in square houses called *hogans*.

The nomadic Plains peoples lived in hide tents called *tepees*. The women planted maize, squash, and beans. The men hunted antelope, deer, and buffalo. Buffalo provided more than food. Their skin was used for clothes and shelter, and their bones were used to make weapons.

In the woodlands of eastern North America lived many Algonquian peoples, who all spoke a similar language. The Cherokee and Iroquois had formal laws and alliances called **federations.** There were five Iroquois nations—the Onondaga, Seneca, Mohawk, Oneida, and Cayuga. They were often at war until, in the 1500s, they formed the Iroquois League, which was organized by clans, or groups of people related. Under the League's constitution, the Grand Council settled disputes.

Southeastern peoples were farmers. The Creek grew corn, squash, and tobacco. The Chickasaw farmed the fertile area where the Mississippi River connects to the sea.

Check for Understanding

What evidence might connect the Mound Builders with the Maya and Aztec?

_____

Name one way each of these Native American groups adapted to their environment:

Hohokam _____

Ancient Puebloans _____

Inuit _____

Plains People _____

Glue Foldable here /////////////////

Describing

10. How did the Southwest people grow crops in such a dry region?

_____

Listing

11. List three things buffalo provided for the Plains peoples.

_____

_____

_____

Analyzing

12. How did the five Iroquois nations come together?

_____

 FOLDABLES®

13. Place a one-tab Foldable along the dotted line to cover Check for Understanding. Create a memory map by writing *Dwellings* in the middle of the tab. Draw arrows to words or phrases you remember about the kinds of shelter Native Americans built. Write additional information on the back.

Exploring the Americas

Lesson 1 A Changing World

ESSENTIAL QUESTION
How do new ideas change the way people live?

GUIDING QUESTIONS
1. **Where did the Renaissance take place?**
2. **What technological advancements paved the way for European voyages of exploration?**
3. **What were the most powerful empires in Africa?**

Terms to Know
Crusade one of a series of expeditions Europeans made to regain control of Christian holy sites in the Middle East from the A.D. 1000s to the 1200s

classical related to the culture of ancient Greece and Rome

Renaissance a reawakening of culture and intellectual curiosity in Europe from the 1300s to the 1600s

technology the use of scientific knowledge for practical purposes

astrolabe an instrument used to plan a course, using the stars

compass an instrument that shows the direction of magnetic north

pilgrimage a journey to a holy place

mosque a Muslim house of worship

When did it happen?

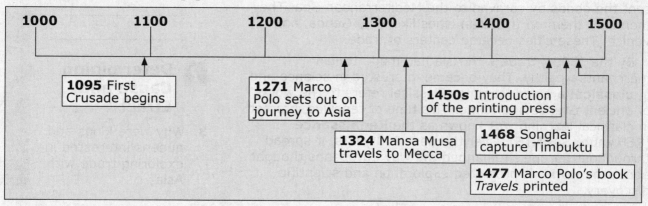

| 1000 | 1100 | 1200 | 1300 | 1400 | 1500 |

1095 First Crusade begins

1271 Marco Polo sets out on journey to Asia

1324 Mansa Musa travels to Mecca

1450s Introduction of the printing press

1468 Songhai capture Timbuktu

1477 Marco Polo's book *Travels* printed

What do you know?

In the first column, answer the questions based on what you know before you study. After this lesson, complete the last column.

Now...		Later...
	What church dominated Europe after the fall of the Roman Empire?	
	What countries in Europe became strong by the 1400s?	
	Which country developed the fastest ships during this period?	

Exploring the Americas

Lesson 1 A Changing World, *Continued*

New Ideas, New Nations

The people of Western Europe were isolated for centuries after the Roman empire fell in A.D. 476. The area was dominated by the Catholic Church. In the early 600s, Islam began to spread across the Middle East and Africa. The rise of Islam led to the end of Europe's isolation.

In 1095 Europeans started the **Crusades**. These were expeditions to gain control of the Christian holy sites from Muslims in the Middle East. There, Europeans came in contact with Arab merchants. These merchants sold them spices, silks, and other goods from faraway China and India. Europeans became interested in Asia.

Interest in Asia grew after an explorer named Marco Polo returned from China. He wrote about his trip in a book called *Travels*. Many Europeans read the book.

Wealthy Europeans wanted silks and spices from Asia. Merchants bought these goods from Arab traders. They sent the goods by caravan to the Mediterranean Sea. They then sent them on to Italian cities like Pisa, Genoa, and Venice. These cities became centers of trade.

By the 1300s, trade with Asia had made Italian merchants wealthy. They became interested in science and in **classical** art and learning. Classical refers to the works of ancient Greece and Rome. This time of renewed interest in classical learning was known as the **Renaissance** (REH•nuh•SAHNTS). Over the next 200 years, it spread throughout Europe. It changed the way Europeans thought about the world. It promoted exploration and scientific discovery.

European merchants were interested in exploration. They wanted to find a way to buy goods directly from Asia. This would be less expensive than buying them from Arab merchants.

By the 1400s, strong kings and queens had come to power in several nations. They set up laws and national armies. They wanted to find ways to increase trade to make their countries richer. Soon, Spain, Portugal, England, and France were competing with the Italian cities which had become rich through trade. This competition encouraged a period of exploration.

? Making Inferences

1. How did the rise of Islam affect Western Europe during this period?

_____
_____
_____

✓ Reading Check

2. What was the Renaissance?

_____
_____

? Determining Cause and Effect

3. Why were kings and queens interested in exploring trade with Asia?

_____
_____

Exploring the Americas

Lesson 1 A Changing World, *Continued*

☑ **Reading Check**

4. What three things helped sailors figure out their location?

_____

_____

_____

🖊 **Marking the Text**

5. Underline the sentences that describe the advantages of the Portuguese caravel.

☑ **Reading Check**

6. How did Islamic religion and culture come to West Africa?

_____

_____

_____

The Effects of New Technology

Advances in **technology** helped pave the way for exploration. Technology is the use of scientific knowledge for practical purposes. The invention of the printing press in the 1450s made it possible for more people to read books and get information.

Mapmakers started to make better maps. They mapped the direction of the ocean currents. They also showed lines of latitude that measured the distance north and south of the Equator. The invention of new instruments helped sailors travel. The **astrolabe** measured the positions of stars. This helped sailors figure out their latitude while at sea. Europeans also began to use the magnetic **compass**, a Chinese invention. The compass helped sailors find their direction when they were far from land.

The design of ships also improved. Sailors were now able to make long ocean voyages. In the late 1400s, the Portuguese created the caravel. It had three masts and could sail into the wind. This ship sailed faster than other ships. It could carry more goods. All of these inventions helped start a new time of exploration. Countries like Portugal began searching for sea routes to Asia. Portugal started by sending ships south along the west coast of Africa.

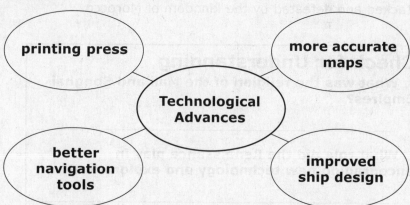

Kingdoms and Empires in Africa

Between A.D. 400 and 1600, several powerful kingdoms prospered in Africa. They became powerful through mining and trade. Arab traders traveled along Africa's east coast. West Africans traded with societies in North Africa. This trade brought wealth and Islamic religion and culture to West Africa. The Portuguese set up trading posts along the west coast of Africa in the mid-1400s.

Exploring the Americas

Lesson 1 A Changing World, *Continued*

Ghana was a trading empire in West Africa. Caravans with gold and other goods from Ghana crossed the Sahara to North Africa. There, Muslim traders loaded the caravans with salt, cloth, and other goods to take back to Ghana. Ghana grew wealthy from the taxes it collected on this trade.

In 1076 people from North Africa attacked Ghana. Trade slowed down. New trade routes were set up that did not go through Ghana. Ghana then began to lose power.

Another powerful kingdom, called Mali, developed in the same region. Like Ghana, it developed trade routes across the desert to North Africa. Mali's greatest king was Mansa Musa. He made Mali famous. In 1324 Musa made a grand **pilgrimage** to the Muslim holy city of Mecca. A pilgrimage is a journey to a holy place. Musa returned to Mali with an Arab architect who built great **mosques** in Timbuktu, the Mali capital. Mosques are Muslim houses of worship. Timbuktu became an important center of Islamic learning.

In 1468 the Songhai (sawng•GEYE) people rose up against Mali rule and captured Timbuktu. Under Askiya Muhammad, the Songhai Empire became strong. Askiya divided Songhai into provinces. Each province had its own officials. He also set up laws for Songhai. These laws were based on Islamic teaching. In the late 1500s, Songhai was attacked and defeated by the kingdom of Morocco.

/ / / / / / / / / / / / / Glue Foldable here / / / / / / / / / / / / /

Check for Understanding
What was the religion of the Mali and Songhai Empires?

_____

What role did the Renaissance play in encouraging new technology and exploration?

_____

_____

FOLDABLES

7. Place a one-tab Foldable along the dotted line to cover Check for Understanding. Draw a large circle on the tab and label it *A Changing World.* Draw two smaller circles inside the large circle. Label the small circles *Marco Polo* and *African Empires*. Use the space inside the circles to list words or short phrases that explain why both were important to the changing world. Use the reverse side to write additional information. Use the Foldable to help answer Check for Understanding.

networks

Exploring the Americas

Lesson 2 Early Exploration

ESSENTIAL QUESTION

Why do people trade?

GUIDING QUESTIONS

1. Which country took the lead in finding a trade route to India?
2. How did Spain and Portugal protect their claims in the Americas?

Terms to Know

cape a point of land that sticks out into water, much like a peninsula

circumnavigate to travel completely around something, usually by water

Where in the world?

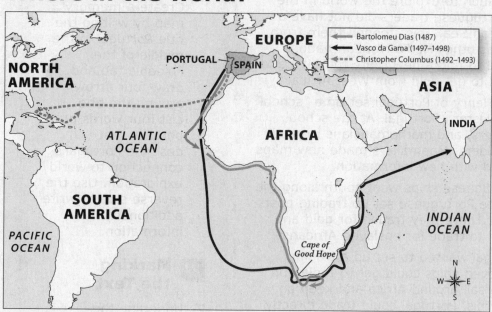

Legend:
- Bartolomeu Dias (1487)
- Vasco da Gama (1497–1498)
- Christopher Columbus (1492–1493)

When did it happen?

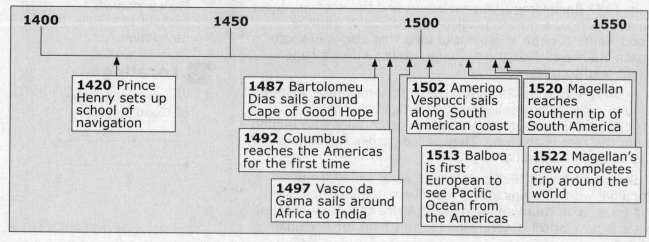

1420 Prince Henry sets up school of navigation

1487 Bartolomeu Dias sails around Cape of Good Hope

1492 Columbus reaches the Americas for the first time

1497 Vasco da Gama sails around Africa to India

1502 Amerigo Vespucci sails along South American coast

1513 Balboa is first European to see Pacific Ocean from the Americas

1520 Magellan reaches southern tip of South America

1522 Magellan's crew completes trip around the world

Lesson 2 Early Exploration, *Continued*

The Search for New Trade Routes

When Columbus began his voyage to America in 1492, he did not know North America existed. The maps that sailors used showed just three continents joined together— Europe, Asia, and Africa. Columbus believed that by sailing west, he would reach the Indies islands near China. Explorers believed that the Atlantic and Pacific Oceans were a single large body of water they called the Ocean Sea.

/ / / / / / / / / / , Glue Foldable here / / / / / / / / / / /

The first European nation to explore the world in the 1400s was Portugal. Portuguese traders did not have a port on the Mediterranean Sea. This stopped them from using the same routes as other Mediterranean nations. Portugal's rulers wanted to find a new route to China and India. They also wanted to get gold from West Africa.

Around 1420, Prince Henry of Portugal set up a "school of navigation" in southwestern Portugal. At the school, astronomers, geographers, and mathematicians worked with sailors and shipbuilders. Mapmakers made new maps when explorers returned with new information.

The route of the Portuguese ships went south along the coast of West Africa. The Portuguese set up trading posts along the African coast. There they traded for gold and ivory. Later, they began to trade for enslaved Africans.

King John II of Portugal wanted to set up a trading empire in Asia. He believed ships could get to India and China. They just had to sail around Africa and keep on going. If they could do this, Portugal could trade directly with Asia. They would not have to rely on caravans to bring goods across Asia and North Africa.

In 1487 Bartolomeu Dias sailed around the southernmost point of Africa. King John called this point the Cape of Good Hope. A **cape** is a point of land that sticks out into water. He hoped that the passage around Africa's cape might lead to a route to India.

In 1497 Vasco da Gama led the first Portuguese voyage around Africa. They sailed around Africa and reached Africa's eastern coast. They met an Indian pilot who guided them the rest of the way. They sailed across the Indian Ocean and on to India.

Six months later, Pedro Álvares Cabral sailed from Portugal with 13 ships. They, too, were headed for India. His route took them so far west of Africa that they reached what is now Brazil. Cabral claimed this land for Portugal.

FOLDABLES

📝 Describing

1. Place a one-tab Foldable along the dotted line to cover the text beginning with "The first European nation ..." Create a memory map by writing the title *Portugal* in the middle of the Foldable tab and draw four arrows around the title. List four words or phrases that describe Portugal's connection to world exploration. Use the reverse side to write additional information.

📝 Marking the Text

2. Underline the groups of people that contributed to Prince Henry's "school of navigation."

👁 Locating

3. Where is the Cape of Good Hope?

_____

_____

networks

Exploring the Americas

Lesson 2 Early Exploration, *Continued*

Identifying

4. Who was the first European to reach the Americas? What date did he do it?

_____

_____

Comparing

5. How were the missions of Spanish and Portuguese explorers similar in the 1400s?

_____

_____

Drawing Conclusions

6. Why did Christopher Columbus name the native people "Indians"?

_____

_____

_____

_____

He went on to India and returned with spices and other goods. The Portuguese continued their voyages to India. Soon, Lisbon, the Portuguese capital, became an important marketplace in Europe.

Columbus Crosses the Atlantic

Columbus was born in Genoa, Italy, in 1451. He became a sailor for Portugal. After many voyages north and south, he came up with a new idea. He planned to reach Asia by sailing west, not east.

Columbus had studied the works of Ptolemy (TAHL•uh•mee). Ptolemy was an ancient Greek astronomer. Based on his works, Columbus thought Asia was 2,760 miles (4,441.8 km) from Europe. However, Ptolemy was incorrect, so Columbus believed Asia was much closer than it is.

Columbus was not the first European to sail to the Americas. Hundreds of years earlier, people from northern Europe, called Vikings, had already sailed there. Norse sagas, or traditional stories, tell of a Viking sailor named Leif Eriksson who explored a land west of Greenland around A.D. 1000. Some ruins in eastern Canada suggest this may be true. But Europeans did not know about Viking voyages.

Spain saw the success of Portugal's sailing voyages. They wanted to trade with Asia as well. Spain's queen, Isabella, agreed to pay for Columbus's voyage. She had two reasons for doing this:

- Columbus promised to bring Christianity to any lands he found.

- If Columbus found a sea route to the Indies, Spain would become very wealthy. Trade would increase.

On August 3, 1492, Columbus set out from Spain. He had a crew of about 90 sailors. They had three ships, the *Niña*, the *Pinta*, and the larger *Santa María*. Columbus was captain of the *Santa María*. They sailed with a six-month supply of food and water. A little over two months later, on October 12, 1492, the ship's lookout saw land. The land he saw was in an island chain now called the Bahamas. When Columbus went ashore, he claimed the island for Spain. He named it San Salvador. Columbus believed he had reached the East Indies near China because of the earliest maps. He named the people he saw "Indians."

Exploring the Americas

Lesson 2 Early Exploration, *Continued*

He returned to Spain. Spain's king and queen, Ferdinand and Isabella, received him with great honor. They agreed to pay for more voyages. He made three more trips: in 1493, 1498, and 1502. He explored the Caribbean islands. These included what are now Haiti, the Dominican Republic, Cuba, and Jamaica. He sailed along the coasts of Central America and part of South America. He made maps of the coastline of Central America.

Spain and Portugal wanted to protect their claims in the new world. With the help of the Pope, they chose a line down the center of the Atlantic Ocean. Portugal would control all new lands east of the line. Spain would control everything to the west. They divided the entire unexplored world between them.

Others followed Columbus. As a result of their voyages, the Spanish built an empire in the Americas. In 1502 Amerigo Vespucci (veh•SPOO•chee) sailed along the coast of South America. He discovered that South America was a continent. "America" is named for him.

In 1513, Vasco Núñez de Balboa (bal•BOH•uh) landed in Panama in Central America. He hiked through the jungle and saw the Pacific Ocean. He was the first European to see it from the Americas.

Ferdinand Magellan was a Portuguese seaman. He wanted to **circumnavigate**, or sail around, the world. In 1520 he reached the southern tip of South America. He sailed through a narrow sea passage to another ocean. He noticed that the waters were very calm. *Pacifico* means "peaceful" in Spanish. Magellan named the ocean the Pacific. Magellan died on the journey, but his crew kept on going. In 1522 they returned to Spain.

/ / / / / / / / / / / Glue Foldable here / / / / / / / / / / /

Check for Understanding

List two reasons Spain chose to pay for Columbus's voyage.

1. _____

2. _____

What effect did the Portuguese school of navigation have on future explorations?

_____

_____

? Evaluating

7. Which voyage of exploration do you think was the most important? Why?

_____

_____

_____

FOLDABLES®

8. Place a one-tab Foldable along the dotted line to cover Check for Understanding. Create a memory map by writing the title *Columbus* in the middle of the tab and drawing four or more arrows. List words or phrases describing Christopher Columbus's first voyage. Use the reverse side to write additional information. Use your Foldable to help answer Check for Understanding.

Exploring the Americas

Lesson 3 Spain in America

ESSENTIAL QUESTION
What are the consequences when cultures interact?

GUIDING QUESTIONS

1. What were the goals of early Spanish explorers?
2. What did Spain hope to find in the Americas?
3. What effect did Spanish rule have on society?

Terms to Know
conquistador Spanish explorer
immunity resistance, such as to a disease
pueblo a town in the Spanish-ruled lands
mission a religious community where farming was carried out and Native Americans were converted to Christianity
presidio a fort
plantation a large farm

Where in the world?

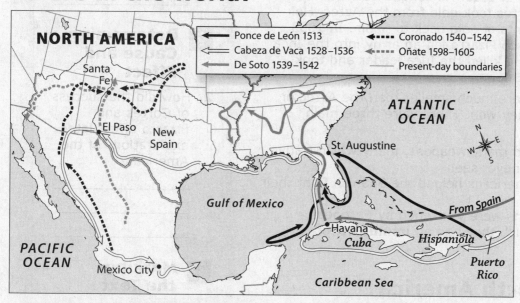

NORTH AMERICA

Ponce de León 1513
Cabeza de Vaca 1528–1536
De Soto 1539–1542
Coronado 1540–1542
Oñate 1598–1605
Present-day boundaries

Santa Fe
El Paso
New Spain
Mexico City
PACIFIC OCEAN
Gulf of Mexico
St. Augustine
ATLANTIC OCEAN
Havana
Cuba
Hispaniola
Puerto Rico
Caribbean Sea
From Spain

When did it happen?

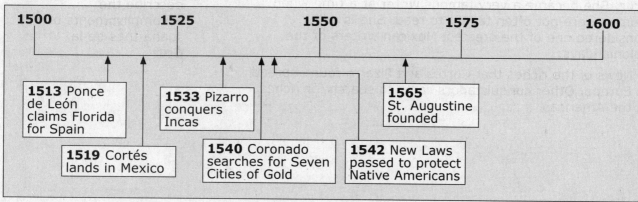

1500 1525 1550 1575 1600

1513 Ponce de León claims Florida for Spain

1519 Cortés lands in Mexico

1533 Pizarro conquers Incas

1540 Coronado searches for Seven Cities of Gold

1542 New Laws passed to protect Native Americans

1565 St. Augustine founded

Exploring the Americas

Lesson 3 Spain in America, *Continued*

European Explorers and Conquerors

Early Spanish explorers were known as **conquistadors,** or conquerors. Their main goal was to find riches. Spanish rulers gave them the right to explore and settle in the Americas. The conquistadors would give the rulers part of the wealth they found.

The Aztec Empire was in the area that is present-day Mexico and Central America. The Inca Empire was in present-day Peru. Both of these empires were very wealthy.

Hernán Cortés was a conquistador. He landed on the east coast of Mexico in 1519. He conquered the Aztec Empire by 1521. Cortés took gold from the Aztec. He shipped great amounts of gold back to Spain. In 1533 conquistador Francisco Pizarro led an army into the Inca capital city, Cuzco. He killed the Inca leader and took control of the Inca Empire.

Spanish armies were much smaller than the Aztec or Inca armies. Still, they won. There were three main reasons for this:

- The Spanish had many weapons, many which Native Americans had never seen
- Many Native Americans helped the Spanish fight their Aztec rulers
- Native Americans were weakened by European diseases for which they had no **immunity,** or resistance.

Spain in North America

Not everyone in the Spanish Empire was a conquistador. One important figure of the time was Juana Inés de la Cruz. She became a very famous writer at a time when women were not often taught to read. She is still considered one of the greatest Mexican writers of the colonial days.

News of the riches that Cortés and Pizarro found spread in Europe. Other conquistadors came to search for riches in the Americas.

✔ **Reading Check**

1. How were the Spanish able to conquer the Aztec Empire and the Inca Empire?

   _____

   _____

   _____

❓ **Determining Cause and Effect**

2. How did the success of Cortés and Pizarro affect later explorations of the Americas?

   _____

   _____

🖋 **Marking the Text**

3. Underline the sentences that describe the accomplishments of Juana Inés de la Cruz

Exploring the Americas

Lesson 3 Spain in America, *Continued*

✓ Reading Check

4. What can you conclude about the Seven Cities of Gold?

_____

_____

_____

❓ Contrasting

5. How was a pueblo different from a mission?

_____

_____

_____

Explorer	Year	Achievement
Juan Ponce de León	1513	• landed on Florida coast • established first Spanish settlement in modern United States • searched for the "Fountain of Youth"
Álvar Núñez Cabeza de Vaca	1528	• sailed south toward Mexico • spent time in present-day Texas • told his eager audience a legend about "Seven Cities of Gold"
Hernando de Soto	1541	• searched for "Seven Cities of Gold" • crossed Mississippi River • got as far west as Oklahoma
Francisco Vásquez de Coronado		• searched for "Seven Cities of Gold" • wound up in present-day Kansas

Life Under Spanish Rule

In 1598 Juan de Oñate (day ohn•YAH•tay) traveled north from Mexico. He started the province of New Mexico. He established Santa Fe in 1607. Santa Fe was the first Spanish city there. It became the province capital in 1610.

Spanish law called for three kinds of settlements in their colonies: **pueblos**, **missions**, or **presidios**.

pueblo	town, trading center
mission	religious community, including a small town, surrounding farmland, a church; goal of the mission was to spread the Catholic religion and the Spanish way of life among the Native Americans
presidio	fort, usually built near a mission

There were different classes, or levels, in Spanish American society:

networks

Exploring the Americas

Lesson 3 Spain in America, *Continued*

- People who were born in Spain were the top class of society. They were called *peninsulares*. Peninsulares owned land and ran the government. They served in the Catholic Church.
- People who were born in America to Spanish parents were next. They were called *creoles*.
- People with one Spanish parent and one Native American parent were called *mestizos*.
- Native Americans and enslaved Africans were at the bottom level of society. The conquistadors could demand taxes or labor from the Native Americans. Therefore, they also became slaves to the Spanish. For example, Native Americans were forced to work in silver mines owned by the Spanish.

A Spanish priest, Bartolomé de Las Casas, helped to convince the Spanish government to pass the New Laws in 1542 to protect Native Americans.

Some Spanish settlers had **plantations**, or large farms. They shipped crops and raw materials to Spain. At first, they made Native Americans do the hard labor. Later, they were replaced by enslaved Africans.

In the 1600s and the 1700s, the Spanish settled the Southwest, including modern California, Texas, and New Mexico. California was the northern border of Spain's empire. Spain wanted more colonists to live there.

The Spanish, with the help of the Native Americans, built missions along the southern coast of California. After the missions were built, Native Americans were made to live and work on the missions. They were forced to become Christians.

Check for Understanding

What were the goals of the Spanish conquistadores?

_____

_____

How did Native Americans contribute to the success of the Spanish American colonies?

_____

_____

? Explaining

6. What was the purpose of the New Laws in 1542?

_____

_____

FOLDABLES®

7. Place a two-tab Foldable along the dotted line to cover Check for Understanding. Write the title *Searching for Riches* on the anchor tab. Label the tabs *Fountain of Youth*, and *Seven Cities of Gold*. Use both sides of the tabs to write two or more facts that you remember about each. Use your Foldable to help answer Check for Understanding.

Glue Foldable here

24

network⊕rks

Exploring the Americas

Lesson 4 Competing for Colonies

ESSENTIAL QUESTION

What are the consequences when cultures interact?

GUIDING QUESTIONS

1. *What were the religious motives behind the Age of Exploration?*
2. *How did French and Dutch settlements compare to the Spanish colonies?*

Terms to Know

Reformation a sixteenth-century religious movement rejecting or changing some Roman Catholic teachings and practices and establishing the Protestant churches

Protestantism a form of Christianity that was in opposition to the Catholic Church

armada a fleet of warships

Northwest Passage a sea passage between the Atlantic and the Pacific along the north coast of North America

tenant farmer settler who pays rent or provides work to a landowner in exchange for the right to use the landowner's land

Where in the world?

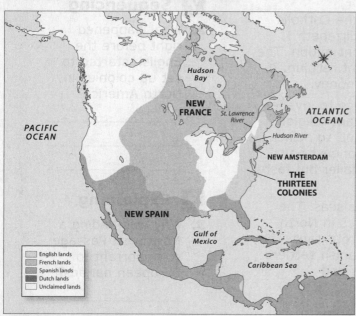

When did it happen?

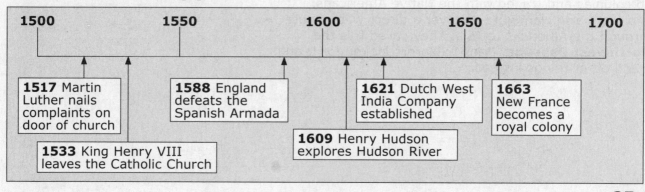

25

Exploring the Americas

Lesson 4 Competing for Colonies, *Continued*

Religious Rivalries

Part of the purpose of exploring the Americas was to spread the Christian religion there. The first explorers were Roman Catholics. In 1517, a new form of Christianity began. It opposed the Catholic Church. It was called **Protestantism**.

Protestantism started with Martin Luther, a German priest. He did not agree with many Catholic Church practices. In 1517, he nailed a list of complaints on the door of the local Catholic Church. He questioned the power and authority of Catholic leaders. His actions led to the **Reformation**. This was a religious movement that took hold in many parts of Europe. It led to widespread conflict within and between the nations of Europe.

In 1533, King Henry VIII of England left the Catholic Church. His daughter ruled later as Queen Elizabeth I. During her rule, England became a Protestant nation. The people were required to follow the Protestant religion. If they didn't, they might lose their land and money.

The king of Spain, a Catholic, saw a chance to invade England. He wanted to wipe out the Protestant religion there. The king sent an **armada**, or war fleet, to attack England. The fleet was huge. It was the strongest naval force in the world. The English fleet was smaller but faster. The British defeated the Spanish.

This meant that Spain no longer ruled the seas. The English decided it was time to set up colonies in North America. English and Dutch settlers were Protestant. They set up colonies along the Atlantic coast. Spanish settlers were Catholic. They settled in southwestern and southeastern North America. The French were also Catholic. They settled in the northeast. Religious differences caused conflicts between the colonies.

Explorers mapped the coast of North America. They set up colonies and traded with the Native Americans. Explorers also wanted to discover a direct water route through the Americas to Asia. They called this the **Northwest Passage**. Many explorers looked for it and found other things instead.

? Determining Cause and Effect

1. What was a major cause of conflict between England and Spain in the 1500s?

_____

_____

? Sequencing

2. What happened right before the English started to set up colonies in North America?

_____

_____

? Explaining

3. Why was finding a Northwest Passage so important to European nations?

_____

_____

net w rks

Exploring the Americas

Lesson 4 Competing for Colonies, *Continued*

📝 Listing

4. Which countries sent explorers to find a Northwest Passage to Asia?

_____

_____

☑ Reading Check

5. What were France's main interests in North America?

_____

_____

📝 Marking the Text

6. Underline the sentences which describe *tenant farmers*.

Searching for the Northwest Passage

Explorer	Sailed For	Year	Found Instead
John Cabot	England	1497	Probably present-day Newfoundland
Giovanni de Verrazano	France	1524	Explored coast of North America from Nova Scotia to the Carolinas
Jacques Cartier	France	1535	Sailed up St. Lawrence River, named the mountain at the site of modern Montreal
Henry Hudson	Netherlands	1609	Discovered Hudson River, sailed as far north as Albany; later discovered Hudson Bay

French and Dutch Settlements

At first, the French were mainly interested in the rich natural resources of North America. They fished and trapped animals for their fur. French trappers and missionaries went far inland into North America. They traded with Native Americans. They built forts and trading posts. They treated the Native Americans with respect. Native Americans did not see them as a threat to their way of life.

In 1663 New France became a colony. New France was made up of estates along the St. Lawrence River. Those who owned estates received land in exchange for bringing settlers. The settlers were known as **tenant farmers**. They paid rent to the estate owner. They also worked for him a certain number of days each year.

The French explored the Mississippi River. In the 1670s, fur trader Louis Joliet and priest Jacques Marquette explored the Mississippi River by canoe. They turned back when they realized the river flowed south, not west to Asia. A few years later, Robert Cavelier de La Salle also traveled the Mississippi. He went all the way to the Gulf of Mexico and claimed the whole area for France. He called it

27

Lesson 4 Competing for Colonies, *Continued*

Louisiana, after France's king, Louis XIV. In 1718, the French established a port city where the Mississippi River meets the Gulf of Mexico. It was named New Orleans.

French explorers had traveled west to the Rocky Mountains and southwest to the Rio Grande. This led to New France claiming that entire territory.

The Netherlands was a small country in Europe. It had few natural resources and a limited amount of farmland. The people of the Netherlands were called the Dutch. They were attracted by the vast lands and natural resources of North America. They already had a large fleet of trading ships. They sailed all over the world. In 1621 the Netherlands set up the Dutch West India Company. Its purpose was to ship goods for the Netherlands between the Americas and Africa. In 1623 this company took control of the country's North American colony, New Netherland.

The center of New Netherland was New Amsterdam. New Amsterdam was located on the tip of Manhattan Island, where the Hudson River enters New York Harbor. Governor Peter Minuit purchased the land from the Manhattoes people in 1626 for about $24 worth of trade goods.

//////////// Glue Foldable here ////////////

Check for Understanding

What started the Protestant Reformation? What was the result of that action?

_____

_____

What were the French hoping to find as they explored the Mississippi River?

_____

_____

? Describing

7. How did the Dutch acquire the land for New Amsterdam?

_____

_____

FOLDABLES

8. Place a one-tab Foldable along the dotted line to cover Check for Understanding. Draw a large circle on the tab and label it *Religion in North America*. Next, draw two smaller circles inside the large circle. Label the small circles *Catholic* and *Protestant.* Use the space inside the circles to list the countries of each religion that established colonies in North America. Use your Foldable to help answer Check for Understanding.

28

networks

Colonial America

Lesson 1 Roanoke and Jamestown

ESSENTIAL QUESTION
How does geography influence the way people live?

GUIDING QUESTIONS
1. **What problems did the Roanoke settlers encounter?**
2. **Why did the Jamestown settlement succeed?**

Terms to Know
charter a document granting the recipient the right to settle a colony

joint-stock company a company in which investors buy stock in return for a share of the company's future profits

headright a 50-acre grant of land given to settlers who came to the colony

burgess an elected representative to an assembly

When did it happen?

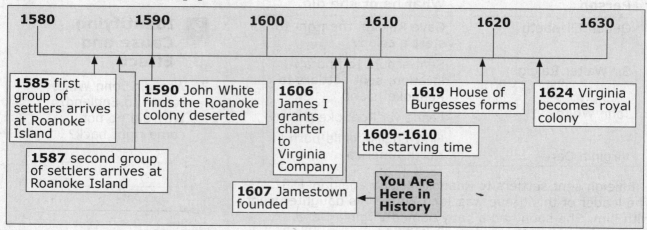

1580 — 1590 — 1600 — 1610 — 1620 — 1630

1585 first group of settlers arrives at Roanoke Island

1587 second group of settlers arrives at Roanoke Island

1590 John White finds the Roanoke colony deserted

1606 James I grants charter to Virginia Company

1607 Jamestown founded

1609-1610 the starving time

You Are Here in History

1619 House of Burgesses forms

1624 Virginia becomes royal colony

What do you know?

In the first column, answer the questions based on what you know before you study. After this lesson, complete the last column.

Now...		Later...
	Who were the Powhatan?	
	Where was Jamestown located?	

Colonial America

Lesson 1 Roanoke and Jamestown, *Continued*

The Mystery of Roanoke

England wanted to settle some people on land it claimed in North America. England's Queen Elizabeth gave Sir Walter Raleigh the right to start a colony there. Raleigh sent scouts to find a good place for the colony. They said Roanoke Island would be a good place. Roanoke Island is just off the coast of what is now North Carolina. The first settlers arrived in 1585. They had a rough winter and gave up and returned to England.

People Involved with Roanoke Colony	
Person	**What he or she did**
Queen Elizabeth	Gave Raleigh the right to start a colony
Sir Walter Raleigh	Sent scouts to find a location; sent settlers to Roanoke Island
John White	Leader of Roanoke Colony
Virginia Dare	First English child born in North America

Raleigh sent settlers to Roanoke Island again in 1587. The leader of this group was John White. His daughter went with him. She soon had a baby named Virginia Dare. Virginia Dare was the first English child born in North America.

The colony needed supplies, so White returned to England to get them. He did not come right back, though. England was fighting a war with Spain. All of England's ships were being used in the war. It took three years for White to get back to Roanoke Island.

When White arrived back at Roanoke Island all the settlers were gone. What happened to them? The only clue was a word carved on a tree trunk. That word was *Croatoan*. Maybe the word meant the settlers went to Croatoan Island. No one knows for sure. They were never seen again.

Success at Jamestown

The Roanoke Colony failed. However, England still wanted a colony in North America. The English decided to try again.

England had a new king, James I. He gave a business a "charter" to start a colony. A **charter** is a document

Identifying

1. Who sent settlers to Virginia?

_____

Mark the Text

2. Circle the date the second group of settlers went to Roanoke Island.

Identifying Cause and Effect

3. Why did John White return to England? Why did he not come right back?

_____

_____

_____

Speculating

4. What do you think happened to the Roanoke colonists?

_____

_____

_____

Reading Check

5. Why did the English decide to settle on Roanoke Island?

_____

_____

Colonial America

Lesson 1 Roanoke and Jamestown, *Continued*

FOLDABLES

📝 Listing

6. Place a one-tab Foldable along the dotted line to cover the text that begins with "The Virginia Company was a joint-stock company." Label the anchor tab *Virginia Company*. Write *Making Money* in the middle of the tab. Draw three arrows around the title. List words or phrases that explain how investors felt they would make money by investing in the Virginia Company.

🔤 Mark the Text

7. Circle the date the settlers built Jamestown.

📝 Identifying

8. Who forced the settlers to work? Who helped the colonists?

_____

_____

that gives someone the right to start a colony. The name of the business that received the charter was the Virginia Company.

/ / / / / / / / / / / Glue Foldable here / / / / / / / / / / /

The Virginia Company was a **joint-stock company**. This meant that many people each owned a small part of the company. If the company made money, each owner would get part of the money the company made.

> **Why is it called a joint-stock company?**
>
> *Joint* means "together." All of the owners owned the Virginia Company together. *Stock* is the word for the part of the company each person owned.

The people who each owned stock, or small parts, of the Virginia Company, wanted to make money. They hoped that a colony in North America would make money for the company. How? They thought the colonists would find gold, or collect and sell furs and fish.

The Virginia Company sent 144 settlers to North America. They sailed from England, across the Atlantic Ocean, and to the coast of North America. They sailed up a river and on its bank built a tiny town in 1607. They named the river the James River. They named their town Jamestown. Both names were to honor King James.

Life was difficult in Jamestown. The colonists suffered from disease and hunger. Captain John Smith forced the settlers to work. He also made friends with the local people. They were Native Americans called the Powhatan. Their chief was also named Powhatan. He gave the colonists food and helped them survive.

Then, things got worse. The colonists and the Powhatan stopped getting along. Powhatan stopped giving the colonists food. The winter of 1609–1610 was called "the starving time." Many colonists died.

Soon after that, new colonists arrived. The colony started to do well. The colonists started growing and selling tobacco. This made money for the owners of the Virginia Company. Then, things got even better. A colonist named John Rolfe married a Powhatan woman. Her name was Pocahontas, and she was the chief's daughter.

Colonial America

Lesson 1 Roanoke and Jamestown, *Continued*

Jamestown Succeeded For Many Reasons

help from Powhatan

leadership of Captain John Smith

John Rolfe marries Pocahontas

tobacco

headright system

→ Jamestown Succeeds

The Virginia Company wanted even more settlers to go to Virginia. They gave 50 acres of land free to each new settler who would go there. This land grant is called a **headright.** The headright system brought many new settlers to the colony.

At first, the Virginia Company and the leaders it appointed made the rules for the colonists. In 1619, the company began letting the colonists make some of the rules themselves. It allowed them to choose representatives called **burgesses** to make the rules for them. These representatives met in a group called the House of Burgesses. The House of Burgesses was the first legislature in North America to be elected by the people.

/ / / / / / / / / / / Glue Foldable here / / / / / / / / / / / /

Check for Understanding

What happened to the colony at Roanoke?

_____

_____

How did the colony at Jamestown survive?

_____

_____

📝 Identifying

9. What was the purpose of the House of Burgesses?

_____

10. Who did the burgesses represent?

_____

✓ Reading Check

11. Why was the House of Burgesses important?

_____

_____

FOLDABLES®

12. Use a three-tab Venn diagram Foldable and write the title *English Colonies* on the anchor tab. Place it along the dotted line to cover the Check for Understanding. Label the tabs— *Roanoke*, *Both*, and *Jamestown*. On both sides of the tabs, list words and short phrases that you remember about each to compare the colonies. Use the Foldable to help do the activity below the tabs.

networks

Colonial America

Lesson 2 The New England Colonies

ESSENTIAL QUESTION

How do new ideas change the way people live?

GUIDING QUESTIONS

1. Why did the Puritans settle in North America?

2. What role did religion play in founding the various colonies?

Terms to Know

dissent to disagree with an opinion

persecute to mistreat a person or group on the basis of their beliefs

tolerance the ability to accept or put up with different views or behaviors

Where in the world?

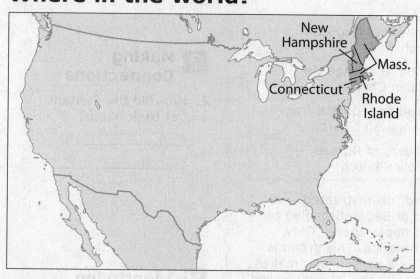

When did it happen?

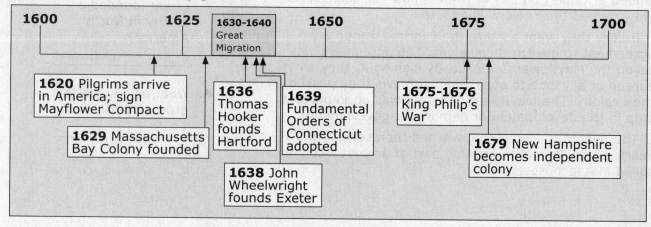

Colonial America

Lesson 2 The New England Colonies, Continued

Seeking Religious Freedom

Many English settlers came to North America to have religious freedom. In England, the main church was the official Anglican Church. The Anglican Church was a Protestant church. Many people who were Catholic did not want to practice the Anglican religion. Even many Protestants were unhappy with the Anglican Church. They **dissented,** or disagreed with, what the church was doing. Members of the Anglican Church who wanted to change or "purify" it were called Puritans. Persons who wanted to leave the Anglican Church, or separate from it, were called Separatists.

English religious groups in 1600s	Anglicans	members of Anglican Church
	Puritans	wanted to change the Anglican Church
	Separatists	wanted to separate from the Anglican Church
	Catholics	members of Roman Catholic Church

The Separatists were **persecuted**, or mistreated because of their beliefs. One group of Separatists fled to the Netherlands, but they were not happy there. They decided to start a colony in North America. This group is known as the Pilgrims. (A "pilgrim" is a person who makes a journey for religious reasons.) In 1620 the Pilgrims sailed to North America aboard a ship called the *Mayflower*. They landed at Cape Cod Bay in what is now Massachusetts. They named their colony Plymouth.

Before they went ashore, the Pilgrims signed an agreement to govern themselves. The agreement was called the Mayflower Compact. By signing it, they all agreed in advance to obey whatever laws they passed for their colony. The Mayflower Compact was an important step in the development of democratic government.

The people of Plymouth governed themselves for 70 years. Later, Plymouth became part of a nearby colony called Massachusetts.

🔤 Defining

1. Write the definition of *dissent* here.

   _____

   _____

❓ Making Connections

2. How did the Puritans get their name?

   _____

   _____

🖌 Identifying

3. Which Separatist group founded a colony in North America?

   _____

4. What colony did this group found?

   _____

Colonial America

Lesson 2 The New England Colonies, *Continued*

Defining

5. What is another word that has the same meaning as *compact?*

_____

Identifying

6. Name three ways that Squanto and Samoset helped the Pilgrims survive.

_____

_____

_____

Reading Check

7. Why is the Mayflower Compact an important document in American history?

_____

_____

_____

Defining

8. What is another word for *tolerance?*

_____

Why was it called the Mayflower Compact?

The Pilgrims named their document the Mayflower Compact because they were on their ship the *Mayflower* when they signed it. *Compact* means "an agreement." So the Mayflower Compact was an *agreement* signed on board the *Mayflower*.

At first life was very difficult in the Plymouth colony. Nearly half of the colonists died during the first winter. Then, in the spring, two Native Americans befriended the Pilgrims: Squanto and Samoset. They showed the Pilgrims how to grow corn and other crops and where to hunt and fish. The Pilgrims might not have survived without their help. Squanto and Samoset also helped the Pilgrims be accepted by other Native Americans nearby. In the fall of 1621, they all celebrated together in a great feast of thanksgiving.

New Colonies

In 1629 another colony was established nearby. This was the Massachusetts Bay Colony. It was founded by Puritans. The leader of the colony was John Winthrop.

In the 1630s, more than 15,000 Puritans left England to settle in Massachusetts. They were escaping persecution and bad economic times. This movement of people is known as the Great Migration (*migration* means "movement").

The Puritans in Massachusetts had no **tolerance**, or acceptance, of different beliefs. This resulted in people leaving Massachusetts to start their own colonies.

New Colonies from Massachusetts			
	Connecticut	**New Hampshire**	**Rhode Island**
Founded in year ...	1636	1638	1644
by founder ...	Thomas Hooker	John Wheelwright	Roger Williams
who left ...	Massachusetts	Massachusetts	Massachusetts
in search of ...	democracy	religious freedom	religious freedom

Colonial America

Lesson 2 The New England Colonies, *Continued*

One man who helped start a new colony was a minister named Thomas Hooker. He and his followers left Massachusetts to form a new colony in what is now Connecticut. In 1639, they wrote out a plan for government. It was called the Fundamental Orders of Connecticut. The Fundamental Orders of Connecticut was the first written constitution, or written plan of government, in America.

In 1638, John Wheelwright also left Massachusetts with a group of religious dissenters. He led them north and founded the town of Exeter in New Hampshire. New Hampshire became an independent colony in 1679.

Another man who helped start a new colony was a minister named Roger Williams. He believed in religious freedom. He also believed in treating Native Americans fairly. When the Puritans expelled him from Massachusetts, he started the colony of Rhode Island in 1644. Rhode Island was the first place in America where people of all faiths could worship freely.

Gradually the colonists created settlements throughout New England. The settlers and Native American peoples traded with each other. Sometimes there was conflict. Usually, it was because settlers moved onto Native American lands without permission.

In 1675, the Wampanoag leader Metacomet fought a war against settlers in Massachusetts, Connecticut, and Rhode Island. He got other Indian groups to help. The settlers called Metacomet "King Philip," so the war became known as King Philip's war. Hundreds of Native Americans and colonists died. In the end, the colonists won the war. They were now free to expand their colonies and take even more land.

/ / / / / / / / / / Glue Foldable here / / / / / / / / / / / /

Check for Understanding

Why did the Pilgrims start a colony in North America?

_____

_____

Why did people form the colonies of Connecticut, Rhode Island, and New Hampshire?

_____

_____

 Identifying

9. What was America's first written constitution?

_____

 Identifying Cause and Effect

10. What was the cause of King Philip's War?

_____

✔ **Reading Check**

11. Which colony let people of all faiths worship freely?

_____

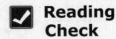

12. Use a two-tab Foldable and place it along the dotted line to cover Check for Understanding. Write the title *New Colonies* on the anchor tab. Label the two tabs—*Pilgrims*, and *Puritans*. Write key words and phrases that you remember about each group. Use the Foldable to help answer Check for Understanding.

netw⊕rks

Colonial America

Lesson 3 The Middle Colonies

ESSENTIAL QUESTION
How does geography influence the way people live?

GUIDING QUESTIONS
1. **Why did the Middle Colonies grow?**
2. **How did Pennsylvania differ from the other English colonies?**

Terms to Know
patroon landowner in the Dutch colonies who ruled over large areas of land
pacifist a person who refuses to use force or fight in wars

Where in the world?

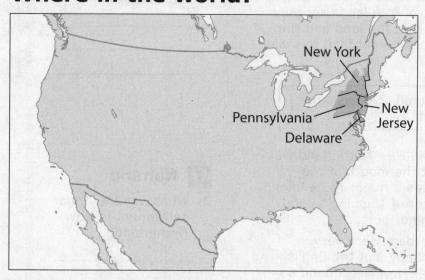

New York

Pennsylvania

New Jersey

Delaware

When did it happen?

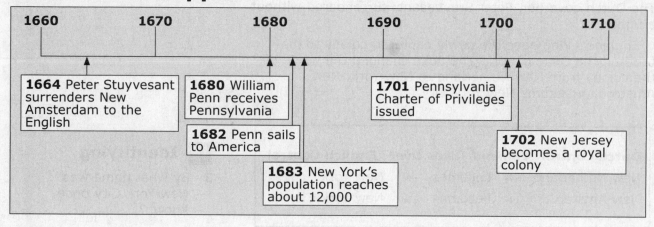

| 1660 | 1670 | 1680 | 1690 | 1700 | 1710 |

1664 Peter Stuyvesant surrenders New Amsterdam to the English

1680 William Penn receives Pennsylvania

1682 Penn sails to America

1683 New York's population reaches about 12,000

1701 Pennsylvania Charter of Privileges issued

1702 New Jersey becomes a royal colony

networks

Colonial America

Lesson 3 The Middle Colonies, Continued

New York and New Jersey

The Middle Colonies were the colonies in the middle of the east coast of North America. Some of these colonies were at first controlled by the European country called the Netherlands. This colony was called New Netherland. People from the Netherlands are called "Dutch." New Netherland was under Dutch control.

The Dutch wanted more people to move to their colony of New Netherland. To get people to move there, they gave away land. The land giveaway worked like this: If someone could bring at least 50 new settlers to New Netherland, the Dutch would give that person a lot of free land. Not only that, but that person would get to rule the land and the settlers like a king. The landowners who got land this way were called **patroons**.

> **patroon** landowner in the Dutch colonies who ruled over large areas of land

The most important settlement in New Netherland was New Amsterdam. It was located at the mouth of the Hudson River. The Hudson River was a major route inland. This made New Amsterdam a center of shipping to and from the Americas. It became a major port.

New Netherland and New Amsterdam were very successful. The Dutch were very happy, but the English were not. They wanted to take over New Netherland so they could have this valuable colony for themselves. In 1664, the English sent warships to attack New Amsterdam. The Dutch governor, Peter Stuyvesant, surrendered without a fight.

England's king gave the newly captured colony to his brother, the Duke of York. The duke changed the name of the colony from New Netherland to New York. New Amsterdam became New York City.

Dutch Control	*England Takes Over*	English Control
New Netherland	→ becomes →	New York
New Amsterdam	→ becomes →	New York City

? Analyzing

1. What was the purpose of the patroon system?

_____

_____

_____

Naming

2. What was the major settlement in New Netherland?

_____

Identifying

3. By what name was New York City once known?

_____

Colonial America

Lesson 3 The Middle Colonies, *Continued*

Abc Defining

4. What is another word for *owner*?

_____

✓ Reading Check

5. Why did no major city develop in New Jersey?

_____

_____

Abc Mark the Text

6. Underline the definition of *pacifist.* What religious group practiced pacifism?

_____

7. Underline the last sentence in the last paragraph on this page. What caused this result?

_____

_____

New York continued to grow and prosper under English rule. When England took over in 1664, the colony was home to about 8,000 people. This included 300 enslaved Africans. By 1683, its population had grown to about 12,000. The residents included many Dutch, Germans, Swedes, and Native Americans. New York was also home to the first Jews to settle in North America.

Before long, the Duke of York decided to divide his colony. He gave part of the land to two other nobles. This land became the colony of New Jersey. The two proprietors, or owners, named their colony after an island off the coast of England called Jersey.

Unlike New York, New Jersey had no natural harbors that could become a good port. So New Jersey did not develop a major city. However, like New York, people of many different racial, religious, and national backgrounds lived in New Jersey. To attract settlers, the proprietors offered large amounts of land. They also promised settlers freedom of religion, trial by jury, and a representative assembly.

Pennsylvania and Delaware

The colony of Pennsylvania was founded by Quakers. The Quakers were a Protestant religious group who had been mistreated in England. They believed that everyone was equal. They were also **pacifists**. Pacifists are people who refuse to use force or fight in wars. Welsh, Irish, Dutch, and German settlers also came to Pennsylvania.

The owner of the colony was named William Penn. (In fact, the name *Pennsylvania* means "Penn's Woods.") Penn founded his colony to put his Quaker ideas into practice.

He designed the colony's main city of Philadelphia. The name means "city of brotherly love." Penn came to America in 1682 to supervise the building of the city. Philadelphia quickly became the most popular port in the colonies.

What really makes Pennsylvania stand out, however, is the way Penn treated Native Americans. He believed that the land belonged to the Native Americans. Instead of just taking their land, he paid them for it. As a result, Pennsylvania had better relations with Native Americans than many other colonies.

Colonial America

Lesson 3 The Middle Colonies, *Continued*

Penn wrote Pennsylvania's constitution and he took an active role in governing his colony. In 1701, Penn issued the Charter of Privileges. This document gave the colonists the right to elect representatives to a legislature, or lawmaking body. The Charter of Privileges was important because it was another step in setting up democracy in America.

When the colonists got the right to elect people to make their laws, some colonists in southern Pennsylvania wanted to have their own legislature. Many of these colonists were from Sweden. Sweden had started a colony there years before the Dutch and then the English took over the region. Penn let these colonists have their own legislature. Eventually this region became a separate colony called Delaware.

/ / / / / / / / / / / / Glue Foldable here / / / / / / / / / / / / / /

Check for Understanding

Name two colonies that were formed from parts of other colonies and the colony from which each was formed.

_____

_____

Name two groups of people, besides the English, who lived in the Middle Colonies.

_____

Defining

8. What does a legislature do?

_____

Reading Check

9. What was William Penn's main reason for founding Pennsylvania?

_____

FOLDABLES®

10. Use a one-tab Foldable and place it along the dotted line to cover *Check for Understanding.* Write *Middle Colonies* in the center of the Foldable tab. Create a memory map by drawing arrows around the title and writing five or more short phrases that you remember about each of the Middle Colonies and the people that lived there. Use the reverse side to list additional information you recall.

networks

Colonial America

Lesson 4 The Southern Colonies

ESSENTIAL QUESTION
How does geography influence the way people live?

GUIDING QUESTIONS
1. **What problems faced Maryland and Virginia?**
2. **What factors contributed to the growth of the Carolinas?**

Terms to Know
indentured servant person who agrees to work without pay for a certain period of time in exchange for passage to America
constitution written plan of government; a set of fundamental laws to support a government
debtor person who owes money to another

Where in the world?

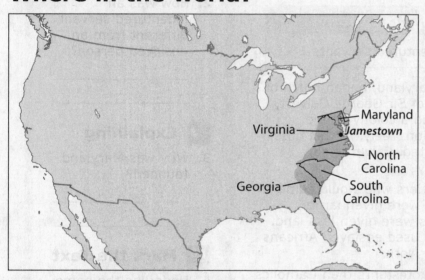

Maryland
Virginia — Jamestown
North Carolina
Georgia — South Carolina

When did it happen?

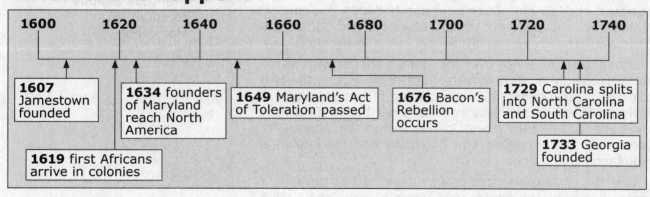

1600   1620   1640   1660   1680   1700   1720   1740

1607 Jamestown founded

1619 first Africans arrive in colonies

1634 founders of Maryland reach North America

1649 Maryland's Act of Toleration passed

1676 Bacon's Rebellion occurs

1729 Carolina splits into North Carolina and South Carolina

1733 Georgia founded

41

Colonial America

Lesson 4 The Southern Colonies, *Continued*

Virginia and Maryland

Jamestown was settled in 1607. Over the years, it grew into a larger colony: the Virginia Colony. The Virginia colonists made their living by growing tobacco. It took a lot of workers to plant, take care of, and harvest this crop. Landowners forced enslaved Africans to do much of this work. The first Africans arrived in Virginia in 1619.

Not all workers were slaves. Many were **indentured servants**. These were people who agreed to work for a certain number of years for no pay. In exchange, their employers paid for their voyage to the colony.

Workers in the Virginia Colony	
enslaved Africans	indentured servants

In 1634, a new colony, called Maryland, began north of Virginia. Maryland was the dream of Sir George Calvert, Lord Baltimore. He wanted to found a colony where Catholics could practice their religion freely. At this time, Catholics in England were persecuted. Calvert's son, Cecilius, worked to start the colony.

Cecilius offered free land to settlers who would come to Maryland. Upper class Englishmen were given large amounts of land. Average colonists were given less land. As in Virginia, wealthy landowners used enslaved Africans and indentured servants to do the work.

Before long, there were more Protestants than Catholics living in Maryland. To protect the Catholics' religious freedom, the colony passed the Act of Toleration in 1649. However, the law did not end tension between the colony's Protestants and Catholics. Eventually Maryland named one Protestant church as the official church of Maryland.

Other tensions arose over Maryland's border with its northern neighbor, Pennsylvania. For many years, the two colonies argued over the exact location of the boundary between them. They finally agreed to settle the dispute once and for all. They hired Charles Mason and Jeremiah Dixon to map the border. This boundary became known as the Mason-Dixon line.

Virginia also experienced troubles during this time. James Berkeley, the governor of Virginia, promised Native Americans that settlers would not go farther west into their lands. Nathaniel Bacon was a farmer in western Virginia. He did not like the promise Governor Berkeley had made.

❓ Analyzing

1. Why might a person agree to become an indentured servant and work for no pay?

_____

_____

❓ Contrasting

2. How was an indentured servant different from an enslaved person?

_____

_____

🖋 Explaining

3. Why was Maryland founded?

_____

_____

ᴬᵇᴄ Mark the Text

4. Underline the name of the law that granted religious freedom in Maryland.

42

networks

Colonial America

Lesson 4 The Southern Colonies, *Continued*

Explaining

5. Why was Bacon's Rebellion important?

_____

_____

_____

Reading Check

6. Why did Nathaniel Bacon oppose the colonial government?

_____

_____

_____

_____

Defining

7. What is a constitution?

_____

_____

Listing

8. List three products that were important in North Carolina.

_____

_____

_____

In fact, many people in western Virginia did not like it. They wanted to be able to move farther west. They felt that the government of the colony was controlled by people from eastern Virginia who did not care about the problems of western Virginia.

In 1676, Bacon led attacks on Native American villages. His army even marched to Jamestown and drove out Berkeley. They burned Jamestown down. Bacon was about to take over the colony when he died. Today, we remember this event as Bacon's Rebellion. Bacon's Rebellion was important in history because it showed that people wanted a government that would listen to their demands.

Bacon's Rebellion

Cause	Effect
• unhappy with promise not to move into Native Americans' land • felt the government was controlled by people in the east	• showed that government must listen to the demands of the people

The Carolinas and Georgia

In 1663, King Charles II created a new colony. It was called Carolina, which is Latin for "Charles's Land." The new colony needed a constitution. A **constitution** is a written plan of government. An English political thinker named John Locke wrote the constitution for Carolina.

Farmers from Virginia settled in the northern part of Carolina. They grew tobacco and sold timber and tar. There was no good harbor in northern Carolina, so the farmers used Virginia's ports. However, southern Carolina did have a good port at Charles Town (later Charleston).

Other crops were more important in southern Carolina. One of these was indigo. Indigo is a blue flowering plant. It was used to dye cloth. The other important crop was rice. Growing rice requires much labor, so the demand for slave labor increased.

netw⊕rks

Colonial America

Lesson 4 The Southern Colonies, *Continued*

In 1729, Carolina split into two separate colonies: North Carolina and South Carolina.

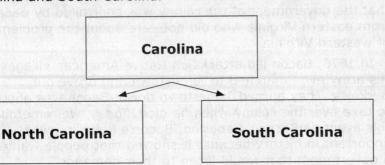

The colony of Georgia was founded in 1733. It was the last colony set up by the English in North America. The founder of Georgia was James Oglethorpe. Georgia was to be a place where poor people and debtors (DEH • tuhrs) could get a fresh start. **Debtors** are people who owe other people money. England also hoped Georgia would protect the colonies from Spain. Spain had a colony in Florida, and Georgia stood between Spain and the other English colonies.

/ / / / / / / / / / / / Glue Foldable here / / / / / / / / / / / / /

Check for Understanding

What two things caused Bacon's Rebellion?

_____

_____

List two problems that Maryland faced.

_____

_____

Mark the Text

9. Underline the definition of *debtors*.

Reading Check

10. Why was Georgia founded?

_____

_____

_____

FOLDABLES®

11. Use a one-tab Foldable and place it along the dotted line to cover *Check for Understanding.* Write the title *Southern Colonies* on the anchor tab. Label the top of the Foldable tab *Problems in Maryland and Virginia.* Recall and record the problems that Southern colonies had to face.

Life in the American Colonies

Lesson 1 Colonial Economy

ESSENTIAL QUESTION
How does geography influence the way people live?

GUIDING QUESTIONS
1. **How did the economic activity of the three regions reflect their geography?**
2. **Why were enslaved Africans brought to the colonies?**

Terms to Know
subsistence farming producing just enough to meet immediate needs
cash crop a crop that can be sold easily in markets
diversity variety, such as of ethnic or national groups
triangular trade trade route between three destinations, such as Britain, Africa, and America
slave code rules focusing on the behavior and punishment of enslaved people

Where in the world?

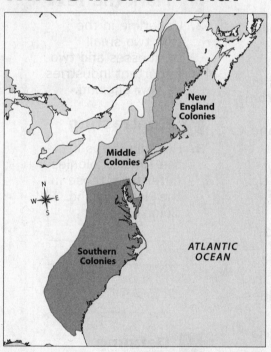

New England Colonies

Middle Colonies

Southern Colonies

ATLANTIC OCEAN

N W E S

When did it happen?

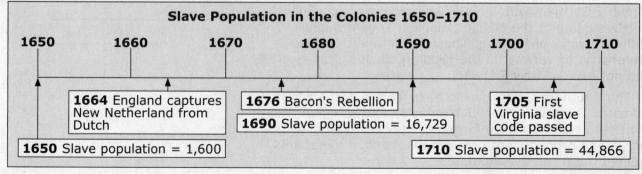

Slave Population in the Colonies 1650–1710

1650   1660   1670   1680   1690   1700   1710

1664 England captures New Netherland from Dutch

1676 Bacon's Rebellion

1690 Slave population = 16,729

1705 First Virginia slave code passed

1650 Slave population = 1,600

1710 Slave population = 44,866

45

networks

Life in the American Colonies

Lesson 1 Colonial Economy, *Continued*

Making a Living in the Colonies

In Colonial America, most colonists were farmers or had a business linked to farming. For example, a farmer who grew wheat would need someone to mill (grind) the wheat into flour. In each region, the colonists learned how to best use the climate and land.

In New England, winters were long. The soil was poor and rocky. This made large-scale farming difficult for the colonists. Instead, farmers practiced **subsistence farming.** This means that they grew only enough crops to feed their families. They did not have crops to sell or trade. On these farms, the whole family worked—milking cows, planting and picking crops, and so forth.

New England also had many small businesses, like mills for grinding grain and sawing lumber. In large towns, blacksmiths, shoemakers, and others set up businesses.

Building ships and shipping were important industries in New England. The wood needed for shipbuilding came from forests in the region. Ships sailed from coastal cities to other colonies and to other parts of the world. Fishing and whaling were also important industries in New England.

In the Middle Colonies, the soil and climate were very good for farming. The soil was richer and the climate milder than in New England. Farmers were able to plant larger areas and grew more crops. In New York and Pennsylvania, farmers grew large amounts of wheat and other **cash crops.** These were crops that could be sold easily in the colonies and overseas. Farmers sent their wheat and livestock (like sheep and pigs) to New York City and Philadelphia to be shipped to other places. These cities became busy ports.

Like the New England Colonies, the Middle Colonies also had industries. Some were home-based crafts like carpentry and flour making. Others were larger businesses like lumber (wood) mills and mining.

Many German, Dutch, Swedish, and other non-English settlers came to the Middle Colonies. They brought different ways of farming. They also brought cultural **diversity,** or variety, to the Middle Colonies. This diversity did not exist in New England.

The Southern Colonies also had rich soil and a warm climate. There was not much industry in the region. Most Southern colonists were farmers. They could plant large areas and produce large cash crops. London merchants helped them sell these crops.

 Explaining

1. Why did New England farmers practice subsistence farming?

_____

_____

_____

Mark the Text

2. Underline in the text two small businesses and two important industries in New England.

 Contrasting

3. How did farms in the Middle Colonies differ from those in the New England Colonies?

_____

_____

_____

_____

Defining

4. What are *cash crops*?

_____

_____

netw⊗rks

Life in the American Colonies

Lesson 1 Colonial Economy, *Continued*

? Contrasting

5. How were plantations in the Southern Colonies different from small farms?

_____

_____

_____

_____

✓ Reading Check

6. Why was agriculture so important to the economy of the Southern Colonies?

_____

_____

_____

_____

A𝖇c Mark the Text

7. Circle in the text two examples of important cash crops grown in the Southern Colonies.

A𝖇c Defining

8. What was the Middle Passage?

_____

_____

_____

Large farms, called plantations, were often located along rivers. This made it easier to ship crops to market by boat. Most large plantations were near the coast. Each plantation was like a small village. It could provide almost everything a person needed to live and work. Some plantations even had a school and a church.

In the hills and forests of the Southern Colonies, smaller farms grew corn and tobacco. There were many more small farms than there were plantations. Even so, the plantation owners had more money and more power. They controlled the economy and politics in the Southern Colonies.

Tobacco was the main crop in Maryland and Virginia. Many workers were needed for growing tobacco and preparing it for sale. It cost a lot of money to hire workers, so Southern farmers began using enslaved Africans.

The main cash crop in South Carolina and Georgia was rice. Growing and harvesting rice was hard work. Many workers were needed, so rice growers also used slave labor. Rice was very popular in Europe. Its price kept rising. Farmers made more money from growing rice than from growing tobacco.

The Growth of Slavery

There was slavery in West Africa before the Europeans came to the Americas.

In the colonies, plantation owners needed workers. West African slave traders had workers to sell and began shipping enslaved people to America. Here, they were traded for goods. Slavery and the slave trade became important parts of the colonial economy.

Enslaved Africans were sent by ship to the Americas. Slave ships traveled from Europe to West Africa to buy or trade for slaves. Next, the ships went to the Americas. Here the slavers sold or traded the enslaved Africans. Finally, the ships returned to Europe, now filled with trade goods. This three-sided route (shaped like a triangle) was called the **triangular trade**. The second, or middle, part across the ocean from West Africa was called the "Middle Passage."

Many Africans died during the Middle Passage. Conditions on the ships were terrible. The slavers chained the enslaved Africans together. They could hardly sit or stand. They had little food or water. If they became sick or died, the slavers threw them into the sea. If they refused to eat, the slavers whipped them.

47

networks

Life in the American Colonies

Lesson 1 Colonial Economy, *Continued*

When the slave ships reached American ports, plantation owners bought the survivors. Slave owners often split up families by selling a husband, wife, or child to another slave owner. Many colonies had **slave codes.** These were rules about the behavior and punishment of enslaved people.

On the plantations, some enslaved Africans worked in the houses, but most worked in the fields. A few learned trades, like weaving. Sometimes they set up shops and shared the money they made with the slaveholders. In this way, some earned enough money to buy their freedom.

In the colonies, there were also people who did not like slavery. They believed no human had the right to own another. Puritans, Quakers, and Mennonites were among those with this point of view.

/ / / / / / / / / / / / / Glue Foldable here / / / / / / / / / / / /

Check for Understanding

Why were New England farmers unable to grow cash crops?

_____

_____

_____

Why were enslaved Africans brought to the colonies?

_____

_____

_____

Ⓐᵇ𝒸 Vocabulary

9. What is a set of rules that says how enslaved people should behave and be punished?

_____

☑ Reading Check

10. What role did enslaved Africans play in the economy of the Southern Colonies?

_____

_____

FOLDABLES®

11. Use a two-tab Foldable and place it along the dotted line to cover Check for Understanding. Write the title *Farming in the Colonies* on the anchor tab. Label the two tabs *Geography* and *Labor Force*. Recall and describe how the land and the work force affected farming in the colonies. Use the Foldable to help answer Check for Understanding.

Life in the American Colonies

Lesson 2 Colonial Government

ESSENTIAL QUESTION

How do new ideas change the way people live?

GUIDING QUESTIONS

1. **Why are protected rights and representative government important principles?**

2. **How did the colonists react to England's economic policies?**

Terms to Know

representative government a system by which people elect delegates to make laws and conduct government

mercantilism an economic theory whose goal is building a state's wealth and power by increasing exports and accumulating precious metals in return

export to sell to other countries

import to bring in from foreign markets

When did it happen?

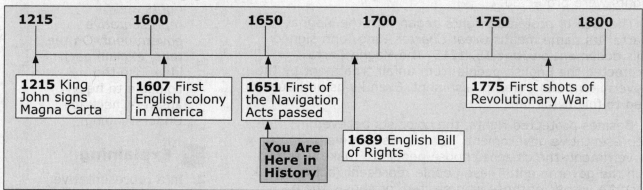

1215	1600	1650	1700	1750	1800

1215 King John signs Magna Carta

1607 First English colony in America

1651 First of the Navigation Acts passed

You Are Here in History

1689 English Bill of Rights

1775 First shots of Revolutionary War

What do you know?

Before you read, decide whether the following statements are true or false. Write a T or an F before each one. After you read, look at your answers again. Were they right or wrong?

_____ **1.** English colonists in America believed the government should respect their rights.

_____ **2.** English colonists in America believed the king should make all the laws.

_____ **3.** The king of England controlled all the English colonies in America.

_____ **4.** Everyone in the colonies could vote.

_____ **5.** England forced the colonists to sell their raw materials to England.

netwrks

English Principles of Government

////////// Glue Foldable here ////////////

English colonists brought their ideas about government with them. Two beliefs were especially important to the English system of government. The first was in protected rights (rights that are protected by law), such as the right to a trial by jury. The second belief was in **representative government.** This is a system where voters elect people to make laws and run the government. Colonists believed that their lawmakers should represent the common people. Later, these two beliefs became important parts of the U.S. Constitution.

The colonists believed that government must respect the rights of the people it governs. Laws made sure these rights were protected.

The idea of protected rights began with the Magna Carta. Its name means *Great Charter*. King John signed this document on June 15, 1215. The Magna Carta protected the English people from unfair treatment by the government and unfair punishment. Even kings and queens had to follow the law.

Besides protected rights, the colonists believed in representative government. In a representative government, the citizens choose people to make laws and run the government. These people represent (act or speak for) the wishes of those who elected, or chose, them.

In England, these representatives gathered in the Parliament. It was made up of two parts, or houses: the House of Lords and the House of Commons. The House of Commons included commoners (everyday people). Most of these were property owners and merchants. The people in the House of Lords were members of the aristocracy— dukes, earls, barons, and so forth. Together, as Parliament, these two houses had the power to make laws.

Parliament was a model for the lawmaking branches of government in America. Like Parliament, the U.S. Congress has two houses: the House of Representatives and the Senate.

In the mid-1600s, King James II and Parliament struggled for control of the government. At last, in 1688, Parliament removed King James II from power. William and Mary became king and queen. The English call this peaceful change the Glorious Revolution. William and Mary promised to rule by the laws agreed upon in Parliament. From then on, no king or queen had more power than Parliament.

FOLDABLES®

Abc Defining

1. Place a two-tab Foldable along the dotted line under the title "English Principles of Government." Write *Colonists Brought Ideas* on the anchor tab. Label the two tabs *protected rights* and *representative government*. On the tabs, explain each idea. Use the Foldable to help answer Check for Understanding.

Explaining

2. In a representative government, whom do the lawmakers represent?

_____

_____

✓ Reading Check

3. How did the Magna Carta influence government in the colonies?

_____

_____

_____

_____

Life in the American Colonies

Lesson 2 Colonial Government, *Continued*

Identifying

4. In the colonies, whose wishes did the upper house usually represent?

_____

Drawing Conclusions

5. Why might a decision by the upper house upset the lower house?

_____

_____

Finding Examples

6. Name two exports from the colonies.

_____

_____

Explaining

7. If a colonist bought cloth from France, what happened to it under the rules of the Navigation Acts?

_____

_____

_____

In 1689, an important document set clear limits on a ruler's power. This was the English Bill of Rights. It limited the ruler's ability to set aside Parliament's laws. Rulers could no longer require taxes without Parliament's say-so. The bill said that members of Parliament would be freely elected. It gave citizens the right to a fair trial by jury. It banned cruel and unusual punishment.

How did these ideas of government work in the colonies? Some of the thirteen colonies were owned by an individual or group. They were called proprietary colonies. These colonies set up most of their own rules. Pennsylvania was a proprietary colony. Other colonies, like Massachusetts, had been started by a company with permission of the English king. They were called charter colonies.

In time, some colonies in America became royal colonies. This put them under direct English control. Virginia was a royal colony. In every royal colony, Parliament appointed (chose) a governor and a council. This was called the upper house. The colonists chose an assembly, called the lower house. The upper house usually did what the king and Parliament told them to do. Often this went against the wishes of the lower house.

Not everyone in the colonies had a voice in government. Only white men who owned property could vote. Even so, a large share of the population did take part in government in some way. In towns, people often met to talk about local issues. In time, town meetings turned into local governments. What they learned was useful when the colonies became independent.

English Economic Policies

In the early 1600s, many European nations followed an idea called **mercantilism.** Mercantilism is a system for building wealth and power by building supplies of gold and silver. To do this, a country must **export,** or sell, to other countries more than it **imports,** or buys, from them. A country must also set up colonies. Colonies have two purposes. They provide raw materials and are a market for exports.

The English followed this system of mercantilism. The American colonies provided raw materials. These raw materials might be crops such as tobacco and rice. They might be natural resources, too, like lumber and fur. The colonies also bought English-made goods such as tools, clothing, and furniture.

51

Life in the American Colonies

Lesson 2 Colonial Government, *Continued*

In the 1650s, the English passed laws to control Colonial trade. These were the Navigation Acts. They forced colonists to sell their raw materials to England. Also, if a colonist bought goods from a country in Europe, those goods went to England first. Here they were taxed, then shipped to the colony. In addition, all ships carrying trade goods had to be built in England or the colonies. The crews on these ships had to be English.

The colonists welcomed the trade laws at first. The laws made sure that the colonists had a place to sell their raw materials. Later, the colonists felt the laws limited their rights. They wanted to make their own products to sell. Also, they wanted to sell their products to countries other than England. Many colonial merchants began smuggling—shipping goods without paying taxes or getting permission from the English government. Later, controls on trade would cause problems between the colonies and England.

/ / / / / / / / / / / Glue Foldable here / / / / / / / / / / /

Check for Understanding

How do people benefit from a limited government?

_____

_____

_____

Why did colonists begin smuggling goods into and out of the colonies?

_____

_____

_____

✍ Explaining

8. How did the trade laws help the colonists?

_____

_____

_____

✓ Reading Check

9. What was the purpose of the Navigation Acts?

_____

_____

_____

FOLDABLES®

10. Use a two-tab Foldable and place it along the dotted line to cover Check for Understanding. Write the title *Colonial Government* on the anchor tab. Label the two tabs— *British Actions* and *Colonial Reactions.* Write one thing that you remember about each. Use the Foldable to help answer Check for Understanding.

netw⊙rks

Life in the American Colonies

Lesson 3 Culture and Society

ESSENTIAL QUESTION

How do new ideas change the way people live?

GUIDING QUESTIONS

1. **What was life like for people living in the thirteen colonies?**

2. **What values and beliefs were important to the American colonists?**

Terms to Know

immigration the permanent movement of people into one country from other countries

epidemic an illness that affects a large number of people

apprentice a young person who learns a trade from a skilled craftsperson

civic virtue the democratic ideas, practices, and values that are at the heart of citizenship in a free society

Where in the world?

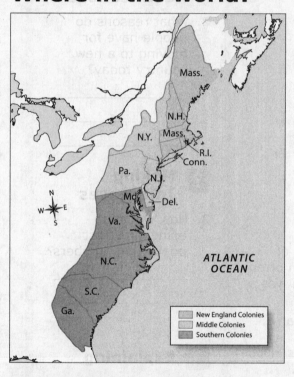

New England Colonies
Middle Colonies
Southern Colonies

When did it happen?

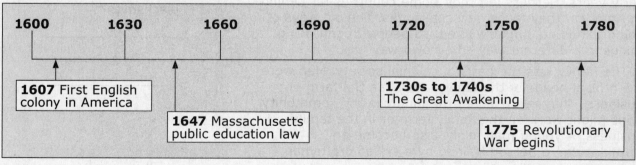

| 1600 | 1630 | 1660 | 1690 | 1720 | 1750 | 1780 |

1607 First English colony in America

1647 Massachusetts public education law

1730s to 1740s The Great Awakening

1775 Revolutionary War begins

53

Life in the American Colonies

Lesson 3 Culture and Society, *Continued*

Life in the Colonies

In 1700, there were about 250,000 people living in the colonies. By the mid-1770s, there were about 2.5 million colonists. The number of African Americans grew from 28,000 to more than 500,000. **Immigration** was important to this growth. Immigration occurs when people move permanently to one country from another.

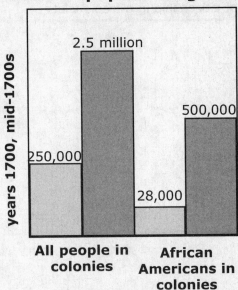

Colonial population growth

There was another reason for the growing number of people in the colonies: large families. Colonial women often married young and had many children. Also, America was a very healthy place to live, especially New England.

Still, there were more threats to life than today. Many women died in childbirth. There were outbreaks of smallpox and other serious diseases. Some outbreaks killed large numbers of people. This is called an **epidemic.**

The American spirit of independence began in these early years. Settlers left their home countries far behind. In America, they faced new challenges. The old ways of doing things no longer worked, so people began doing things in a different way—their own way.

The family was the basis of colonial society. Men were the official heads of the family. They ran the farm or business. They represented the family in the community. Sons might work on the family farm or in the family business. A young man might also become an **apprentice**—a person trained by a skilled craftsman.

54

Identifying

1. List two reasons why the population of the colonies was growing.

   1. _____

   2. _____

Making Connections

2. What reasons do people have for moving to a new country today?

   _____

   _____

   _____

Making Inferences

3. How would an epidemic affect population numbers?

   _____

   _____

Explaining

4. How could a young man learn to be a blacksmith?

   _____

   _____

   _____

Life in the American Colonies

Lesson 3 Culture and Society, *Continued*

✔ Reading Check

5. What was the role of the family in colonial life?

_____

_____

❓ Determining Cause and Effect

6. Why was there such a high level of literacy in New England?

_____

_____

_____

🖊 Listing

7. List three different groups that might run a school.

_____

_____

_____

✔ Reading Check

8. In what ways did the Great Awakening influence religion in the colonies?

_____

_____

_____

Women ran their homes and cared for the children. On farms, many worked in the fields with their husbands. A young, unmarried woman might work as a maid or cook for a wealthy family. A widow (a woman whose husband has died) might sew, teach, or nurse for a living. Widows and unmarried women also could run businesses and own property.

Even children worked. By the time they were four or five years old, they often had jobs. Even so, they did have time to play. Their games and toys were simple.

American Beliefs

Life in the colonies was built upon a strong, two-part foundation: the spirit of independence and the family.

Americans valued education. Parents often taught their children to read and write at home.

In New England and Pennsylvania, people set up schools. In 1647, Massachusetts passed a public education law. It said that communities with 50 or more homes must have a school. The result of this was a high level of literacy (the ability to read and write) in New England. By 1750, about 85 percent of the men and half of the women could read.

In the Middle Colonies, most schools were private. Widows and unmarried women ran many of them. Religious groups, such as Quakers, ran others.

Another kind of school was run by craftspeople. In these schools, apprentices learned a skill. Colleges in the colonies had a special purpose: to train ministers (people who lead religious worship).

Religion shaped much of colonial life. In the 1730s and 1740s, ministers were asking people to renew their faith—to return to the strong faith of earlier days. This renewal of religious faith was called the Great Awakening.

The Great Awakening inspired many new types of churches. These churches stressed personal faith rather than church ceremonies. The most important effect of the Great Awakening was greater religious freedom. More colonists began to choose their own faith. The older, more established churches lost power within the colonies.

The Great Awakening also broke down walls between the colonies. From north to south, the colonists were united by this revival of faith. This helped to spread other ideas—political ideas. In time, the colonies would also share the ideas of revolution and independence.

55

Life in the American Colonies

Lesson 3 Culture and Society, *Continued*

By the mid-1700s, another movement spread from Europe to the colonies—the Enlightenment. With it came the idea that knowledge, reason, and science could improve society. In the colonies, interest in science grew. People, like Benjamin Franklin, began to study nature, do experiments, and write about their findings. The Enlightenment also brought ideas about freedom of thought and expression, equality, and popular government.

Freedom of the press became important. Newspapers carried news about politics. Often the government did not like what the newspapers wrote and told them not to publish the information. The publishers fought this censorship. Their battle helped a free press to grow in the United States.

How should a citizen think, feel, and act in a free society? This is a question that colonists were beginning to think about. They began to wonder what **civic** (public or community) **virtues** (values) would be important to a free and democratic society.

/ / / / / / / / / / / / Glue Foldable here / / / / / / / / / / / /

Check for Understanding

How did respect for education influence colonial life in New England?

_____

_____

_____

Which of the following values and beliefs were important to the colonists?

_____ **a.** free press

_____ **b.** religious freedom

_____ **c.** immigration

_____ **d.** education

_____ **e.** workers' rights

? **Contrasting**

9. How was the Enlightenment different from the Great Awakening?

_____

_____

_____

? **Critical Thinking**

10. Why is censorship an important issue in a free society?

_____

_____

_____

FOLDABLES®

11. Use a one-tab Foldable and place it along the dotted line to cover Check for Understanding. Write the title *Beliefs That Shaped America* on the anchor tab. Create a memory map by drawing five small arrows from the title to the tab and writing five words or phrases that you remember about the values and beliefs that influenced the colonies. Use the back to list other information.

Life in the American Colonies

Lesson 4 Rivalry in North America

ESSENTIAL QUESTION
Why does conflict develop?

GUIDING QUESTIONS

1. *How did competition for land in North America lead to the French and Indian War?*

2. *What was the turning point in the French and Indian War?*

3. *How did the American colonists react to new British policies?*

Where in the world?

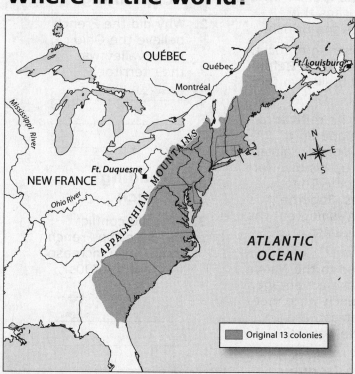

Terms to Know
militia a military force made up of ordinary citizens
alliance partnership
Iroquois Confederacy six Native American nations that joined together in North America

When did it happen?

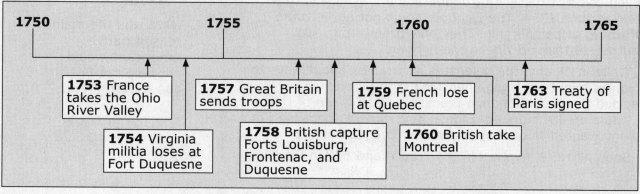

| 1750 | 1755 | 1760 | 1765 |

1753 France takes the Ohio River Valley

1754 Virginia militia loses at Fort Duquesne

1757 Great Britain sends troops

1758 British capture Forts Louisburg, Frontenac, and Duquesne

1759 French lose at Quebec

1760 British take Montreal

1763 Treaty of Paris signed

57

Life in the American Colonies

Lesson 4 Rivalry in North America, *Continued*

Rivalry Between the French and the British

In the 1700s, Britain and France were top world powers. They competed for colonies all over the world, including North America.

West of the thirteen English colonies were the Appalachian mountains. Beyond them was the Ohio River valley. This large area had many natural resources. Both the British and French wanted the region. The French were already trading for fur with the Native Americans there. They did not want to share this business with the British.

To protect their claims, the French built a string of forts. The British then started to build a fort of their own. Before it was finished, the French took it over, built their own fort, and called it Fort Duquesne (doo•KAYN).

In the spring of 1754, Virginia colony sent its **militia** to Fort Duquesne. A militia is a military force made up of everyday citizens. This militia was led by a young Virginian named George Washington. Washington set up his own fort near Fort Duquesne and called it Fort Necessity. The French attacked, helped by Native Americans. Together, they defeated the Virginia militia. Even so, Washington was called a hero. He had struck the first blow against the French.

Now both the French and the British looked to the Native Americans for help. In this, the French had the advantage. The Native Americans trusted them. The French were more interested in fur trading than in land. In contrast, the British had already taken much land from the Native Americans and could not be trusted.

The British tried to make a treaty with the **Iroquois Confederacy,** the most powerful group of Native Americans in eastern North America. Representatives from seven colonies met with Iroquois leaders at Albany, New York, in June 1754. The Iroquois would not agree to an **alliance,** or partnership. They only promised to stay neutral—to take no side in the fighting.

While in Albany, the delegates also talked about ways the colonies might work together against the French. They decided to adopt Benjamin Franklin's Albany Plan of Union. It would create a united colonial government. Because no colony wanted to give up any power, the plan failed.

Soon all were involved in the French and Indian War.

 Describing

1. What geographical area separated the colonies from the Ohio River valley?

_____

Explaining

2. Why did the French believe the Ohio River valley was their territory?

_____

_____

✓ **Reading Check**

3. Why did conflict between the French and British increase in the mid-1700s?

_____

_____

_____

_____

❓ **Finding Main Ideas**

4. What was the main reason Native Americans would not help the British against the French?

_____

_____

58

Life in the American Colonies

Lesson 4 Rivalry in North America, Continued

✔ **Reading Check**

5. Why was William Pitt successful at managing the war for Britain?

_____

_____

_____

🖐 **Mark the Text**

6. Underline William Pitt's goals in the war with the French.

🖐 **Explaining**

7. What event marked the turning point in the war?

_____

_____

? **Drawing Conclusions**

8. How could the Proclamation of 1763 calm the fighting between colonists and Native Americans?

_____

_____

_____

The French and Indian War

Early in the war, the French were winning. They captured several British forts. Their Native American allies were attacking colonists along the frontier, or edges, of the colonies.

In 1757, William Pitt became the leader of the British government. He was a great military planner. He decided to send more trained British soldiers to fight in North America. He also decided that Great Britain would pay the high cost of fighting the war—for now. Higher taxes on the colonies would pay for it later.

In North America, Pitt had two goals. The first was to open the Ohio River valley to the British. The second was to take over French Canada.

The British had a number of victories in 1758. The first was at Fort Louisburg, in present-day Nova Scotia. They also took Fort Frontenac at Lake Ontario and Fort Duquesne. This they renamed Fort Pitt.

In September 1759, the British won a major victory. They captured Quebec—the capital of New France. The following year, the British took Montreal. This ended the war in North America. The war continued in Europe until it finally ended with the Treaty of Paris in 1763.

In the treaty, Great Britain received Canada, Florida, and French lands east of the Mississippi. French lands west of the Mississippi—the Louisiana Territory—went to Spain.

New British Policies

The British now controlled the Ohio River valley. They would not pay for the use of Native American land and raised the price of their trade goods. Worst of all, British settlers began moving west.

In 1763, Pontiac, chief of an Ottawa village near Detroit, decided to fight back. His forces attacked British forts and killed settlers along the Pennsylvania and Virginia frontiers. This was called Pontiac's War.

Then something surprising happened in Britain. King George III ruled that colonists could not settle west of the Appalachian Mountains. This Proclamation of 1763 was useful to the British. It calmed the fighting between colonists and Native Americans. It also stopped colonists from leaving their colonies on the coast, where the important markets and businesses were. Britain sent ten thousand British troops to America to enforce the new rule.

Life in the American Colonies

Lesson 4 Rivalry in North America, *Continued*

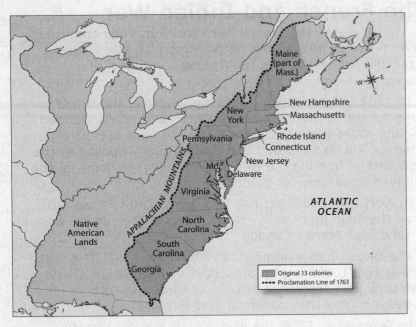

Maine
(part of
Mass.)

New Hampshire
New
York
Massachusetts

Pennsylvania
Rhode Island
Connecticut

Md.
New Jersey
Delaware

APPALACHIAN MOUNTAINS

Virginia

ATLANTIC
OCEAN

Native
American
Lands

North
Carolina

South
Carolina

Georgia

Original 13 colonies
Proclamation Line of 1763

N
W   E
S

Colonists were alarmed. The proclamation limited their freedom of movement. British troops might take away their liberties. They began to distrust their British government.

//////////////////// Glue Foldable here ////////////////////

Check for Understanding

Number these events in the French and Indian War in the order in which they happened.

_____ British capture Quebec

_____ Treaty of Paris signed

_____ Prime Minister Pitt sends British troops to North America

_____ French defeated at Montreal

How might William Pitt defend the decision to tax the colonies to pay for the war?

_____

_____

_____

_____

☑ **Reading Check**

9. Why were some colonists angered by the Proclamation of 1763?

_____

_____

❓ **Critical Thinking**

10. Why did the Proclamation of 1763 cause colonists to distrust Britain?

_____

_____

FOLDABLES®

11. Use a three-tab Foldable and place it along the dotted line to cover Check for Understanding. Write the title *French and Indian War* on the anchor tab. Write the following questions on the three tabs: *What led to the war? What was the turning point? What was the reaction of Americans to the war?* Use both sides to record your answers. Use the Foldable to help complete Check for Understanding.

The Spirit of Independence

Lesson 1 No Taxation Without Representation

ESSENTIAL QUESTION
Why does conflict develop?

GUIDING QUESTIONS
1. *Why did the British government establish new policies?*
2. *How did the American colonists react to British policies?*

Terms to Know

revenue money raised from taxes or other sources

writ of assistance legal paper that allows officers to enter a place to search for smuggled goods

resolution a group's official expression of opinion

effigy a doll-like figure that is meant to stand for an unpopular individual

boycott protest by refusing to buy items

repeal cancel

Where in the world?

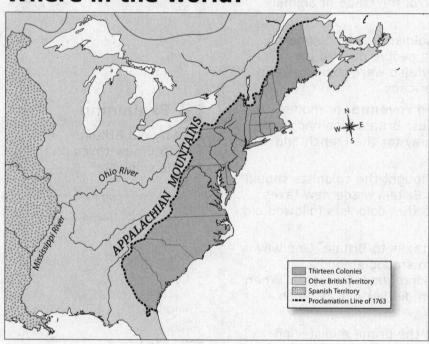

Ohio River

APPALACHIAN MOUNTAINS

Mississippi River

Thirteen Colonies
Other British Territory
Spanish Territory
Proclamation Line of 1763

When did it happen?

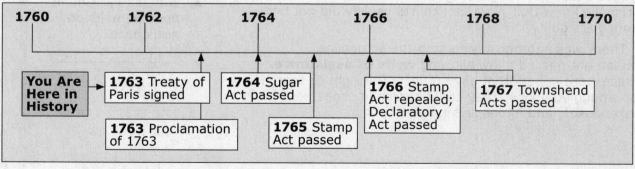

1760   1762   1764   1766   1768   1770

You Are Here in History

1763 Treaty of Paris signed

1763 Proclamation of 1763

1764 Sugar Act passed

1765 Stamp Act passed

1766 Stamp Act repealed; Declaratory Act passed

1767 Townshend Acts passed

61

networks

The Spirit of Independence

Lesson 1 No Taxation Without Representation, *Continued*

Dealing With Great Britain

The French and Indian War was over. Now, the British controlled a lot of land in North America. They had to protect this land. To pay the costs of protecting the land, King George III made the Proclamation of 1763. A proclamation is an important announcement. These are the rules of the Proclamation of 1763.

- Colonists could not live on Native American lands that were west of the Appalachian Mountains. This would keep peace between settlers and Native Americans.

- This also made the colonists live close to the coast. It was easier for the British to control them that way. It also allowed Britain to control the trade of animal furs.

- King George sent 10,000 soldiers to the colonies. Their job was to make sure people obeyed the Proclamation of 1763. They also were there to keep peace with the Native Americans.

The British government needed **revenue,** or money, to give the soldiers food and supplies. Britain also had to pay back money it had borrowed to pay for the French and Indian War.

King George and Parliament thought the colonists should help to pay for these things. So, Britain made new taxes for the colonies. They made sure that colonists followed old tax laws, too.

Colonists did not want to pay taxes to Britain. One way to keep from paying taxes was to smuggle goods. Smuggling means bringing or taking goods in secret. When colonists smuggled goods, Britain did not get as much money from taxes.

In 1763, George Grenville was the prime minister of Britain. He wanted to stop the smuggling. Parliament passed a new law. The law said if a smuggler was caught, judges chosen by King George would hear the case. Grenville knew that American courts usually did not find smugglers guilty.

There was another way to stop the smuggling. Parliament passed a law allowing **writs of assistance.** These were papers that gave officers the right to search for smuggled goods. They could search in shops, in warehouses, and in people's homes.

Listing

1. State three reasons that Britain issued the Proclamation of 1763.

_____

_____

_____

Explaining

2. Why did Britain place new taxes on the colonists?

_____

_____

Making Inferences

3. Why did Parliament approve writs of assistance?

_____

_____

_____

The Spirit of Independence

Lesson 1 No Taxation Without Representation, *Continued*

✔️ **Reading Check**

4. Why did Parliament pass the Sugar Act?

_____

_____

❓ **Making Generalizations**

5. Why didn't the colonists like the laws Parliament passed?

_____

_____

In 1764, Parliament passed a law called the Sugar Act. This law lowered the tax on molasses, a kind of sweetener. The British government hoped that colonists would pay a lower tax instead of smuggling. The law also allowed officers to take smuggled goods without getting permission.

Colonists were angry about the Sugar Act. They knew that they were British citizens. They knew that British citizens had certain rights:

- They had the right to a jury trial.

- According to law, they were innocent until proven guilty.

- They had the right to feel safe in their homes without soldiers coming in to search for smuggled goods.

New Taxes on the Colonies

In 1765 Parliament passed the Stamp Act. This law taxed printed items, such as newspapers. Colonists did not like the Stamp Act at all.

In Virginia, a representative named Patrick Henry did not like the law. He convinced the House of Burgesses to act against the law. They passed a **resolution** against the Stamp Act. A resolution is an official statement.

The resolution said that only the Virginia assembly had the power to tax Virginia citizens.

In Boston, Samuel Adams worked against the Stamp Act. He helped to start a protest group called the Sons of Liberty. The Sons of Liberty burned **effigies** (EH•fuh•jeez), or large, stuffed dolls. The dolls were made to look like tax collectors.

In October 1765, delegates from nine colonies met in New York. The meeting was called the Stamp Act Congress. The delegates wrote a resolution. They sent it to the British Parliament and to King George. Colonial businessmen decided to **boycott,** or refuse to buy, British goods. Many businessmen promised not to buy or use goods that came from Britain.

People followed the boycott. Not enough people were buying British goods. As a result, British merchants lost a lot of money. British merchants asked Parliament to **repeal,** or cancel, the Stamp Act.

The Spirit of Independence

Lesson 1 No Taxation Without Representation, *Continued*

In 1766, Parliament canceled the law. It passed another law instead. This law was the Declaratory Act. It said that Parliament had the right to tax the colonists.

In 1767 Parliament passed the Townshend Acts. The Townshend Acts taxed goods that were imported, or brought into, the colonies. By now, any British taxes made colonists angry. Groups of women protested. They told colonists to make cloth at home and wear it. This way, they would not have to buy cloth from Britain. Some of these groups called themselves the Daughters of Liberty.

/ / / / / / / / / / / / Glue Foldable here / / / / / / / / / / / / /

Check for Understanding

List two laws that taxed colonists.

_____

_____

Name three ways that colonists protested the tax laws passed by Parliament.

_____

_____

Mark the Text

6. Circle the words that explain what the Daughters of Liberty encouraged people to do to protest the taxes.

Reading Check

7. How did the Townshend Acts differ from the Stamp Act?

_____

_____

_____

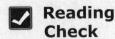

8. Use a three-tab Foldable and place it along the dotted line to cover Check for Understanding. Write the title *Taxes* on the anchor tab. Label the tabs *Sugar Act*, *Stamp Act*, and *Townshend Acts*. Use both sides of the tabs to list facts you remember about taxes placed on the colonists. Use the Foldable to help answer Check for Understanding.

The Spirit of Independence

Lesson 2 Uniting the Colonists

ESSENTIAL QUESTION
Why does conflict develop?

GUIDING QUESTIONS
1. **How did the American colonists react to the Boston Massacre?**
2. **How did the British government react to the actions of the colonists?**

Terms to Know
rebellion open defiance of authority
propaganda ideas or information spread to harm or help a cause
committee of correspondence an organization that spread political ideas and information through the colonies

When did it happen?

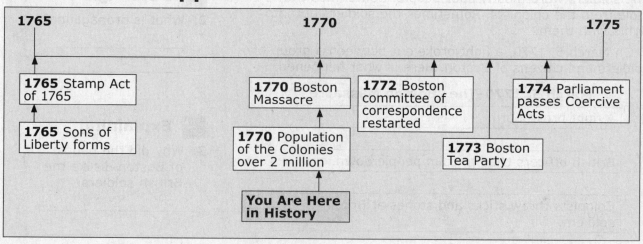

| 1765 | 1770 | 1775 |

1765 Stamp Act of 1765

1765 Sons of Liberty forms

1770 Boston Massacre

1770 Population of the Colonies over 2 million

1772 Boston committee of correspondence restarted

1773 Boston Tea Party

1774 Parliament passes Coercive Acts

You Are Here in History

What do you know?

In the first column, answer the questions based on what you know before you study. After this lesson, complete the last column.

Now...		Later...
	Who was Crispus Attucks?	
	How did the colonists use propaganda?	

The Spirit of Independence

Lesson 2 Uniting the Colonists, *Continued*

Trouble in Massachusetts

Colonists kept on protesting. This made British officials nervous. In 1768 they sent a message to Britain. The message said the colonies were close to **rebellion.** Rebellion means to reject the rules and authority of Britain.

Parliament sent soldiers, called "redcoats," to the city of Boston, Massachusetts. These redcoats set up camp in the center of Boston.

Now, the colonists decided the British had gone too far. Besides, British soldiers were rude to the people of Boston. The soldiers were mostly poor people. Sometimes they stole from the colonists. Sometimes the soldiers got into fights with them.

On March 5, 1770, a fight broke out between a group of soldiers and citizens of Boston. Here is what happened.

March 5, 1770–The "Boston Massacre"

A fight broke out.

↓

British officers tried to calm people down.

↓

Colonists threw sticks and stones at British soldiers.

↓

The soldiers became afraid. They fired their guns into the crowd.

↓

Five colonists were killed.

One of the colonists was Crispus Attucks. He was a worker on the docks. He was part African and part Native American.

The colonists called the event the "Boston Massacre." A massacre is when a large number of people are killed. Colonists used the killings as **propaganda.** Propaganda is using information to make people think or feel a certain way. Samuel Adams put up posters to make people angry at the British. The posters showed soldiers killing the citizens of Boston.

Many colonists called for stronger boycotts. Parliament repealed, or took away, most of the Townshend Acts, but they kept the tax on tea. As a result, colonists ended most of their boycotts. They still kept the boycott on tea.

Mark the Text

1. Locate and underline the definition of *rebellion*.

Defining

2. What is propaganda?
_____
_____

Explaining

3. Why did the people of Boston dislike the British soldiers?
_____
_____
_____

Reading Check

4. What changed after the Boston Massacre?
_____
_____
_____

66

The Spirit of Independence

Lesson 2 Uniting the Colonists, *Continued*

? Understanding Cause and Effect

5. Why did Parliament pass the Tea Act?

_____

_____

6. Why did Parliament pass the Coercive Acts?

_____

_____

In 1772 Samuel Adams restarted a group called the **committee of correspondence.** The group wrote their complaints about Britain and the British. They sent these writings around to many places. More committees of correspondence started in other colonies. These groups brought protesters together and made them stronger against the British.

Crisis in Boston

There was a British company called the British East India Company. It was not doing well. The reason was that colonists were not importing their tea. They were nearly out of business.

Parliament passed a law to help save the company. The law was the Tea Act. The Tea Act gave the company almost total control of the tea market in the colonies. The Tea Act also took away some, but not all, of the taxes on tea. Colonists did not want to pay any taxes on tea. They also did not want Parliament telling them what tea to buy.

Colonists called for a new boycott. They decided to stop ships from the British East India Company from unloading their tea. The Daughters of Liberty put out a booklet. It said that rather than part with freedom, "We'll part with our tea."

Still, the British East India Company kept on shipping tea to the colonies. Colonists in New York and Philadelphia made the ships turn back.

In 1773, three tea ships arrived in Boston Harbor. The royal governor ordered the ships to be unloaded. On the night of December 16, 1773, the Sons of Liberty in Boston took action. They dressed up as Native Americans and boarded the ships. They threw 342 large boxes of tea overboard. This event became known as the "Boston Tea Party." King George III heard about the Boston Tea Party. He saw that Britain was losing control of the colonies.

In 1774, Britain passed the Coercive (co • UHR • sihv) Acts. *Coercive* means "for the purpose of forcing someone." These laws were passed to punish the colonies. One of the laws forced colonists to let British soldiers live among them.

Massachusetts was punished the hardest. There could be no more town meetings there. Boston Harbor was closed until colonists paid for the tea they had thrown overboard.

The Spirit of Independence

Lesson 2 Uniting the Colonists, *Continued*

With the harbor closed, no other food or supplies could get into Boston. The Coercive Acts united the colonists. They sent food and clothing to Boston.

Parliament then passed the Quebec Act. This law created a government for Canada. Canada's border was the Ohio River, much further south than present-day Canada.

Colonists said all these laws violated their rights as English citizens. Colonists called these laws the Intolerable Acts. *Intolerable* means "unbearable."

////////// Glue Foldable here //////////////

Check for Understanding

What kinds of propaganda were used in reporting about the "Boston Massacre"?

_____

_____

_____

How are the Boston Tea Party and the Intolerable Acts connected?

_____

_____

_____

✓ Reading Check

7. List the effects of the Coercive Acts on the citizens of Boston.

_____

_____

FOLDABLES®

8. Use a one-tab Foldable and place it along the dotted line to cover Check for Understanding. Write the title *Memory Map* on the anchor tab. Write *Colonists React* in the middle of the Foldable tab and draw arrows from the title. Write terms you remember that explain the actions of the colonists. Define the terms on the back of the tab. Use the Foldable to help answer Check for Understanding.

The Spirit of Independence

Lesson 3 A Call to Arms

ESSENTIAL QUESTION

What motivates people to act?

GUIDING QUESTIONS

1. **What role did key individuals play in the movement toward independence?**

2. **Why were the battles at Lexington and Concord important?**

3. **What were the beliefs of the Loyalists and Patriots?**

Terms to Know

minutemen people who could be ready to fight as soldiers with one minute's notice

Loyalists American colonists who remained loyal to Britain and were against the war for independence

Patriots American colonists who wanted American independence

When did it happen?

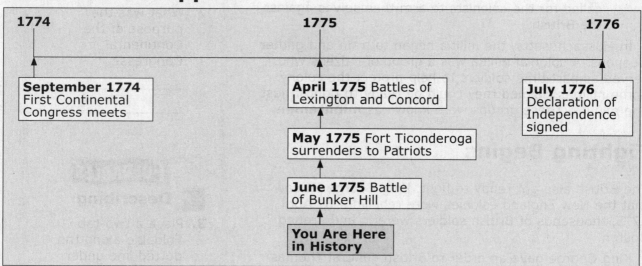

1774   1775   1776

September 1774 First Continental Congress meets

April 1775 Battles of Lexington and Concord

May 1775 Fort Ticonderoga surrenders to Patriots

June 1775 Battle of Bunker Hill

You Are Here in History

July 1776 Declaration of Independence signed

What do you know?

In the first column, answer the questions based on what you know before you study. After this lesson, complete the last column.

Now...		Later...
	Who was Thomas Gage?	
	Where is Breed's Hill? What happened there?	

A Meeting in Philadelphia

Fifty-five delegates met in Philadelphia. They came from every colony except Georgia. They met to discuss how the colonies could challenge British control. The meeting was called the Continental Congress. John Adams, Samuel Adams, and Patrick Henry were delegates. John Jay, Richard Henry Lee, and George Washington were also delegates.

The delegates to the Continental Congress:

- **issued** a statement asking Parliament to repeal several laws that violated colonists' rights.

- **voted** to boycott trade with Britain. This included all goods coming into and going out of the colonies.

- **decided** to approve the Suffolk Resolves. This called for the colonists to arm themselves against the British.

In Massachusetts, the militia began to train and gather weapons. A colonial militia was a group of citizens who served as part-time soldiers to help protect the colony. Some militias claimed they could be ready to fight in just one minute. These groups were known as **minutemen.**

Fighting Begins

/ / / / / / / / / / / ,Glue Foldable here / / / / / / / / / /

The British also got ready to fight. King George III saw that the New England colonies were rebelling. By April 1775, thousands of British soldiers were in and around Boston.

King George gave an order to British general Thomas Gage. He told General Gage to get rid of the militia's weapons. He ordered General Gage to arrest the militia's leaders. General Gage heard that the militia kept its weapons in a town near Boston. The name of the town was Concord. On April 18, 1775, Gage sent 700 soldiers to Concord to destroy the weapons.

Colonists in Boston saw the soldiers march out of town. Paul Revere and William Dawes, members of the Sons of Liberty, rode to Lexington. Lexington was a town near Concord. They warned colonists that the British were coming.

About 70 minutemen met the British at Lexington. Someone fired a shot, and then both sides began firing.

Listing

1. List three things the Continental Congress did.

_____

_____

_____

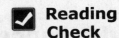
Reading Check

2. What was the purpose of the Continental Congress?

_____

_____

FOLDABLES
Describing

3. Place a two-tab Foldable along the dotted line under the heading "Fighting Begins." Write the title *Fighting Begins* on the anchor tab. Label the two tabs *Lexington* and *Concord*. On both sides of the tabs, list words and phrases to describe each encounter.

Lesson 3 A Call to Arms, *Continued*

? Sequencing

4. Number the events in the order in which they happened.

____ Revere and Dawes warn that the British are coming.

____ Battle of Concord

____ British soldiers ordered to destroy the Massachusetts militia's weapons.

____ Battle of Lexington

✓ Reading Check

5. Why did British troops march to Concord?

_____

_____

✓ Reading Check

6. What did the British learn from the Battle of Bunker Hill?

_____

_____

Eight minutemen were killed. The British moved on to Concord. They found that most of the militia's gunpowder had been taken away. They destroyed all the supplies that were left. Then the minutemen fought with the British soldiers. They forced the soldiers to turn back.

Word quickly spread that the British were on the move. Along the road from Concord to Boston, colonists hid behind trees and fences. As British troops marched back to Boston, the colonists fired. By the time the British reached Boston, 73 of their soldiers had been killed. At least 174 soldiers had been wounded.

More Military Action

After what happened at Lexington and Concord, many colonists joined militias. Benedict Arnold was an officer in the Connecticut militia. He got 400 men to join his militia.

Benedict Arnold and his army set out to capture Fort Ticonderoga on Lake Champlain. He joined forces with Ethan Allen and the Vermont militia. The Vermont militia were called the Green Mountain Boys.

Together, the two groups attacked the British soldiers. It was a surprise attack. The British surrendered Fort Ticonderoga on May 10, 1775.

Later, Benedict Arnold turned against the Patriot cause. He sold military information to the British. When he was found out, he fled to New York City. New York City was controlled by the British. Arnold commanded British soldiers. He led attacks against the Americans.

More American soldiers began joining colonial militias. Before long, there were about 20,000 militiamen around Boston. On June 16, 1775, Colonel William Prescott had his militia set themselves up on Bunker Hill and Breed's Hill. These places were across the harbor from Boston. The British decided to force the colonists from the hills.

The next day, British soldiers charged up Breed's Hill. (However, this battle is called the Battle of Bunker Hill.) The Americans were running out of ammunition, and Prescott is said to have shouted, "Don't fire until you see the whites of their eyes."

The militia fired. They stopped the British attack. Twice more the British attacked, but were stopped. Finally, the Americans ran out of gunpowder. They had to retreat. The British won this battle, but more than 1,000 of their soldiers were killed or wounded. The British were learning that it was going to be a hard fight against the Americans.

71

The Spirit of Independence

Lesson 3 A Call to Arms, *Continued*

News about the battles spread. Colonists had to decide whether to join the rebels or stay loyal to Britain. Colonists on the British side were called **Loyalists.** They did not think that unfair taxes and unfair laws were good reasons to fight. Many believed the British would win and did not want to be on the losing side. Colonists who supported the war for independence were called **Patriots.** They felt they could no longer live under British rule. The American Revolution was not just a war between the British and the Americans. It was also a war between American Patriots and American Loyalists.

/ / / / / / / / / / / Glue Foldable here / / / / / / / / / / /

Check for Understanding

Identify each battle.

The first shot of the American Revolution is fired.

_____

The Green Mountain Boys catch the British by surprise.

_____

The British attack uphill.

_____

What is the difference between a Loyalist and a Patriot?

_____

_____

FOLDABLES®

7. Place a three-tab Foldable along the dotted line to cover *Check for Understanding.* Write *Loyalist or Patriot* on the anchor tab. Label the tabs *Paul Revere, Both,* and *Benedict Arnold.* On the reverse sides, write words and phrases that you remember about each to compare and contrast the men. Use the Foldable to help answer Check for Understanding.

networks

The Spirit of Independence

Lesson 4 Declaring Independence

ESSENTIAL QUESTION

What motivates people to act?

GUIDING QUESTIONS

1. **How did individuals and events impact efforts for independence?**
2. **Why did the American colonies declare independence?**

Terms to Know

petition a formal request
preamble the introduction to a formal document that often tells why the document was written

When did it happen?

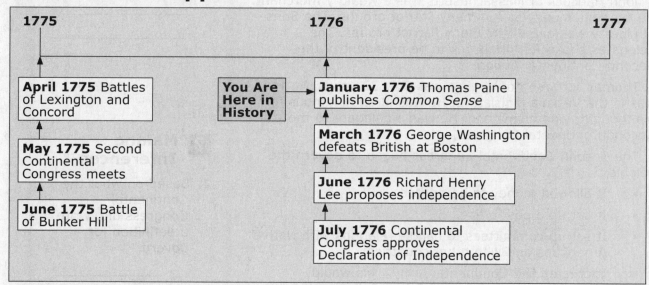

1775   1776   1777

April 1775 Battles of Lexington and Concord

May 1775 Second Continental Congress meets

June 1775 Battle of Bunker Hill

You Are Here in History

January 1776 Thomas Paine publishes *Common Sense*

March 1776 George Washington defeats British at Boston

June 1776 Richard Henry Lee proposes independence

July 1776 Continental Congress approves Declaration of Independence

What do you know?

In the first column, answer the questions based on what you know before you study. After this lesson, complete the last column.

Now...		Later...
	What was the Second Continental Congress?	
	What was the booklet, *Common Sense*?	
	What did Jefferson have to do with the Declaration of Independence?	

73

Lesson 4 Declaring Independence, *Continued*

The Second Continental Congress

On May 10, 1775, the Second Continental Congress met. The delegates included some of the greatest leaders in America. Among them were John and Samuel Adams, Patrick Henry, Richard Henry Lee, and George Washington. Several new delegates came as well.

Benjamin Franklin of Pennsylvania was well respected. He had been a leader in the Pennsylvania legislature. In 1765 he had gone to London and worked to have the Stamp Act repealed.

John Hancock of Massachusetts was a wealthy merchant. He used his money to run many Patriot groups. The Sons of Liberty was one of the many Patriot groups. The delegates chose John Hancock to be president of the Second Continental Congress.

Thomas Jefferson of Virginia was only 32 years old. He was in the Virginia legislature. He was already famous for his thoughts and his writing. He was a delegate to the Second Continental Congress.

The Second Continental Congress began to govern the colonies.

- It allowed money to be printed.
- It set up a post office.
- It set up committees to handle relations with Native Americans and with other countries.
- It created the Continental Army. This would allow colonists to fight the British in a more organized way.
- It chose George Washington to command the army.

The Congress gave Britain one more chance to avoid war. It sent a **petition,** a formal request, to King George III. The request was called the Olive Branch Petition. It said that the colonists wanted peace. It asked King George to protect their rights. King George would not accept the petition. Instead, he got ready for war.

The Americans found out that British soldiers were planning to attack New York from Canada. The Americans decided to attack first. They sent soldiers northward from Fort Ticonderoga and captured Montreal.

In July 1775, George Washington arrived in Boston. He found the militia was not well organized, so he trained them. He brought many cannons from far away.

Listing
1. Name five delegates to the Second Continental Congress.
_____
_____
_____
_____
_____

Making Inferences
2. Based on what the Continental Congress did, write a definition for *govern*.
_____
_____
_____

Reading Check
3. What was the purpose of the Olive Branch Petition?
_____
_____

The Spirit of Independence

Lesson 4 Declaring Independence, *Continued*

Mark the Text

4. Underline the name of the booklet and the author who encouraged independence from Britain.

Specifying

5. Who was chosen to write the Declaration of Independence?

_____

_____

Reading Check

6. According to John Locke, what is the purpose of government?

_____

_____

In March 1776, Washington decided the soldiers were ready to fight. He moved the soldiers and the cannons to the hills overlooking Boston while the British soldiers slept.

The British were surprised. British General William Howe commanded his soldiers to sail away from Boston. On March 17, Washington led his soldiers into the city.

Colonist Thomas Paine wrote a booklet called *Common Sense*. It explained why complete independence from Britain would be a good thing. Paine's words had a great effect on colonists and how they felt.

Declaring Independence

The delegates at the Second Continental Congress argued back and forth. Some wanted the colonies to declare independence. Others did not. In June 1776, Richard Henry Lee of Virginia came up with a resolution. The resolution stated that the United Colonies should be free and independent states, a new nation.

Congress chose a committee to write a Declaration of Independence. John Adams, Benjamin Franklin, Thomas Jefferson, Robert Livingston, and Roger Sherman were on the committee. Adams asked Jefferson to write it.

Jefferson was inspired by the ideas of an English philosopher named John Locke.

John Locke's Ideas
People have the right to life, liberty and property.
• People are born with these rights.
• People form a government to protect their rights.
• If the government does not protect their rights, people can get rid of the government.

The delegates discussed Jefferson's Declaration of Independence. They made some changes. Then they approved it on July 4, 1776. John Hancock signed first. He said he wrote his name large enough for King George to read without his glasses. Eventually 56 delegates signed the document announcing the birth of the United States.

Copies were made and sent to the states. George Washington had the Declaration read to his soldiers.

The Spirit of Independence

Lesson 4 Declaring Independence, *Continued*

The Declaration of Independence has four main parts.

1. First is a **preamble,** or introduction. It says that people who wish to form a new country should explain their reasons.

2. and **3.** The next two parts list the rights that the colonists believed they should have and their complaints against Britain.

4. The last section announces that they have formed a new nation.

John Adams thought July 2, 1776, should be the holiday that celebrated independence. This was the day that the Congress voted for independence. Instead, July 4 is celebrated today as Independence Day. This is the day the Declaration was approved.

//////////////// Glue Foldable here ////////////////

Check for Understanding

Explain the connection between John Locke, Thomas Jefferson, and the Declaration of Independence.

_____

_____

_____

What was the most important result of the Declaration of Independence??

_____

_____

Copyright by The McGraw-Hill Companies.

FOLDABLES

7. Use a one-tab Foldable and place it along the dotted line to cover Check for Understanding. Write *Declaration of Independence* in the middle of the Foldable tab and draw arrows from the title to words and short phrases that you recall about the Declaration of Independence. Use the Foldable to help answer Check for Understanding.

The American Revolution

Lesson 1 The War for Independence

ESSENTIAL QUESTION

Why does conflict develop?

GUIDING QUESTIONS

1. Who were the opposing sides in the American Revolution?

2. What were significant battles in the early years of the American Revolution?

3. Was the British plan for victory successful?

> **Terms to Know**
> **mercenary** hired soldier
> **recruit** to enlist in the military

Where in the world?

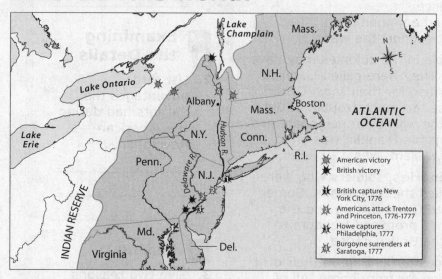

When did it happen?

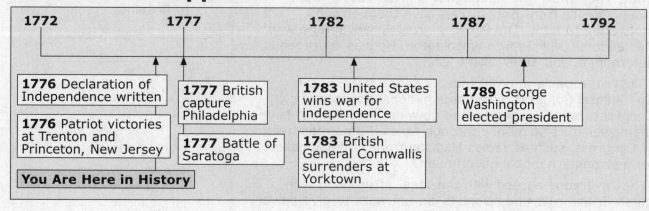

| 1772 | 1777 | 1782 | 1787 | 1792 |

1776 Declaration of Independence written

1776 Patriot victories at Trenton and Princeton, New Jersey

You Are Here in History

1777 British capture Philadelphia

1777 Battle of Saratoga

1783 United States wins war for independence

1783 British General Cornwallis surrenders at Yorktown

1789 George Washington elected president

77

The American Revolution

Lesson 1 The War for Independence, *Continued*

The Two Armies Face Off

The British felt they would crush the colonists. The colonists thought Great Britain would give up quickly after losing a few battles.

The British were confident because they had:
- the strongest navy in the world
- a well-trained army
- great wealth from their worldwide empire
- a large population (over 8 million people)

In comparison, the colonists had
- a weak navy
- no regular army, just local militia groups
- a lack of fighting experience
- a shortage of weapons and ammunition
- some people who did not support the war.

As many as one in three people in the colonies may have remained loyal to Great Britain. They were called Loyalists, or Tories. Some relied on the British for their jobs. Others thought a revolution would cause too much trouble or did not agree with the reasons for the war. Even neighbors and family members disagreed. Benjamin Franklin was an important Patriot while his son, William, was a Loyalist.

Great Britain also had **mercenaries**, soldiers who were paid to fight. The Americans called them Hessians. Some African Americans also supported Great Britain and the Loyalists. Great Britain sometimes promised freedom to African Americans who helped the British cause.

The Patriots had the advantages of fighting on their own land. The British would be fighting far from home. All of the British supplies and soldiers had to come from far away. They were also fighting for a great cause—their independence from Britain. This gave them strong motivation to fight. The Patriots' greatest advantage was the leadership of George Washington. He was courageous, determined, and an excellent leader.

After the Declaration of Independence in 1776, the Continental Congress acted as a national government. Congress, however, had limited powers. They did not have the power to raise money through taxes. Some members of Congress, such as James Madison from Virginia, called for a stronger national government.

Not everyone agreed with this idea. After living with harsh British rule, the colonists did not want to give power to the new government. This made it hard for Congress to raise money and **recruit**, or enlist, soldiers.

 Reading Check

1. What disadvantages did the Patriots face in fighting the British?

_____

_____

_____

_____

 Examining the Details

2. List three advantages the Patriots had during the American Revolution.

_____

_____

_____

Listing

3. Give two reasons that people in the colonies stayed loyal to Britain.

_____

_____

The American Revolution

Lesson 1 The War for Independence, *Continued*

? Critical Thinking

4. Why did Congress need to establish the Continental Army?

_____

_____

✐ Identifying

5. Name three women who were involved in the fighting.

_____

_____

_____

✐ Comparing

6. How did the number of British troops compare with the number of American troops?

_____

_____

✓ Reading Check

7. About how many African Americans fought in the war?

_____

_____

Many of the troops were members of a local militia, or people who are called to fight when needed. Many needed to tend to their farms to support their families. Congress established the Continental Army so that soldiers could be trained and paid. At first, soldiers signed up for a year at a time. General Washington, however, felt soldiers should agree to stay until the war was over. It was also difficult to find good leaders. Some were capable young men from the army. Others had experience in earlier wars.

A few women were involved in the fighting. Margaret Corbin went with her husband, then took his place when he died in battle. A legend says that a woman called "Molly Pitcher" fought in the war and brought pitchers of water to the soldiers. Deborah Sampson disguised herself as a man so she could join the fight, too.

Early Campaigns

Early battles of the American Revolution were fought by smaller numbers of soldiers. At Bunker Hill, in Massachusetts, about 2,200 British soldiers fought about 1,200 Americans. The British outnumbered the Americans and won the battle, but lost many more troops. They quickly realized more troops were needed to fight the war.

In 1776, Great Britain sent 32,000 more troops to help fight the war. The Patriots did not have a large army, about 20,000 soldiers, but they were very determined. In August 1776, the two armies met in the Battle of Long Island in New York. The British caught a Patriot spy, Nathan Hale. Before he was hanged, Hale supposedly said, "I only regret that I have but one life to lose for my country."

The British had more men and more supplies. Many Patriot soldiers had no shoes, socks, or jackets. The Battle of Long Island was a serious defeat for the Continental Army. The British leader chased the Continental Army across New Jersey into Pennsylvania. He could have probably captured all of the Patriot troops, but he was satisfied that Washington was defeated, and he let him go.

This was a difficult time for the Continental Army. Even General Washington worried. They needed more men and more supplies. Many African Americans wanted to join the Army but were not allowed to. Washington asked Congress to reconsider. Historians estimate that around 5,000 African Americans eventually fought.

General Washington did not give up. On Christmas night, he and his troops crossed the icy Delaware River. He

networks

The American Revolution

Lesson 1 The War for Independence, *Continued*

surprised a Hessian force camped in Trenton, New Jersey. After this victory, they marched on to Princeton, New Jersey. Washington pushed back the British troops they met there. The battles encouraged the troops to believe they could win.

British Strategy

The British had a plan to win in 1777. They wanted to cut off New England from the Middle Colonies. They needed to take Albany, New York, and control the Hudson River. The British plan involved coming in to Albany from three directions at the same time. General Burgoyne would move south from Canada, Lieutenant Colonel St. Leger would move east from Lake Ontario, and General Howe would move north up the Hudson River.

General Howe changed his plans, capturing Philadelphia instead. The Continental Congress was forced to escape. Howe stayed in Philadelphia for the winter. St. Leger also lost a battle to the Americans and did not reach Albany.

General Burgoyne captured Fort Ticonderoga in July 1777, but needed supplies. He sent troops to Vermont, but the local militia, called the Green Mountain Boys, attacked. Burgoyne's troops retreated to Saratoga, New York. There, American general Horatio Gates surrounded them and Burgoyne surrendered on October 17, 1777.

The British plan to take Albany and the Hudson River had failed. The Americans had won a huge victory at Saratoga. The American win at the Battle of Saratoga changed the course of the war.

/ / / / / / / / / / / Glue Foldable here / / / / / / / / / / / /

Check for Understanding

List two important American wins in the early days of the American Revolution.

1. _____

2. _____

Give two reasons that the British plan to take Albany failed.

1. _____

2. _____

? Critical Thinking

8. What was the British plan in 1777?

_____

_____

✓ Reading Check

9. How did Howe's victory in Philadelphia lead to Burgoyne's defeat at Saratoga?

_____

_____

FOLDABLES®

10. Place a one-tab Foldable along the dotted line to cover Check for Understanding. Write the title *Factors that led to Independence* on the anchor tab. Create a memory map by drawing five small arrows from the title to the tab and writing what you remember about the advantages the Patriots had that helped them win their independence. Use the Foldable to help answer Check for Understanding.

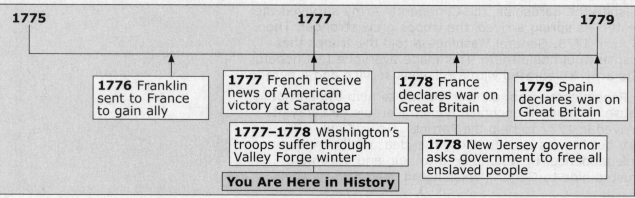

networks

The American Revolution

Lesson 2 The War Continues

ESSENTIAL QUESTION

Why does conflict develop?

GUIDING QUESTIONS

1. **How did America gain allies?**
2. **What was life like on the home front during the American Revolution?**

Terms to Know

desert to leave without permission or intent to come back

inflation when it takes more and more money to buy the same amount of goods

---

Where in the world?

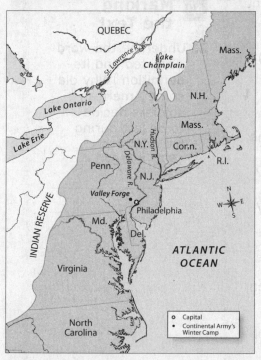

When did it happen?

1775	1777	1779

1776 Franklin sent to France to gain ally

1777 French receive news of American victory at Saratoga

1777–1778 Washington's troops suffer through Valley Forge winter

You Are Here in History

1778 France declares war on Great Britain

1778 New Jersey governor asks government to free all enslaved people

1779 Spain declares war on Great Britain

81

The American Revolution

Lesson 2 The War Continues, *Continued*

Gaining Allies

The United States needed help to win the American Revolution. The Continental Congress sent Benjamin Franklin to France in 1776. Franklin was a charming, skilled statesman and was very popular in France. The Continental Congress hoped he would be able to win French support for the American war. Early on, the French secretly gave the Americans money for their cause. They did not want to openly take sides against Great Britain.

Some news arrived in 1777, however, that ended up changing the French position. The Continental Congress sent Jonathan Austin of Boston to France with news of the American victory at Saratoga. When Austin arrived, Benjamin Franklin asked him if the British had taken Philadelphia. "Yes sir ... but sir, I have greater news than that," Austin answered. "General Burgoyne and his whole army are prisoners of war!"

This information about the Patriot win at Saratoga was very important. France and other nations now saw that the Patriots might win the war. Soon after, in February 1778, France declared war on Great Britain. They agreed to help the Americans with money, equipment, and troops.

News that the French had joined the war traveled slowly back to the United States. Over the winter of 1777–1778, the Continental Army suffered through a hard winter. General Washington and his troops were camped in Valley Forge, Pennsylvania. This city was about 20 miles away from Philadelphia. There, British General Howe and his men were comfortable and warm. Washington's troops were miserable and cold. They did not have enough food, clothing, or medicine. General Washington had to use all of his skills to keep his army together at Valley Forge.

Many soldiers got sick. Many died. Some soldiers quit. Other soldiers **deserted**, or left without permission. Despite the hardships, the Continental Army survived the winter. As spring arrived, the troops grew stronger. Then, in April 1778, General Washington told the troops that France would help them. This made everyone feel hopeful. The army celebrated with a religious service and a parade.

People came from all over Europe to help the Patriot cause. A young Frenchman named Marquis de Lafayette arrived in 1777 to help the Patriots. He was only 19 years old, but he was excited about the ideas of liberty and independence. He volunteered to help and became a trusted aide to General Washington.

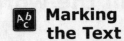

Explaining

1. Why was the Battle of Saratoga an important victory for the Patriots?

_____

_____

Marking the Text

2. Underline the word *deserted* and its definition. Why did some American soldiers decide to desert during the winter of 1777–1778?

_____

_____

The American Revolution

Lesson 2 The War Continues, *Continued*

? Critical Thinking

3. Why would foreign-born people come to help the Patriots in their fight for freedom?

_____

_____

✓ Reading Check

4. How did Lafayette help the Patriot cause?

_____

_____

✓ Reading Check

5. What help did the Patriots receive from Spain?

_____

_____

Two Polish men were also important in the war effort: Thaddeus Kosciuszko and Casimir Pulaski. Kosciuszko helped build important defenses for the Americans. Pulaski was promoted to general. He was wounded in battle, and later died in 1779.

Friedrich von Steuben from Prussia was another foreign-born person who helped the Patriots. Through the harsh winter at Valley Forge, von Steuben trained the Continental Army. This made them a better fighting force.

Some people did important work off the battlefield as well. Juan de Miralles came from Spain. He helped persuade Spain, Cuba, and Mexico to help the United States by sending money to support the war.

Marquis de Lafayette	French nobleman and Patriot volunteer; became trusted aide to General Washington
Thaddeus Kosciuszko	Polish nobleman who helped build important defenses for the Americans
Casimir Pulaski	Polish man who rose to rank of general in Continental Army, died fighting for the Patriot cause
Friedrich von Steuben	Former army officer from Prussia who helped train the Continental Army
Juan de Miralles	Spanish supporter who persuaded Spain, Cuba, and Mexico to send money to help the Patriots

Even with help from many countries and individuals, the fight for independence was still not over. More battles and challenges were yet to come.

Life on the Home Front

The war affected the lives of everyone in the United States. Getting money to pay for the war was a challenge for the government. It printed millions of dollars of paper money. But the paper money lost value. The economy suffered from **inflation**. It took more and more money to buy the same amount of goods.

Women raised their children and took care of their homes on their own. They also ran businesses and farms while their fathers, husbands, and brothers were away at war. Children lived without their fathers present.

networks

The American Revolution

Lesson 2 The War Continues, *Continued*

This caused some people to think differently about women's roles. Abigail Adams, the wife of Congressman John Adams, wrote to ask him to think about the rights of women as he helped form the new nation.

For others, the fight for freedom made them change their thoughts about slavery. In 1778, the governor of New Jersey, William Livingston, asked his state government to free all enslaved people. He felt that slavery went against the ideas of Christianity. African Americans also spoke up for their freedom. The conflict over slavery would continue for many years to come.

The war also affected another group of people in the United States. These people were Loyalists, or American settlers who supported Great Britain. Some Loyalists joined the British troops and fought against the Patriots in the war. Some were spies for Great Britain. Others fled to Canada or went back to Great Britain.

The people who stayed faced trouble. Many were treated badly by their neighbors. Some were attacked or hurt. Those caught spying could be arrested or even put to death.

/ / / / / / / / / / / / Glue Foldable here / / / / / / / / / / / / /

Check for Understanding

Name two people from other nations who helped the United States gain freedom. Describe what each contributed.

1. _____

_____

2. _____

_____

Name two groups of people who sought greater freedom as a result of the Revolution and how people's thinking changed.

1. _____

_____

2. _____

_____

☑ Reading Check

6. How were Loyalists treated by the Patriots during the war?

_____

_____

FOLDABLES®

7. Place a two-tab Foldable along the dotted line to cover Check for Understanding. Write the title *Foreign Allies* on the anchor tab. Label the two tabs *France* and *Spain*. Recall and list ways that each helped the Patriots during their fight for independence. Use the Foldable to help answer Check for Understanding.

The American Revolution

Lesson 3 Battlegrounds Shift

ESSENTIAL QUESTION
Why does conflict develop?

GUIDING QUESTIONS

1. **How did the war in the West develop?**

2. **What was the result of the war at sea?**

3. **What was the result of the war in the South?**

Terms to Know

blockade measure that keeps a country from communicating and trading with other nations

privateer privately owned ship outfitted with weapons

When did it happen?

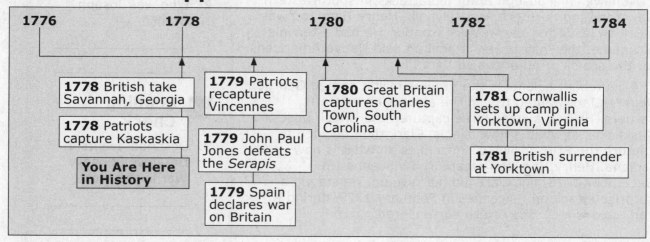

1776   1778   1780   1782   1784

1778 British take Savannah, Georgia

1778 Patriots capture Kaskaskia

You Are Here in History

1779 Patriots recapture Vincennes

1779 John Paul Jones defeats the *Serapis*

1779 Spain declares war on Britain

1780 Great Britain captures Charles Town, South Carolina

1781 Cornwallis sets up camp in Yorktown, Virginia

1781 British surrender at Yorktown

What do you know?

In the first column, answer the questions based on what you know before you study. After this lesson, complete the last column.

Now ...		Later ...
	On which side did most Native Americans fight during the Revolution?	
	How did Americans fight back against the British naval blockade?	
	What area of the United States did the British focus on winning?	

The American Revolution

Lesson 3 Battlegrounds Shift, *Continued*

Fighting in the West

There were many Native American nations in the different colonies. Some of these nations took sides in the war between the Patriots and the British. Some helped the Patriots. More Native Americans decided to help the British. The Patriots had fought against them, taken land that belonged to them, and changed their way of life. To Native Americans, the British seemed like less of a threat.

The American Revolution was fought in many areas. One important area was along the western frontier, or land west of the Appalachian Mountains. The British and some Native Americans raided American settlements.

Mohawk chief Joseph Brant led attacks in southwestern New York and northern Pennsylvania. Henry Hamilton was a British leader on the western frontier. He had a terrible nickname: the "hair buyer." Hamilton paid Native Americans for the scalps of American settlers.

A lieutenant colonel in the Virginia militia named George Rogers Clark wanted to end the attacks on western settlers. He and a small force captured the British post of Kaskaskia, in what is now Illinois. Clark then decided to capture the British town of Vincennes, in what is now Indiana. Henry Hamilton recaptured Vincennes in December 1778, but Clark did not give up. He staged a surprise attack on Vincennes in February 1779, during a very cold winter. The British surrendered.

The War at Sea

The war was also fought at sea. The United States did not have a strong navy. Congress called for building 13 warships, but only two ever sailed. Great Britain had a very powerful navy. Its many ships blocked American ports and harbors. This stopped ships from coming or going with people or supplies. This is known as a **blockade**.

Something had to be done to break the blockade. So Congress gave special permission to about 2,000 privately owned merchant ships to have weapons attached. The ships could then capture enemy ships and take their cargo. These ships were called **privateers**. They played an important role in the American Revolution because they captured more British ships than the American navy.

A very famous battle at sea took place in 1779 off the coast of Great Britain. It was between a British ship called the *Serapis* and an American ship called the *Bonhomme*

 Explaining

1. Why did more Native Americans side with the British than with the Patriots?

_____

_____

 Identifying

2. Who was Joseph Brant?

_____

_____

✔ **Reading Check**

3. Describe events in the Revolutionary War in the West.

_____

_____

_____

_____

 **Marking the Text**

4. Underline the word *blockade* and its definition. What did Americans do to combat the blockade?

_____

_____

The American Revolution

Lesson 3 Battlegrounds Shift, *Continued*

 Identifying

5. Who was John Paul Jones?

_____

6. What did he do?

_____

 Explaining

7. What special method of fighting did Francis Marion use in his attacks on the British?

_____

 Identifying

8. Who was Bernardo de Gálvez and how did he help the Americans?

_____

_____

Richard. The American captain was John Paul Jones. The ships fought for hours. Eventually, the British captain asked Jones if he wanted to surrender. Jones refused and said, "I have not yet begun to fight." John Paul Jones and his crew captured the *Serapis.* The victory was the first time an American ship had captured a British ship in British waters. John Paul Jones became a Patriot hero.

Fighting in the South

The British had more troops and supplies during the American Revolution, but they realized that they would not be able to win quickly. They came up with a new strategy. They wanted to win the South.

The Americans won some important early battles in the South. The Patriots beat Loyalist forces at Wilmington, North Carolina. They also kept the British from capturing Charles Town, now called Charleston, South Carolina. They were small battles, but had a big impact on the war.

The British also had some successes in the South. They took the city of Savannah, Georgia. In 1780, they finally captured Charles Town. Thousands of troops were taken prisoner by the British. This was the worst American defeat of the war. The British success would not last, however.

The British believed they could use strong Loyalist support and their naval power to help them win the South. The British did not get the Loyalist support they hoped for. They also had to deal with American hit-and-run tactics. Patriot forces would attack the British by surprise, and then disappear again. Francis Marion, called the "Swamp Fox," was a successful Patriot leader in the South. He was quick and smart, and he hid from the British easily in the eastern South Carolina swamps.

Other countries were also keeping Great Britain distracted in the South. In 1779, Spain declared war on Great Britain. At that time, Louisiana had a Spanish governor named Bernardo de Gálvez. He helped the Patriots a great deal. He did this by giving them money and allowing them to use the Port of New Orleans. He also shipped tons of supplies and ammunition up the Mississippi River. Gálvez also fought the British in the South. This fighting with Spain weakened the British.

The British gained a big victory at Camden, South Carolina. General Cornwallis led the British troops, and General Horatio Gates led the Patriot forces. The British

networks

The American Revolution

Lesson 3 Battlegrounds Shift, *Continued*

won the battle but could not control the area. British forces under Cornwallis moved north.

Some settlers in the South were neutral, meaning they did not take sides. The British told these local people that they must support them. The British said if the locals did not help them, they would hang their leaders and destroy their land. This angered the Americans who lived in the mountains of the South. They formed a militia.

They clashed with a Loyalist force at Kings Mountain. The Patriots surrounded the Loyalist forces. They killed or captured nearly all of the 1,000 Loyalist troops. This victory won more support from Southern settlers.

More victories followed. Nathaniel Greene took command of the Continental Army in the South. He decided to split his troops into two sections. One part had success against the British at Cowpens, South Carolina. The other part of the army helped in raids with Francis Marion.

Later in 1781, the two sections met Cornwallis' army at what is now Greensboro, North Carolina. The Patriots did not win, but the British suffered great losses. General Cornwallis decided to give up the fight in the Carolinas.

Cornwallis and his troops went north into Virginia. Cornwallis set up camp with his men at Yorktown on the Virginia coast. Both Marquis de Lafayette and Anthony Wayne went south into Virginia to push Cornwallis back. The battle for the South was entering its final phase.

/ / / / / / / / / / / Glue Foldable here / / / / / / / / / / /

Check for Understanding

Identify each of these people.

1. John Paul Jones _____

2. Francis Marion _____

3. General Charles Cornwallis _____

How did the treatment of neutral settlers in the South hurt British chances for success?

_____

_____

? Critical Thinking

9. Why do you think neutral Americans decided to fight against the British?

_____

_____

_____

✓ Reading Check

10. What effect did the Patriot victory at Kings Mountain have?

_____

_____

11. Place a three-tab Foldable along the dotted line to cover Check for Understanding. Label the three tabs *War in the West*, *War at Sea*, and *War in the South*. List the key words, dates, names, and events that you remember about each. Use the Foldable to help answer Check for Understanding.

88

The American Revolution

Lesson 4 The Final Years

ESSENTIAL QUESTION
Why does conflict develop?

GUIDING QUESTIONS
1. **What events occurred in the victory at Yorktown?**
2. **What helped the Patriots win independence?**

Terms to Know
siege an attempt to force surrender by blocking the movement of people or goods into or out of a place
ratify to approve officially
ambush an attack in which the attacker hides and surprises the enemy

Where in the world?

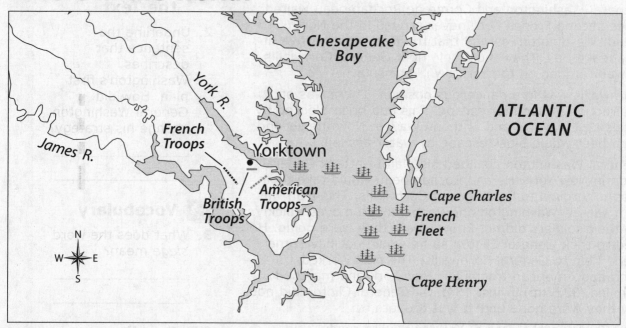

When did it happen?

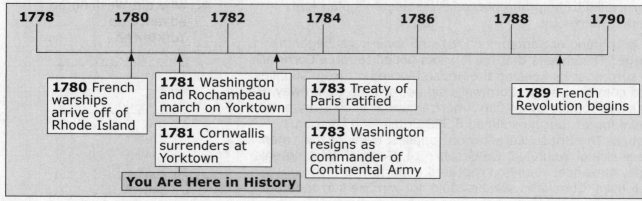

1780 French warships arrive off of Rhode Island

1781 Washington and Rochambeau march on Yorktown

1781 Cornwallis surrenders at Yorktown

1783 Treaty of Paris ratified

1783 Washington resigns as commander of Continental Army

1789 French Revolution begins

You Are Here in History

networks

The American Revolution

Lesson 4 The Final Years, *Continued*

Victory at Yorktown

While battles were going on in the South, General Washington and his troops were in New York. In July 1780, French warships arrived off of Rhode Island to help the Americans. They carried thousands of French troops led by Comte de Rochambeau. They joined General Washington and waited for a second French fleet to arrive.

General Washington had a plan. He wanted to attack an army base in New York commanded by British general Clinton. A second fleet of French ships was expected. The attack would happen when that force arrived.

General Washington and Comte de Rochambeau waited, but the second French fleet never arrived in the North. Instead, Washington learned that the fleet would arrive at Chesapeake Bay. They could help fight General Cornwallis, who was camped on the Yorktown Peninsula.

Cornwallis was in a dangerous position. There was only one direction on land for escape. This had been blocked by Marquis de Lafayette and Anthony Wayne. Now the second French fleet would block escape by water as well.

General Washington changed his plan to attack General Clinton in New York. He and Rochambeau would take their troops to Virginia to fight against Cornwallis. This plan was kept a secret. Washington and Rochambeau moved quickly. Even their soldiers did not know where they were going. He hoped to trick General Clinton so he would not have time to send help to General Cornwallis. The plan worked. French and American troops left New York and marched 200 miles (322 km) in just 15 days. General Clinton did not know they were gone until it was too late.

The Continental forces at Yorktown were ready. Washington, Rochambeau, Lafayette, and the French fleet had Cornwallis cornered. British ships could not reach Cornwallis to help him escape. Washington's plan had worked perfectly.

At the end of September 1781, the Americans began a **siege**. This means that the Patriots hoped to force Cornwallis to surrender by keeping the British blocked off from supplies and communication. Cornwallis did not give up right away. He was surrounded by 14,000 American and French army and naval forces, but he still had 8,000 British and Hessian troops. The British were low on supplies. Many of their men were sick or wounded. On October 14, General Washington's aide, Alexander Hamilton captured important British defenses. Cornwallis saw he could not win. He surrendered.

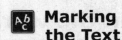 **Describing**

1. Explain how General Cornwallis was trapped on the Yorktown Peninsula.

_____

_____

Marking the Text

2. Underline the sentence that describes Washington's first plan. How did General Washington change his strategy?

_____

_____

Vocabulary

3. What does the word *siege* mean?

_____

_____

Reading Check

4. Why did Washington advance on Yorktown?

_____

_____

_____

90

The American Revolution

Lesson 4 The Final Years, *Continued*

? **Critical Thinking**

5. Why was the Treaty of Paris important?

_____

_____

✓ **Reading Check**

6. Why did Washington take action to end the soldier's threat in Newburgh?

_____

_____

The Patriots won the Battle of Yorktown. The French band played the song "Yankee Doodle" which the British had used to make fun of the Americans. In response, the British band played a children's tune called "The World Turned Upside Down."

Independence Achieved

Yorktown was not the last battle of the American Revolution. The British still held cities such as Savannah, Charles Town, and New York. Yet the British realized that the fight was finished. The war was too costly to continue.

Both sides sent representatives to France to work out a peace agreement. Benjamin Franklin, John Adams, and John Jay represented the United States. The first draft of the Treaty of Paris was **ratified**, or approved, by Congress. The final agreement was signed in September 1783.

The treaty was a success for the Patriots. Great Britain agreed to recognize the United States as an independent nation along with other agreements.

United States	Great Britain
Recognized as independent nation	British merchants could collect debts from Americans
Promised that Congress would advise state governments to return Loyalist property	British agree to withdraw troops
	Americans granted permission to fish off of Canada

Some time passed between the end of the war and the signing of the treaty. The Continental Army was kept active during this time in Newburgh, New York. The soldiers wanted to get paid. They were angry because they were owed money. Some thought they should use force against Congress if they were not paid. General Washington stepped in to settle the dispute. He understood the threat was very serious for the new nation. He asked the soldiers to be patient. He also asked Congress to meet the soldiers' demands. Congress agreed. General Washington showed his superior leadership once again.

91

networks

The American Revolution

Lesson 4 The Final Years, *Continued*

When the last of the British troops left New York City in November 1783, Washington decided to resign. He wanted to retire to Virginia and live a quiet life with his family.

Even though the British were strong, the Americans won the war because they had certain advantages. They fought on their own land for a cause they believed in. They knew the land and how to use it, often using **ambushes** to surprise the enemy. The British, on the other hand, fought a war far from home. Their troops and supplies had to be shipped in. They also had a hard time controlling the Americans even when they captured major cities.

The Americans also had help from many others. The French supplied soldiers and naval support as well as money. The Spanish gave aid when they attacked Britain. Individuals from other countries came to help the Americans fight and build their defenses.

Most of all, the British could not fight against the power of independence. Americans fought hard because they believed in what they were fighting for. They wanted to protect their land, their families, and their freedom.

This spirit spread to other places in the world as well. Shortly after the American Revolution, French rebels fought for freedom. They fought for the ideals of "Liberty, Equality, and Fraternity." These ideas also took root in the French colony of Saint Domingue, which is now Haiti. Led by a man named Toussaint L'Ouverture, enslaved Africans fought for their freedom. In 1804, Saint Domingue became the second nation in the Americas to win its freedom.

///////////////// Glue Foldable here ///////////////

Check for Understanding

Give two reasons that General Cornwallis was defeated at Yorktown.

1. _____

2. _____

List two elements that helped the Patriots win the war.

1. _____

2 _____

Explaining

7. How did France and Spain help the Americans win the war?

_____

_____

FOLDABLES

8. Use a two-tab Foldable and place it along the dotted line to cover Check for Understanding. Write *American Independence* on the anchor tab. Label the two tabs *Patriots Win* and *British Defeated*. Recall and list reasons for the Patriots' victory and the defeat of the Loyalists. Use the Foldable to help answer Check for Understanding.

A More Perfect Union

Lesson 1 The Articles of Confederation

ESSENTIAL QUESTION

Why do people form governments?

GUIDING QUESTIONS

1. What kind of government was created by the Articles of Confederation?

2. What process allowed new states to join the union?

3. In what ways was the Confederation government weak?

Terms to Know

bicameral having two separate lawmaking organizations

republic a government in which citizens rule through elected representatives

ordinance law

depreciate lose value

Where in the world?

When did it happen?

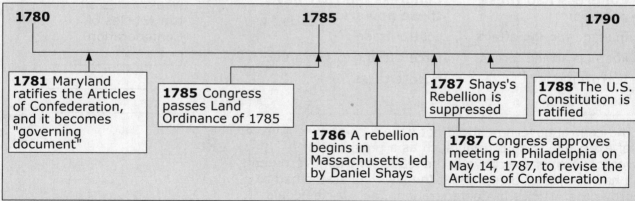

1780

1781 Maryland ratifies the Articles of Confederation, and it becomes "governing document"

1785 Congress passes Land Ordinance of 1785

1785

1786 A rebellion begins in Massachusetts led by Daniel Shays

1787 Shays's Rebellion is suppressed

1787 Congress approves meeting in Philadelphia on May 14, 1787, to revise the Articles of Confederation

1788 The U.S. Constitution is ratified

1790

netw⬤rks

Lesson 1 The Articles of Confederation, *Continued*

The Making of a Republic

In May 1776, the Continental Congress asked each state to set up its government. Each state wrote a constitution. A constitution is a plan of government.

Americans did not want to give too much power to one ruler or one branch of government. State constitutions solved that problem. They split the power between the governor and legislature. The governor had less power than the legislature. Most states set up two-house, or **bicameral,** legislatures. This divided the power even more.

Americans had to set up a national government, too. Americans wanted their country to be a **republic.** In a republic, citizens elect people to represent them and make decisions based on what they want.

People could not agree on what powers the national government should have. Americans felt the central government should have only the power to fight wars and to deal with other countries.

In 1776 the Second Continental Congress had a group of people make a plan for a central government. This group created the Articles of Confederation. The Articles called for a weak central government. They also let states keep most of their powers. Congress accepted the Articles of Confederation in November, 1777.

The Articles of Confederation gave Congress certain powers, but there were important powers that Congress did not have. For example, if Congress needed to raise money or an army, it had to ask the states. The states did not have to say yes.

Powers of Congress Under The Articles of Confederation	
Congress had these powers:	**Congress did NOT have these powers:**
manage foreign affairs	control trade
keep up armed forces	force citizens to join army
borrow money	impose taxes
issue money	

The central government did not have a chief executive. A chief executive is an official, such as a president or a governor. A chief executive is the leader of the government and has the job of carrying out the laws. All states had to approve the Articles of Confederation. The Articles could

 Mark the Text

1. Underline the meaning of a *constitution*.

 Analyzing

2. What might be one result of state constitutions that limited the power of the governor?

_____

_____

 Mark the Text

3. Circle the meaning of *republic*.

 Listing

4. What were three weaknesses of the Articles of Confederation?

_____

_____

A More Perfect Union

Lesson 1 The Articles of Confederation, *Continued*

✓ **Reading Check**

5. How many votes did each state have in the new Congress?

_____

_____

Mark the Text

6. Underline how a western district could apply to become a state.

✓ **Reading Check**

7. What did the Northwest Ordinance say about slavery?

_____

_____

not be changed unless all states agreed to change it. Each state had one vote.

The states also did not agree on what to do with land in the West. Some states believed land west of the Appalachian Mountains belonged to them. Maryland did not want to approve the Articles until other states gave up claims to this land. The states finally agreed and approved the Articles. On March 1, 1781, the Articles of Confederation became the government of the United States of America.

The new national government was weak. This made it difficult for the government to handle the nation's problems. Congress could not pass a law unless 9 states voted for it. Congress also did not have the power to change the Articles of Confederation. Any plan to change the Articles needed to be approved by all 13 states.

Even so, America's government did some important things. America made a peace treaty with Britain. It expanded foreign trade. It set up plans for people to settle lands to the west.

Policies for Western Lands

The Articles of Confederation did not tell how to add new states. Settlers were already living west of the Appalachian Mountains. This was outside the United States. Western settlers wanted to form new states and join the Union. Congress needed to give people a way to settle the Western lands and form new states.

In 1785, the Confederation Congress passed an **ordinance,** or law, about western lands. This law set up a way to divide and then sell the western lands. Land was divided into townships. Land in the township was divided into smaller sections. These sections were sold to settlers.

In 1787, the Northwest Ordinance created the Northwest Territory. This territory included lands north of the Ohio River and east of the Mississippi River. The lands were divided into three to five smaller territories. A territory could apply to become a state when 60,000 people lived there. New states would have the same rights as the original 13 states. Settlers had a bill of rights. They had freedom of religion and trial by jury. The bill of rights said there could be no slavery in the Northwest Territory.

The Land Act of 1800 was passed to make it easier for people to buy land in the Northwest Territory. Some settlers did not have all of the money needed to buy land.

A More Perfect Union

Lesson 1 The Articles of Confederation, *Continued*

The Act made it possible for people to pay for the land over a period of four years.

Problems at Home and Abroad

The national government had problems paying its bills. By 1781, American dollars, called Continentals, had **depreciated,** or lost value. They were worth almost nothing. The War for Independence left the Continental Congress with a large debt. Congress did not have the power to raise taxes to pay these debts.

In 1781, Congress created a department of finance, led by Robert Morris. Morris made a plan to charge a 5 percent tax on goods brought in from other countries to help pay the debts. All 13 states had to approve Morris' plan for it to pass, but Rhode Island voted no. The plan did not pass.

The new government faced other problems. The British did not let Americans trade in the West Indies and other British areas. British soldiers were still in several important forts in the Great Lakes region.

The American government had problems with Spain, too. Spain controlled Florida and lands west of the Mississippi River. Spain wanted to stop America's growth in Spanish territory. In 1784, Spain closed the lower Mississippi River to American shipping. Western settlers could no longer use the river for trade.

It became clear that the Confederation was not able to deal with major problems. Americans came to agree that their new country needed a stronger government.

/ / / / / / / / / / / / Glue Foldable here / / / / / / / / / / / /

Check for Understanding

What kind of government was created by the Articles of Confederation?

_____

List three problems the Confederation government faced in its relations with other countries.

_____

_____

_____

? Analyzing

8. Why did Robert Morris's plan to pay the country's war debts fail?

_____

☑ Reading Check

9. Why did Spain close the lower Mississippi River to American shipping in 1784?

_____

FOLDABLES®

10. Glue a three-tab Foldable behind a two-tab Foldable along the anchor tabs to cover *Check for Understanding.* Write *Articles of Confederation* on the anchor tab. Label the two-tabs— *Strengths*, *Weaknesses*. Label the three-tabs— *Problems at Home*, *Problems with Britain*, and *Problems with Spain*. Write two words or phrases you remember about each.

networks

A More Perfect Union

Lesson 2 Forging a New Constitution

ESSENTIAL QUESTION

How do new ideas change the way people live?

GUIDING QUESTIONS

1. **What problems did the government face under the Articles of Confederation?**

2. **How did leaders reshape the government?**

3. **What compromises were reached in the new Constitution?**

Terms to Know

depression a period when economic activity slows and unemployment increases

manumission when a slaveholder frees an enslaved person

proportional having the proper size in relation to other objects or items

compromise an agreement between two or more sides in which each side gives up some of what it wants

When did it happen?

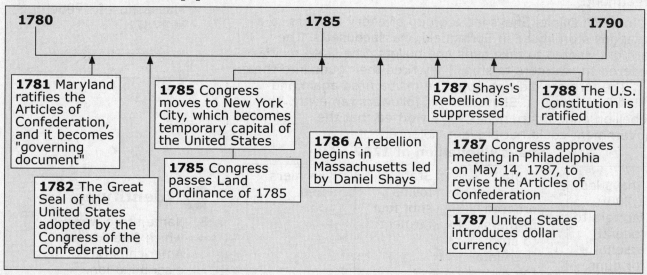

1780   1785   1790

1781 Maryland ratifies the Articles of Confederation, and it becomes "governing document"

1782 The Great Seal of the United States adopted by the Congress of the Confederation

1785 Congress moves to New York City, which becomes temporary capital of the United States

1785 Congress passes Land Ordinance of 1785

1786 A rebellion begins in Massachusetts led by Daniel Shays

1787 Shays's Rebellion is suppressed

1787 Congress approves meeting in Philadelphia on May 14, 1787, to revise the Articles of Confederation

1787 United States introduces dollar currency

1788 The U.S. Constitution is ratified

What do you know?

In the first column, answer the questions based on what you know before you study. After this lesson, complete the last column.

Now...		Later...
	What was Shays's Rebellion?	
	What was the Constitutional Convention?	
	What was the Great Compromise?	

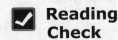

Lesson 2 Forging a New Constitution, *Continued*

The Need for Change

The Articles of Confederation created a weak national government. This made it difficult for the government to deal with the nation's problems. The United States went through a **depression** after the American Revolution. A depression is a period of time when business slows down and many people lose their jobs.

The government had little money. The money it had was used to pay debts, or money owed, to foreign countries. There was not enough money in the United States.

The slow economy meant farmers sold less of their goods. Some farmers could not pay taxes and other debts. As a result, state officials took over their land and put many of them in jail. Farmers grew angry over this treatment.

In 1787, Daniel Shays led a group of angry farmers to a weapons storehouse in Springfield, Massachusetts. The farmers wanted to take guns and bullets. The state militia ordered the farmers to stop. They fired their guns into the air. The farmers did not stop. The militia fired again and killed four farmers. Shays and his followers ran away. The rebellion ended. Americans were worried that the government could not prevent violence.

Shays's Rebellion of 1787

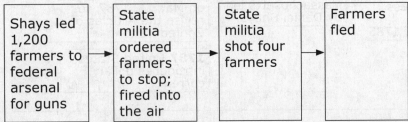

Shays led 1,200 farmers to federal arsenal for guns → State militia ordered farmers to stop; fired into the air → State militia shot four farmers → Farmers fled

The American Revolution was based on freedom. This caused some Americans to believe that slavery should be outlawed. Several northern states began passing laws to end slavery. Free African Americans faced discrimination even in states that did not have slavery. They were not allowed to go to many public places. Few states gave them the right to vote. The children of most free African Americans could not go to school with white children.

Some slaveholders freed their slaves after the American Revolution. Virginia passed a law that encouraged **manumission**, the freeing of individual enslaved persons. The number of free African Americans grew in that state. Even with these efforts, slavery was still a key part of life in Southern states. Southern plantations depended on

Mark the Text

1. Underline the meaning of *depression*.

Reading Check

2. Why did farmers in Massachusetts rebel in 1787?

_____

_____

Identifying

3. Name three ways in which free African Americans faced discrimination.

_____

_____

_____

Defining

4. What was *manumission*?

_____

_____

_____

98

A More Perfect Union

Lesson 2 Forging a New Constitution, *Continued*

slave labor. Many white Southerners were afraid that their economic system would die without slavery. The issue of slavery began to divide Northerners and Southerners.

The American Revolution and Slavery

North		South
American Revolution led to gradual end of slavery in the North.		Economy in South continued to depend heavily on slave labor.

The Constitutional Convention

The American Revolution had not created a united country. Some leaders liked strong, independent state governments. Other leaders wanted a strong national government. They wanted to change the Articles of Confederation. Two of these leaders were James Madison and Alexander Hamilton.

In September 1786, Hamilton called for a convention in Philadelphia to talk about trade issues. He also suggested that people at the convention should talk about how to change the Articles of Confederation.

The convention began in May 1787. George Washington and Benjamin Franklin were among those who attended. This helped people trust the convention's work. Trust was important because the convention's purpose was to create an entirely new constitution. The delegates chose George Washington to lead the meetings.

Edmund Randolph of Virginia surprised the delegates at the convention. He proposed a plan created by James Madison, called the Virginia Plan. The Virginia plan would set up a strong national government. It would create a government with three branches. There would be a two-house legislature, a chief executive chosen by the legislature, and a court system.

The plan also called for the number of members in both houses of the legislature to be **proportional**. The number of members would be based on each state's population. States with more people would have more representatives than states with fewer people.

Delegates from small states were against the Virginia Plan. They wanted all states to have equal representation. They supported the New Jersey Plan. Under the New Jersey plan, the legislature would be a one-house legislature. Each state would have one vote in the legislature.

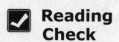 **Analyzing**

5. Why was it important for the American people to trust the work of the Constitutional Convention?

_____

_____

Identifying

6. How many representatives would each state have under the Virginia Plan?

_____

_____

☑ **Reading Check**

7. Why did New Jersey's delegates object to the Virginia Plan?

_____

_____

A More Perfect Union

Lesson 2 Forging a New Constitution, *Continued*

Agreeing to Compromise

The delegates agreed to create a new constitution based on the Virginia Plan. The delegates still needed to deal with the issue of representation.

Roger Sherman came up with an agreement called the Great Compromise. A **compromise** is an agreement between two or more sides. Each side gives up some of what it wants. The Great Compromise called for a two-house legislature. Each state would have two members in the Senate. The number of members in the House of Representatives would be based on the size of each state's population.

Southern states wanted to count enslaved people as part of their population. This would raise their population. It would give them more seats in Congress, and it would raise their taxes. Northern states did not want the South to count its enslaved people. The delegates agreed to the Three-Fifths Compromise. Each enslaved person would count as three-fifths of a free person. Northerners also agreed not to block the slave trade until 1808.

George Mason wanted more protection for citizens' rights. He asked for a bill of rights to part of the Constitution. Many delegates felt that the Constitution already protected people's rights.

On September 17, 1787, the delegates gathered to sign the new Constitution. The Constitution was then sent to the states for approval. The new Constitution would take effect when 9 of the 13 states approved it.

//////////////////// Glue Foldable here ////////////////////

> ## Check for Understanding
>
> **List the three branches of government created by the new Constitution.**
>
> _____   _____
>
> _____
>
> **What two things did the delegates disagree about that forced them to make compromises?**
>
> _____
>
> _____

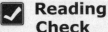

Reading Check

8. What compromises were made on the issue of slavery?

_____

_____

FOLDABLES®

9. Place a two-tab Foldable along the dotted line to cover *Check for Understanding.* Write the title *Constitutional Convention* on the anchor tab. Label the two tabs— *Agreed* and *Disagreed.* Recall and write about issues of agreement and disagreement. Use your notes to help answer the *Check for Understanding.*

networks

A More Perfect Union

Lesson 3 A New Plan of Government

ESSENTIAL QUESTION
How do governments change?

GUIDING QUESTIONS

1. **From where did the Framers of the Constitution borrow their ideas about government?**
2. **How does the Constitution limit the power of the government?**
3. **How was the Constitution ratified?**

Terms to Know

federalism sharing power between the federal and state governments

legislative branch lawmaking branch of government

executive branch branch of government headed by the president

Electoral College group chosen by each state to vote for president and vice president

judicial branch branch of government made up of courts that settle questions of law and disagreements

amendment a change, correction, or improvement added to a document

checks and balances system in which the branches of government can limit each others' powers

When did it happen?

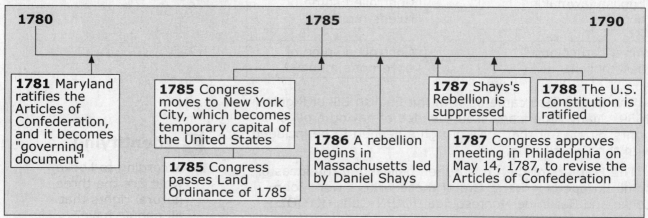

1780	1785	1790

1781 Maryland ratifies the Articles of Confederation, and it becomes "governing document"

1785 Congress moves to New York City, which becomes temporary capital of the United States

1785 Congress passes Land Ordinance of 1785

1786 A rebellion begins in Massachusetts led by Daniel Shays

1787 Shays's Rebellion is suppressed

1787 Congress approves meeting in Philadelphia on May 14, 1787, to revise the Articles of Confederation

1788 The U.S. Constitution is ratified

What do you know?

In the first column, answer the questions based on what you know before you study. After this lesson, complete the last column.

Now...		Later...
	What gave American delegates some of their ideas for the Constitution?	
	What are the three branches of government?	
	What does it mean to ratify the Constitution?	

101

A More Perfect Union

Lesson 3 A New Plan of Government, *Continued*

The Constitution's Sources

The delegates in Philadelphia created a new constitution. The delegates liked ideas from European political groups and writers. Some of these ideas are in the Constitution.

Even though Americans broke away from Britain, they still respected many British traditions. Traditions are cultural ideas and practices. Individual rights are part of the British system. The Framers of the Constitution felt it was important to have individual rights.

An English law, the Magna Carta, limited the power of the king or queen. He or she had to accept the laws of the lawmaking body. The lawmaking body paid for wars and the royal government. American colonies worked the same way. American lawmaking bodies controlled their colonies' funds. They also had some control over colonial governors.

Magna Carta as a Model

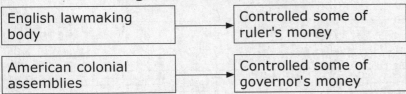

| English lawmaking body | → | Controlled some of ruler's money |
| American colonial assemblies | → | Controlled some of governor's money |

The British also came up with the English Bill of Rights in 1689. Many Americans liked the idea of having a bill of rights. Some felt that a bill of rights needed to be included with the Constitution.

The Framers of the Constitution believed in the ideas of some European writers. Two of these writers were John Locke and Baron de Montesquieu (MAHN•tuhs•KYOO).

The English writer, Locke, believed that all people have natural rights. These rights include the rights to life, liberty, and property. Locke wrote that government is based on an agreement, or contract. This agreement is between the people and the ruler. The Constitution would also be a contract. It would limit the government's power. This would help protect people's natural rights.

Montesquieu was a French writer. He believed that the government's power should be divided and balanced. This would make it difficult for one person or group to have too much power. The Framers of the American Constitution carefully described and divided the powers of government.

The Articles of Confederation had given most power to the states. The Constitution changed this. States had to

 Marking the Text

1. Underline the sources, or starting places, of many ideas in the Constitution.

 Identifying

2. According to Locke, what are the three natural rights that all people have?

_____

_____

A More Perfect Union

Lesson 3 A New Plan of Government, *Continued*

📝 Identifying

3. List three powers the U.S. Constitution gives to the states.

_____

_____

☑ Reading Check

4. What is federalism?

_____

_____

_____

📝 Marking the Text

5. Circle the three branches of government.

A$_c^b$ Defining

6. What is the Electoral College?

_____

_____

_____

give up some of their powers to the federal, or national, government. The Constitution was set up so federal and state governments share power. This is called **Federalism.**

The Constitution gave new powers to the federal government. It could tax, manage trade, control the supply of money, form an army, and declare war. The federal government could pass laws it decided were "necessary and proper."

The Constitution let states keep some important powers. The states could still control trade inside their borders. They had the power to set up local governments and schools. States also made laws about marriage and divorce.

The Constitution allows some powers to be shared by the federal and state governments. Both the federal and state governments may tax their citizens. Both governments may arrest and punish criminals.

The Constitution is the supreme, or highest, law of the land. Any disagreement between the federal government and the states was to be settled by the federal courts. They make decisions based on what the Constitution says.

Government Structure

The Framers of the Constitution divided the federal government into three branches. These are the legislative, executive, and judicial branches. The first three articles, or sections, of the Constitution explain the powers and tasks of these branches of the federal government.

Article I says the **legislative** (LEH•juhs•lay•tiv) **branch,** or lawmaking branch of the federal government is Congress. Congress has two parts: the Senate and the House of Representatives. Congress's powers include such tasks as deciding how much taxes will be, minting coins, and controlling trade.

Article II describes the **executive branch.** The president is in charge of this branch. The president's job is to carry out the nation's laws. A group called the **Electoral** (ee•lehk•TAWR•uhl) **College** elects the president and vice president. Its members are called electors. Electors are chosen by the voters of each state.

Article III describes the **judicial** (joo•DIH•shuhl) **branch**, or the court system. The Supreme Court is the top court in the nation. Congress sets up federal courts under the Supreme Court. Federal courts make decisions

A More Perfect Union

Lesson 3 A New Plan of Government, *Continued*

on cases that have to do with the Constitution, with federal laws, and with problems between states.

The Framers built in a system of **checks and balances.** Each branch of government has ways to check, or limit, the power of the others. This way, no branch can have too much control in the government.

Debate and Adoption

The Constitution could take effect after nine states ratified, or approved, it. People who supported the Constitution were called Federalists. James Madison, Alexander Hamilton, and John Jay were among the Federalists. They wrote a set of essays, called the Federalist Papers. The Federalist Papers explained and defended the Constitution.

People who did not like the new Constitution were called Anti-Federalists. They were afraid that a strong national government would take away freedoms. Anti-Federalists wanted local governments to have more power.

By June 21, 1788, the ninth state ratified the Constitution. That meant the new government could go into effect. New York and Virginia, the two largest states, still had not approved the Constitution.

People worried that the new government would not succeed if those states did not ratify the Constitution. Virginia ratified after it was promised that there would be a bill of rights **amendment.** The Bill of Rights was added in 1791. New York, North Carolina, and Rhode Island also ratified the Consitution.

Check for Understanding

Explain the principle of Federalism.

_____

_____

Why is the system of checks and balances important?

_____

_____

✓ **Reading Check**

7. How is power divided among the branches of government?

_____

_____

✓ **Reading Check**

8. Why was it important that the largest states ratify the constitution?

_____

_____

FOLDABLES

9. Place a three-tab Venn diagram Foldable along the line to cover Check for Understanding. Write *A New Plan for Government* on the anchor tab. Label the tabs—*Federal Government*, *Shared Powers*, and *State Government*. On both sides of the tabs, list facts about each to compare the federal and state governments. Use your notes to help answer the questions below the tabs.

The Constitution

Lesson 1 Principles of the Constitution

ESSENTIAL QUESTION

Why do people form governments?

GUIDING QUESTIONS

1. **What basic principles of government are set forth by the Constitution?**
2. **How is the Constitution able to change over time?**

Terms to Know

popular sovereignty belief that the government is subject to the people's will

limited government a government with limited powers strictly defined by law

enumerated power power belonging only to the federal government

reserved power power belonging only to the states

concurrent power power shared by the federal and state governments

separation of powers division of powers among the branches of government to make sure no branch has too much power

implied power power not specifically stated in the Constitution, but suggested in its language

Where in the world?

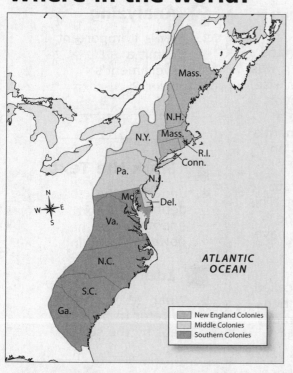

New England Colonies
Middle Colonies
Southern Colonies

Mass.
N.H.
N.Y.
Mass.
R.I.
Conn.
Pa.
N.J.
Md.
Del.
Va.
N.C.
S.C.
Ga.

ATLANTIC OCEAN

When did it happen?

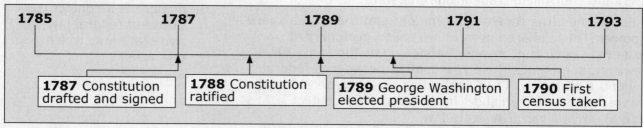

1785   1787   1789   1791   1793

1787 Constitution drafted and signed

1788 Constitution ratified

1789 George Washington elected president

1790 First census taken

The Constitution

Lesson 1 Principles of the Constitution, *Continued*

Our Constitution

The United States Constitution sets up our country's government. It is based on seven main ideas: (1) popular sovereignty, (2) a republican form of government, (3) limited government, (4) federalism, (5) separation of powers, (6) checks and balances, and (7) individual rights.

The Constitution begins with the words "We the People." Those words, "We the People," are the basic idea of our government—that the people have the right to govern themselves. The idea that the people control the powers of government is known as **popular sovereignty.**

The Constitution sets up a system of government in which the people rule by electing, or choosing, representatives. This is called a republic. The elected representatives make laws and carry out other government functions for all the people.

The people who wrote the Constitution knew the United States needed a strong government. They also knew it was important to limit the power of the government. Otherwise, the government might take away people's rights or favor certain groups. To avoid this, the Constitution sets up a **limited government,** which means that the government's powers are clearly defined. A limited government has only the powers that the people give it.

The Constitution also divides power between the state governments and the national, or federal, government. This system is called federalism. Under the Constitution, the federal government has some powers, and the states have other powers. Certain powers are shared by both the federal and the state governments.

Powers that belong to the federal government are called **enumerated powers.** These include coining—or printing—money, regulating interstate commerce and foreign trade, maintaining armed forces, and creating federal courts.

All powers not given to the federal government are kept by the states. These are called **reserved powers.** These include setting up schools, creating marriage and divorce laws, and controlling trade inside the state.

Sometimes, the federal government and the states share a power. These shared powers are called **concurrent powers.** Concurrent means "happening at the same time." However, sometimes there is a conflict between a federal law and a state law. The Constitution makes federal law the "supreme Law of the Land." In the event of a conflict, federal law will win over state law.

Explaining

1. What is the purpose of the U.S. Constitution?

_____

_____

Defining

2. What is a *republic*?

_____

Analyzing

3. Why is it important to limit a government's powers?

_____

_____

Mark the Text

4. Underline the definition of *enumerated powers.*

Identifying

5. What term is used to refer to powers kept by the states?

_____

Analyzing

6. If there is a conflict between federal law and state law, which one wins?

_____

The Constitution

Lesson 1 Principles of the Constitution, *Continued*

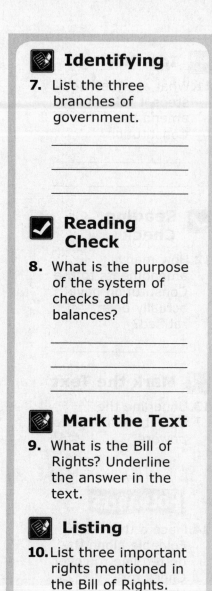

Identifying

7. List the three branches of government.

_____

_____

_____

Reading Check

8. What is the purpose of the system of checks and balances?

_____

_____

_____

Mark the Text

9. What is the Bill of Rights? Underline the answer in the text.

Listing

10. List three important rights mentioned in the Bill of Rights.

_____

_____

_____

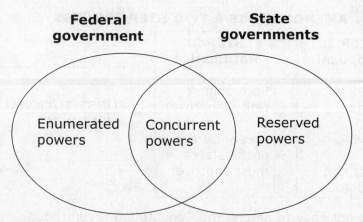

The Constitution also includes rules to make sure that no person or group gets too much power. One rule is called the **separation of powers.** This refers to the way the Constitution divides powers among three branches of government: legislative, executive, and judicial. Each branch has a different role.

Another constitutional protection comes from a system of **checks and balances.** This means each branch can prevent the other branches from becoming too powerful. Each branch is given certain powers that can limit the other branches.

The Constitution also protects **individual rights.** These rights are the basic freedoms that Americans enjoy every day. The Bill of Rights, which is the first 10 amendments to the Constitution, lists many of these important freedoms. These include freedom of religion, freedom of speech, the right to a speedy and public trial, and freedom from "cruel and unusual" punishment.

Amending the Constitution

The Constitution can be amended, or changed. One part of the Constitution describes the process for amending the document. As a result, the Constitution can be updated as time passes and society changes.

It takes two steps to amend the Constitution. In the first step, Congress or the states—either one—can propose, or suggest, an amendment. In the second step, the states ratify, or approve, the amendment. Three-fourths of the states must approve the amendment in order for it to become part of the Constitution.

The Constitution

Lesson 1 Principles of the Constitution, *Continued*

AMENDMENT IS A TWO-STEP PROCESS

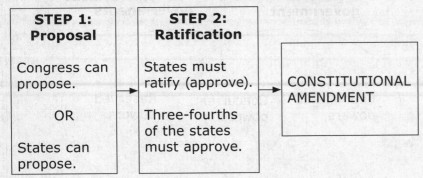

STEP 1: Proposal	STEP 2: Ratification	
Congress can propose. OR States can propose.	States must ratify (approve). Three-fourths of the states must approve.	CONSTITUTIONAL AMENDMENT

It is not easy to amend the Constitution. Even though people have proposed hundreds of amendments, only 27 have been ratified.

Among those 27, there have been many important amendments. Some of them have given more people the right to vote. For example, the Fifteenth Amendment said that African American men can vote. The Nineteenth Amendment gave women the right to vote. The Twenty-Sixth Amendment changed the voting age to 18.

The Constitution can also change in another way. Its words can be interpreted, or understood, in different ways. For example, one section says that Congress may "make all Laws which shall be necessary and proper" to carry out its duties. Another allows Congress to "regulate Commerce with foreign Nations, and among the several States." These clauses give Congress **implied powers**—powers that are suggested even though they are not stated clearly.

/ / / / / / / / / / / / Glue Foldable here / / / / / / / / / / / / /

Check for Understanding

What words would you use to describe the main ideas, or principles, of the Constitution?

_____

_____

List the two ways that the Constitution can be changed. How many changes have been added to the Constitution?

_____

_____

Identifying

11. What are the two steps it takes to amend the Constitution?

_____

_____

Reading Check

12. How many amendments to the Constitution have actually been ratified?

_____

Mark the Text

13. Underline the definition of *implied powers*.

FOLDABLES

14. Place a three-tab Foldable along the dotted line to cover Check for Understanding. Write the title *The Constitution* on the anchor tab. Label the three tabs *Main Ideas*, *Making Changes*, and *Bill of Rights*. Write key words or phrases that you remember about each.

networks

The Constitution

Lesson 2 Government and the People

ESSENTIAL QUESTION

How do new ideas change the way people live?

GUIDING QUESTIONS

1. **What are the three branches of government?**
2. **What are the rights and elements of participation of American citizens?**

Terms to Know

judicial review allows the Supreme Court to look at the actions of the other two branches and decide if the Constitution allows those actions

due process rules and processes the government must follow before it takes a person's life, liberty, or property

equal protection the right of all people to be treated equally under the law

naturalization the process of becoming a citizen of another country

Where in the world?

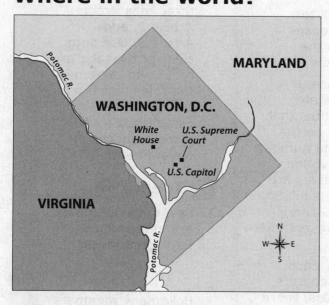

WASHINGTON, D.C.

White House

U.S. Supreme Court

U.S. Capitol

MARYLAND

VIRGINIA

Potomac R.

When did it happen?

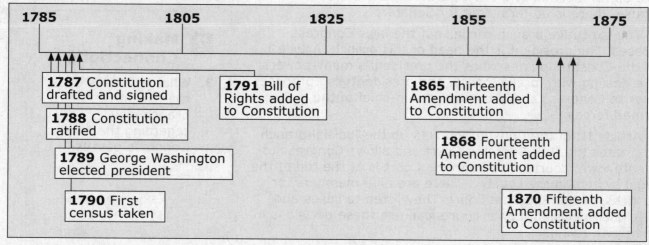

1785   1805   1825   1855   1875

1787 Constitution drafted and signed

1788 Constitution ratified

1789 George Washington elected president

1790 First census taken

1791 Bill of Rights added to Constitution

1865 Thirteenth Amendment added to Constitution

1868 Fourteenth Amendment added to Constitution

1870 Fifteenth Amendment added to Constitution

109

The Constitution

Lesson 2 Government and the People, Continued

The Federal Government

The federal government is divided into three branches: legislative, executive, and judicial. This ensures a separation of powers.

/ / / / / / / / / / / Glue Foldable here / / / / / / / / / / / /

The legislative branch is called Congress. Article I of the Constitution describes what Congress does. Congress makes laws for the nation. These laws can create taxes, permit government spending, and set up government programs. Congress can also declare war.

Congress is made up of two houses: the House of Representatives and the Senate. In order for a bill to become a law, most of the members from both houses must agree on the bill. After that, the bill goes to the president. If the president signs it, the bill becomes a law.

The House of Representatives is the larger house of Congress. The number of representatives that a state sends to the House is based on its population. States that have more people have more representatives. When the population of a state goes up or down, so does the number of its representatives. Today, the House has 435 voting members and 6 nonvoting delegates. Representatives are elected for a term of two years. Every two years, all 435 House seats are up for election at the same time. There are no limits on how many two-year terms a representative can serve.

The Senate has fewer members—100 senators. Each state is represented equally with two senators. Senators are elected for a term of six years. Every two years, there are elections for the Senate. Only one-third of the senators are up for election at a time. As with members of the House, there is no term limit for Senators.

The executive branch carries out the laws Congress passes. The president is the head of this branch. Article II of the Constitution describes the president's many powers, like dealing with foreign policy. The president also proposes laws to Congress and is commander-in-chief of the armed forces.

Article III of the Constitution sets up the judicial branch. It creates the U.S. Supreme Court and allows Congress to create lower courts. The Supreme Court is at the top of the legal system in the country. There are nine members, or justices, of the Supreme Court. They listen to cases and give their decision. Lower courts can use these decisions in their own rulings.

FOLDABLES

Explaining

1. Place a three-tab Foldable along the dotted line to cover the text that begins with "The legislative branch is called Congress." Label the three tabs *Article I*, *Article 2*, and *Article 3*. Use both sides of the tabs to recall and explain the roles that the three Articles established for the three branches of government.

Identifying

2. How many members are in the House of Representatives?

_____

How many members are in the Senate?

_____

Making Connections

3. What two roles does the executive branch play regarding the laws Congress passes?

_____

_____

110

The Constitution

Lesson 2 Government and the People, *Continued*

 Mark the Text

4. Underline the definition of *judicial review*.

✓ **Reading Check**

5. What parts of the Constitution establish the three branches of our federal government?

_____

_____

_____

Defining

6. What is *due process*?

_____

_____

_____

Identifying

7. What right guarantees that we must be treated the same as everyone else under the law?

_____

The Supreme Court has an important power called **judicial review.** Judicial review allows the Supreme Court to look at the actions of the other two branches and decide if those actions follow the rules of the Constitution. The justices are chosen by the president and approved by Congress.

Constitution, Article I	Constitution, Article II	Constitution, Article III
Defines: Legislative branch	**Defines:** Executive branch	**Defines:** Judicial branch
Headed by: Congress	**Headed by:** The president	**Headed by:** The Supreme Court
Made up of: * House of Representatives * The Senate	**Made up of:** * Vice president and cabinet *Government departments	**Made up of:** * The federal court system * Other lower courts

What It Means to Be a Citizen

As U.S. citizens, our rights fall into three main categories:

• The right to be protected from unfair government actions

• The right to be treated equally under the law

• The right to enjoy basic freedoms

Due process is a right guaranteed by the Fifth Amendment. The amendment states that no one shall "be deprived of life, liberty, or property, without due process of law." This means that the government must follow certain rules before it takes a right or freedom away from a citizen. For example, a person accused of a crime has the right to a trial before his freedom is taken away.

Equal protection is a right guaranteed by the Fourteenth Amendment. Equal protection means that the law must treat all people in the same way—no matter what race, religion, or political group they belong to.

The First Amendment describes many of our basic freedoms. These include freedom of speech, freedom of the press, and freedom of assembly. These freedoms allow us to share ideas, which is necessary in a free society.

111

Copyright by The McGraw-Hill Companies.

netw✷rks

The Constitution

Lesson 2 Government and the People, *Continued*

Our rights and freedoms also have some limits. For example, we cannot exercise our rights or freedoms if it hurts others or takes away their rights or freedoms.

A citizen is a person who owes loyalty to a country and receives its protection. There are several ways to become an American citizen. One way is to be born on American soil. Another is to have a parent who is a citizen. People born in other countries can become citizens by following a process called **naturalization.**

Citizenship comes with duties and responsibilities. A duty is something you must do. U.S. citizens must pay taxes, follow laws, and sit on a jury when called. A responsibility is something you should do even though you do not have to. If citizens do not take care of their responsibilities, it lowers the quality of their government. Voting is a citizen's most important responsibility.

A CITIZEN'S	
DUTIES	**RESPONSIBILITIES**
• Obey the law • Pay taxes • Sit on a jury when called	• Vote • Take part in government • Respect the rights of others

/ / / / / / / / / / / / /Glue Foldable here/ / / / / / / / / / / / /

Check for Understanding
List three duties and responsibilities of a citizen.

1. _____

2. _____

3. _____

What do you not have the right to do?

_____

_____

🔍 Examining Details

8. List three ways a person can become a U.S. citizen.

_____

_____

_____

✓ Reading Check

9. What is the difference between a duty and a responsibility? Why is it important for a citizen to do both?

_____

_____

_____

_____

FOLDABLES®

10. Place a two-tab Foldable along the dotted line to cover Check for Understanding. Label the anchor tab *Citizens*, and label the two tabs *must* and *should*. List words and phrases about the duties and responsibilities of citizens.

The Federalist Era

Lesson 1 The First President

ESSENTIAL QUESTION
What are the characteristics of a leader?

GUIDING QUESTIONS
1. **What decisions did Washington and the new Congress have to make about the new government?**
2. **How did the economy develop under the guidance of Alexander Hamilton?**

Terms to Know
precedent something done or said that becomes an example for others to follow
cabinet a group of advisers to a president
bond certificate that promises to repay borrowed money in the future—plus an additional amount of money, called interest

Where in the world?

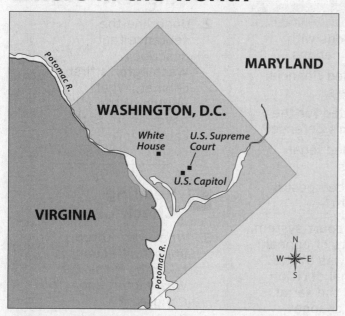

When did it happen?

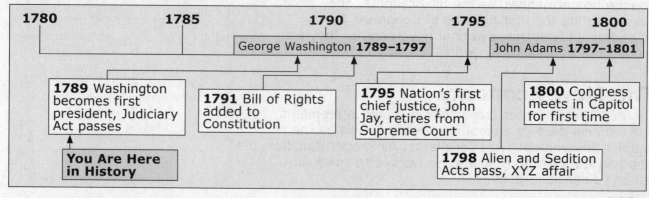

1780   1785   1790   1795   1800

George Washington **1789–1797**   John Adams **1797–1801**

1789 Washington becomes first president, Judiciary Act passes

1791 Bill of Rights added to Constitution

1795 Nation's first chief justice, John Jay, retires from Supreme Court

1800 Congress meets in Capitol for first time

You Are Here in History

1798 Alien and Sedition Acts pass, XYZ affair

113

networks

Lesson 1 The First President, *Continued*

Washington Takes Office

George Washington was the first president of the United States. He knew that the **precedents**, or traditions, he started would be important. They would shape the future of the country and the government. With Congress, Washington set up departments within the executive branch. Washington and Congress also set up the court system. Congress added the Bill of Rights to the Constitution.

The executive branch began with three departments and two offices. These advisors were called the **cabinet**:

Department or Office	Head	Function
State Department	Thomas Jefferson	Relations with other nations
Department of the Treasury	Alexander Hamilton	Handled financial matters
Department of War	Henry Knox	Provided for the nation's defense
Attorney General	Edmund Randolph	Handled legal affairs
Postmaster General	Benjamin Franklin	Managed postal system

The Judiciary Act of 1789 created a federal court system. It had district courts at the lowest level. Courts of appeal were at the middle level. The Supreme Court was at the top of the court system. It would make the final decision on many issues. State courts and laws stayed the same. However, the federal courts had the power to change state decisions.

The first ten amendments, or changes, to the Constitution are known as the Bill of Rights. They were passed during the first meeting of Congress. The amendments limit the powers of government. They also protect the rights of the people.

The New Economy

The new United States faced serious financial problems. The national debt—the amount of money owed by the nation's government—was very large. Alexander Hamilton was secretary of the treasury. He worked to solve the nation's financial problems.

? Critical Thinking

1. Why do you think it was important to set up a federal court system?

_____

_____

✎ Marking the Text

2. Underline the sentence that describes Washington's first cabinet. What branch of the government is the cabinet in?

_____

✓ Reading Check

3. What were three important actions taken by President Washington and Congress?

_____

_____

networks

The Federalist Era

Lesson 1 The First President, *Continued*

? Analyzing

4. Why do you think Alexander Hamilton wanted to pay back the bonds from the confederation government?

_____

_____

_____

✎ Describing

5. Why did some people oppose Hamilton's plan to pay off government bonds?

_____

_____

_____

✓ Reading Check

6. Why did Hamilton support locating the United States capital in the South?

_____

_____

During the Revolutionary War, the confederation government had borrowed a large amount of money. It had issued **bonds**. These are certificates promising to pay back money in a certain length of time. Hamilton argued that the United States should pay back money borrowed from other countries and from American citizens. Hamilton believed that the national government should also pay the war debts of the states.

Some people did not like Hamilton's plan. Many people who bought bonds were worried that they would never be paid back. To get some money for their bonds, many people sold their bonds to speculators for less than the bonds were worth. Speculators hoped to make money later if the government finally paid back the bonds. The original bondholders saw that speculators would get rich and the bondholders would get nothing. Southern states also complained about the plan to pay state war debts. They had built up much less debt than the Northern states. They argued that the plan would make them pay more than their share.

Hamilton worked out a deal with Southern leaders. If they voted for his plan, he would support putting the new capital in the South. A new district called Washington, D.C., would be created between Virginia and Maryland.

To help build a strong national economy, Hamilton asked Congress to start a national bank. It would issue a single type of money for use in all states. Some people were against the idea, but Washington agreed with Hamilton. A national bank called the Bank of the United States was started.

Hamilton also proposed a tariff that would help protect American products. A tariff is a tax on goods bought from foreign countries. It makes products from other nations more expensive than those made at home. This tariff would help American companies compete against foreign companies.

Hamilton's Actions
• Paid back bonds
• Created Bank of the United States
• Introduced a protective tariff to help U.S. companies
• Supported putting the nation's capital in the South

The Federalist Era

Lesson 1 The First President, *Continued*

Check for Understanding

List the 3 departments that were part of Washington's executive branch.

1. _____

2. _____

3. _____

List 4 important actions taken by Alexander Hamilton.

1. _____

2. _____

3. _____

4. _____

FOLDABLES

7. Place a two-tab Foldable along the dotted line to cover Check for Understanding. Write the title *George Washington* on the top tab and *Alexander Hamilton* on the bottom. On both sides of the tabs, list three things you remember about *both* as they helped form the new nation. Use the Foldable to help answer Check for Understanding.

networks

The Federalist Era

Lesson 2 Early Challenges

ESSENTIAL QUESTION

Why does conflict develop?

GUIDING QUESTIONS

1. What challenges on the frontier did the new government face?

2. Why did Washington want to remain neutral in foreign conflicts?

Term to Know

impressment seizing people against their will and forcing them to serve in the military or other public service

Where in the world?

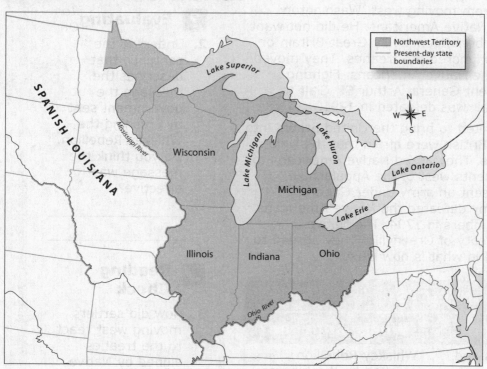

Northwest Territory
— Present-day state boundaries

SPANISH LOUISIANA

Lake Superior

Mississippi River

Wisconsin

Lake Michigan

Lake Huron

Michigan

Lake Ontario

Lake Erie

Illinois

Indiana

Ohio

Ohio River

When did it happen?

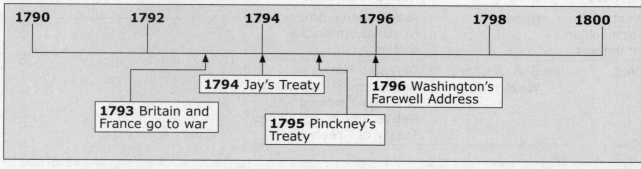

1790   1792   1794   1796   1798   1800

1794 Jay's Treaty

1796 Washington's Farewell Address

1793 Britain and France go to war

1795 Pinckney's Treaty

The Federalist Era

Lesson 2 Early Challenges, *Continued*

Trouble in the New Nation

The new government faced many problems. In western Pennsylvania farmers opposed a tax on whiskey. In 1794, an armed mob attacked tax collectors. They burned down buildings. This armed protest was called the Whiskey Rebellion. It worried government leaders. President Washington and his advisers decided to crush the protest using the army. This sent a message to people: the government would use force when necessary to maintain, or keep, order.

In the Northwest Territory, Native Americans tried to stop American settlers from moving west. Washington signed treaties with the Native Americans. He did not want the Native Americans to be influenced by Great Britain or Spain. American settlers ignored the treaties. They moved into lands promised to the Native Americans. Fighting broke out. Washington sent General Arthur St. Clair to restore order, but St. Clair was defeated in 1791.

Britain and France wanted to bring the United States into their own conflicts. The British were afraid that the United States would help France. They asked Native Americans to attack American settlements west of the Appalachian Mountains. Washington sent an army under General Anthony Wayne. The army defeated the Native Americans at the Battle of Fallen Timbers in 1794. The Native Americans signed the Treaty of Greenville. They agreed to give up most of the land in what is now Ohio.

CONFLICTS		
Where?	**Who?**	**What happened?**
Western Pennsylvania	Farmers and others	Whiskey Rebellion crushed by Washington
Northwest Territory	Gen. Arthur St. Clair	U.S. troops defeated by Native Americans
West of Appalachian mountains	British	Asked Native Americans to attack American settlers
Ohio	Gen. Anthony Wayne	Defeated Native Americans at the Battle of Fallen Timbers; Native Americans signed Treaty of Greenville

🔁 Identifying

1. What three European countries were involved in American affairs?

_____

_____

_____

❓ Evaluating

2. Underline the sentence that describes the message the government sent by crushing the Whiskey Rebellion. Do you think the message was effective?

_____

_____

☑ Reading Check

3. How did settlers moving west react to the treaties signed by Native Americans?

_____

_____

The Federalist Era

Lesson 2 Early Challenges, *Continued*

Vocabulary

4. What was *impressment*?

_____

_____

Determining Cause and Effect

5. What was the result of Pinckney's Treaty?

_____

_____

Reading Check

6. What did the Proclamation of Neutrality do?

_____

_____

Problems with Europe

Britain and France went to war in 1793. Some Americans sided with France and others supported Britain. Washington hoped that the United States could stay neutral. Neutral means not taking sides in a conflict.

The French tried to get American volunteers to attack British ships. In response, President Washington issued a Proclamation of Neutrality. It declared that American citizens could not fight in the war. It also stopped French and British warships from using American ports. The British captured American ships that traded with the French. They forced the American crews into the British navy. This practice was called **impressment**. It angered the Americans.

Washington sent John Jay to work out a peaceful solution with Britain. Jay proposed a treaty. In Jay's Treaty, the British would agree to leave American soil. But the treaty did not deal with the problems of impressment. It also did not deal with the British interfering with American trade. Jay's Treaty was unpopular, but the Senate approved it.

Spanish leaders feared that the United States and Great Britain would work together against them in North America. Thomas Pinckney went to Spain to settle the differences between the United States and Spain. In 1795 he proposed a treaty that said Americans could travel on the Mississippi River. Pinckney's Treaty also gave Americans the right to trade at New Orleans.

Jay's Treaty	Pinckney's Treaty
• British agreed to leave American soil	• Between Spain and the U.S.
• Did not deal with impressment	• Gave Americans right to travel the Mississippi River
• Did not deal with British interfering with American trade	• Gave Americans right to trade at New Orleans
• Unpopular	

Washington decided to retire and not run for a third term as president. In his last speech, he warned the country not to get involved in foreign problems. He also warned against creating political parties.

119

The Federalist Era

Lesson 2 Early Challenges, *Continued*

/ / / / / / / / / / / Glue Foldable here / / / / / / / / / / / / /

Check for Understanding

List four challenges faced by the new government within the United States.

1. _____

2. _____

3. _____

4 _____

List the two treaties that the United States signed with foreign countries to resolve conflicts.

1. _____

2. _____

FOLDABLES®

7. Place a two-tab Foldable along the dotted line to cover Check for Understanding. Write the title *Challenges* on the anchor tab. Label the tabs—*Conflicts in U.S.* and *Foreign Conflicts*. Use both sides of the tabs to record what you recall about each and write facts about who was involved and what happened. Use the Foldable to help answer Check for Understanding.

The Federalist Era

Lesson 3 The First Political Parties

ESSENTIAL QUESTION

How do governments change?

GUIDING QUESTIONS

1. *How did different opinions lead to the first political parties?*
2. *What important events occurred during the presidency of John Adams?*

Terms to Know

partisan firmly favoring one party or faction

caucus a meeting of members of a political party to choose candidates for upcoming elections

alien a person living in a country who is not a citizen of that country

sedition activities aimed at weakening the established government by inciting resistance or rebellion to authority

nullify to legally overturn

states' rights the idea that states should have all powers that the Constitution does not give to the federal government or forbid to the states

When did it happen?

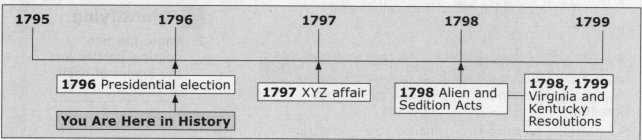

1795	1796	1797	1798	1799

1796 Presidential election

You Are Here in History

1797 XYZ affair

1798 Alien and Sedition Acts

1798, 1799 Virginia and Kentucky Resolutions

What do you know?

In the first column, answer the questions based on what you know before you study. After this lesson, complete the last column.

Now...		Later...
	How did people feel about political parties when Washington was president?	
	What were the first two political parties in America?	
	Did President John Adams and Vice President Thomas Jefferson have similar views about government?	
	Why were Americans suspicious of aliens during this period?	
	Why did some states believe they had the power to overturn federal laws?	

Lesson 3 The First Political Parties, *Continued*

Opposing Parties

President Washington warned against political parties. He was afraid that political parties would divide the nation. Others thought that it was natural for people to disagree about issues. By 1796, Americans were beginning to split into two different groups.

In Washington's cabinet, Alexander Hamilton and Thomas Jefferson often disagreed. They disagreed about economic policy and foreign relations. They disagreed about how much power the federal government should have. They also disagreed on the rules of the Constitution. Even Washington was **partisan**—favoring one side of an issue. Washington usually supported Hamilton's positions. These disagreements caused both Hamilton and Jefferson to resign from, or leave, the cabinet. The two political parties that formed were called Federalists and Republicans.

Federalists	Republicans
Headed by Alexander Hamilton	Headed by Thomas Jefferson
Supported government by representatives	Feared strong central government controlled by only a few people
Believed government had broad powers implied by the Constitution	Believed government only had powers specifically stated in the Constitution

In 1796, there was a presidential election. Before the election, the two parties held meetings called **caucuses.** At the caucuses, members of Congress and other leaders chose their parties' candidates for office.

The Federalists chose John Adams for president. The Republicans chose Thomas Jefferson. This was the first time candidates identified themselves as members of political parties.

Adams received 71 electoral votes to win the election. Jefferson finished second with 68 votes. Under the Constitution at that time, the person with the second-highest number of electoral votes became vice president. Jefferson became the new vice president. The new government in 1797 had a Federalist president and a Republican vice president.

122

? Defending

1. Underline the sentences that describe two opinions about political parties. Which opinion do you agree with? Why?

_____

_____

_____

✍ Identifying

2. Name the two political parties and the leader of each.

_____

_____

✓ Reading Check

3. What was different about the election of 1796?

_____

_____

The Federalist Era

Lesson 3 The First Political Parties, *Continued*

FOLDABLES

📝 Describing

4. Place a four-tab Foldable along the dotted line to cover the text beneath the title *John Adams as President*. Write the title *John Adams* on the anchor tab. Label the four tabs—*Who*, *What*, *When*, and *Where*. On both sides of the tabs, write what you recall about President John Adams and how he handled the capture of American ships by the French.

📝 Identifying

5. Who were the people that President Adams referred to as X, Y, and Z?

_____

_____

✅ Reading Check

6. What was important about the Virginia and Kentucky Resolutions of 1798 and 1799?

_____

_____

John Adams as President

/ / / / / / / / / / Glue Foldable here / / / / / / / / / /

When Adams became president, France and the United States could still not agree. The French thought that Jay's Treaty allowed Americans to help the British. The French captured American ships that carried goods to Britain.

In 1797, Adams sent a team to Paris to try to end the disagreement. The French officials refused to meet with the Americans. Instead, they sent three agents. They demanded a bribe from America and a loan for France. Adams was angry at the French actions. He called the French agents "X, Y, and Z." Adams urged Congress to prepare for war. This was called the XYZ affair.

XYZ Affair

- French captured American ships carrying goods to Britain

- Adams sent a team to France

- Three French agents, known as X, Y, and Z, tried to get a bribe and a loan from Americans

---

People were angry with France. Americans became more suspicious of aliens. **Aliens** are immigrants living in a country who are not citizens of that country. Federalists passed laws to protect the nation's security. In 1798, they passed a group of laws known as the Alien and Sedition Acts. **Sedition** means activities that weaken the government. The Alien Act allowed the president to put aliens in prison. He could also send them out of the country if he thought they were dangerous. Later, France and the United States signed a treaty which stopped French attacks on American ships.

The Virginia and Kentucky Resolutions were passed in 1798 and 1799. They claimed that the Alien and Sedition Acts did not follow the rules of the Constitution. They also said the states should not put them into action. The Kentucky Resolutions said that states might **nullify**, or legally overturn, federal laws if they thought the laws went against the Constitution.

The resolutions supported the idea of **states' rights**. This idea says that the powers of the federal government should be limited. Its powers should be only those clearly given to it in the Constitution. The states should have all other powers. The issue of states' rights would be important in the future.

Lesson 3 The First Political Parties, Continued

Alien and Sedition Acts

↓

Inspired

↓

Virginia and Kentucky Resolutions

/ / / / / / / / / / / Glue Foldable here / / / / / / / / / /

Check for Understanding

List the president and vice president elected in 1796 and the political parties they belonged to.

1. _____

2. _____

List the two states that passed resolutions opposing the Alien and Sedition Acts.

1. _____

2. _____

FOLDABLES

7. Place a one-tab Foldable along the dotted line to cover Check for Understanding. Write the title *Alien and Sedition Acts* in the middle of the Foldable tab. Create a memory map by drawing arrows from the title. List three words or phrases that you recall about the Alien and Sedition Acts. Use the Foldable to help answer Check for Understanding.

The Jefferson Era

Lesson 1 A New Party in Power

ESSENTIAL QUESTION
How do governments change?

GUIDING QUESTIONS
1. **What did the election of 1800 show about the nature of politics?**
2. **What did Jefferson want to accomplish during his presidency?**

Terms to Know
customs duty tax collected on imported goods
jurisdiction the power or right to interpret and apply a law

Where in the world?

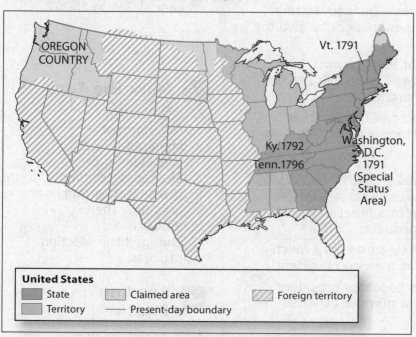

United States
- State
- Territory
- Claimed area
- Present-day boundary
- Foreign territory

OREGON COUNTRY

Vt. 1791

Ky. 1792

Tenn. 1796

Washington, D.C. 1791 (Special Status Area)

When did it happen?

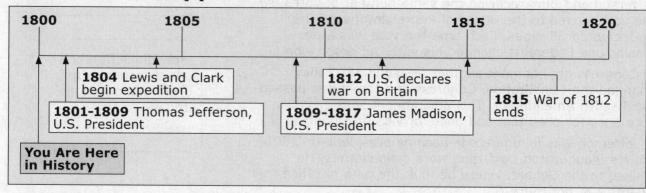

1800   **1805**   **1810**   **1815**   **1820**

1804 Lewis and Clark begin expedition

1801-1809 Thomas Jefferson, U.S. President

1812 U.S. declares war on Britain

1809-1817 James Madison, U.S. President

1815 War of 1812 ends

You Are Here in History

The Jefferson Era

Lesson 1 A New Party in Power, *Continued*

The Election of 1800

These were the choices in the election of 1800:

Party	President	Vice President
Federalists	John Adams	Charles Pinckney
Republicans	Thomas Jefferson	Aaron Burr

In 1800, presidential campaigns were not like they are today. The candidates did not travel around the country to ask people to vote for them. Instead, letters were sent to important people and newspapers to give the candidates' views.

Still, in 1800, the two sides fought hard to win. Federalists said Jefferson was "godless." Republicans said Federalists would bring back a monarchy.

In the United States, it is the Electoral College that elects the president. Today, the system is much like it was in 1800.

The Election Process in 1800
1. People choose electors. The electors meet in the Electoral College to elect the president.
2. Electors vote for two people. They do not say which vote is for president and which is for vice president.
3. The person with the most votes becomes president. The person with the next highest number of votes becomes vice president.
4. If there is a tie, the House of Representatives votes.

When the electors voted in 1800, there was a tie. Jefferson and Burr received the same number of votes, so the vote moved to the House of Representatives. The House voted 35 times. Each time the vote was a tie. Finally, one Federalist changed his vote. Jefferson won.

Congress did not want another tie, so in 1803 they changed the Constitution. Congress and the states passed the Twelfth Amendment. This amendment says electors vote once for president and once for vice president.

Jefferson was inaugurated—became president—in 1801. For his inauguraton, Jefferson wore plain clothes. He walked to the Senate, where he took the oath of office. Adams was not there.

 Listing

1. Who were the presidential candidates in 1800?

_____

_____

Who were the vice presidential candidates in 1800?

_____

_____

 Mark the Text

2. The Twelfth Amendment changed how the president was elected. Underline the sentence that tells how the amendment changed the election process.

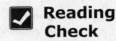 **Reading Check**

3. How did political campaigns in 1800 differ from today?

_____

_____

How did Jefferson's inauguration differ from inaugurations today?

_____

_____

126

networks

The Jefferson Era

Lesson 1 A New Party in Power, *Continued*

 Mark the Text

4. Circle four changes Jefferson made to the federal government.

Identifying

5. Name two ways the government collected money when Jefferson was president.

_____

_____

? **Critical Thinking**

6. Who controlled the courts during Jefferson's presidency?

_____

How did they gain control?

_____

_____

✓ **Reading Check**

7. Why was the *Marbury* v. *Madison* ruling important?

_____

_____

_____

Jefferson also made a speech called an inaugural address. In his speech, Jefferson said that he wanted to limit the power and size of the federal government. He thought states should have more power. He thought states could protect freedom better than a large federal government. He also wanted to cut government spending.

Jefferson as President

Jefferson chose to work with people who agreed with his ideas. Together, they made many changes to the federal government. These included:

• lowering the national debt.

• cutting military spending.

• cutting the number of government workers to only a few hundred.

• getting rid of most federal taxes.

The government still needed money, though. Jefferson's government got money from two sources:

• **customs duties** (taxes on imported goods).

• selling land in the West.

Before Jefferson became President, Congress passed a law called the Judiciary Act of 1801. This act set up a system of courts. President Adams moved fast. He appointed, or chose, hundreds of people to be judges in these new courts. Adams used these appointments to keep Jefferson from choosing judges. In this way, Adams made sure the Federalists controlled the courts.

There was a problem, though. These people could not become judges until they got special papers. Some of the judges Adams appointed did not receive their papers before Jefferson became president. Jefferson told Secretary of State James Madison not to deliver them.

One judge who did not receive his papers was William Marbury. Marbury wanted to get his papers. He took his case to the Supreme Court. The court decided it did not have the **jurisdiction**—the legal power—to force Madison to deliver the papers. This case was called *Marbury* v. *Madison*.

Marbury v. *Madison* was a very important case. It set up the three principles of judicial review. Principles are basic ideas.

127

The Jefferson Era

Lesson 1 A New Party in Power, *Continued*

The head of the Supreme Court was Chief Justice John Marshall. Marshall wrote the court's opinion. In it he said:

1. The Constitution is the supreme, or highest, law in the country.

2. If the Constitution says one thing and another law says something else, people have to follow the Constitution.

3. The judicial branch (courts) can say laws are unconstitutional.

Marbury v. *Madison* made the Supreme Court more powerful. Chief Justice Marshall made the Supreme Court stronger in other cases, too. This chart shows three of these cases. It also shows the effect of each case.

Case	Effect
McCulloch v. *Maryland*	Congress can do more than the Constitution specifically says it can do. States cannot tax the federal government.
Gibbons v. *Ogden*	Federal law takes priority over state law when more than one state is involved.
Worcester v. *Georgia*	States cannot make rules about Native Americans. Only the federal government can.

With these decisions, Chief Justice Marshall also strengthened the federal government and weakened the states.

/ / / / / / / / / / / Glue Foldable here / / / / / / / / / / /

Check for Understanding

State two facts about the election of 1800.

1. _____

2. _____

List two changes Jefferson made to the federal government during his presidency.

1. _____

2. _____

Identifying

8. What three powers did states lose in the three cases listed in the chart?

_____

_____

_____

Drawing Conclusions

9. Do you think Jefferson was pleased with the decisions in these three cases? Why?

_____

_____

FOLDABLES®

10. Place a three-tab Venn diagram Foldable along the dotted line to cover the Check for Understanding. Write *Election of 1800* on the anchor tab. Label the tabs *Federalist Candidate*, *Both*, and *Republican Candidate*. List facts about each to compare the candidates and the election's outcome. Use the Foldable to help answer Check for Understanding.

The Jefferson Era

Lesson 2 The Louisiana Purchase

ESSENTIAL QUESTION

How does geography influence the way people live?

GUIDING QUESTIONS

1. **How did Spain and France play a role in Americans moving west?**

2. **How did the Louisiana Purchase open an area of settlement?**

Term to Know

secede break away from a country or group

Where in the world?

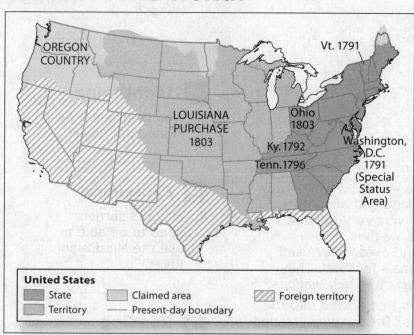

OREGON COUNTRY

Vt. 1791

LOUISIANA PURCHASE 1803

Ohio 1803

Ky. 1792

Tenn. 1796

Washington, D.C. 1791 (Special Status Area)

United States

■ State   ■ Claimed area   ▨ Foreign territory

■ Territory   — Present-day boundary

When did it happen?

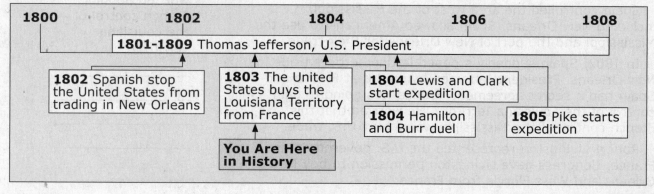

1800   1802   1804   1806   1808

1801–1809 Thomas Jefferson, U.S. President

1802 Spanish stop the United States from trading in New Orleans

1803 The United States buys the Louisiana Territory from France

1804 Lewis and Clark start expedition

1804 Hamilton and Burr duel

1805 Pike starts expedition

You Are Here in History

129

The Jefferson Era

Lesson 2 The Louisiana Purchase, *Continued*

Westward, Ho!

The Mississippi River was the western boundary of the United States in 1800. The area west of the river was called the Louisiana Territory. The Louisiana Territory went west to the Rocky Mountains. It went south to New Orleans. It did not have a clear border to the north.

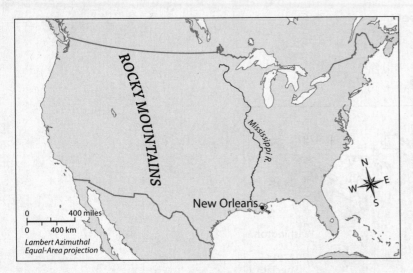

New Orleans

0   400 miles
0   400 km
*Lambert Azimuthal
Equal-Area projection*

In the early 1800s, many Americans moved west. They were called pioneers. They wanted land and adventure. Many pioneers were farmers. Travel was very difficult. Settlers often traveled in Conestoga wagons. Two important possessions were rifles and axes. They used rifles for protection and to hunt animals for food. They used axes to cut paths through forests for their wagons.

Many pioneers settled along rivers that flowed into the Mississippi River. They started farms. The farmers shipped their crops along the rivers to markets. They shipped many goods down the Mississippi River to New Orleans. From New Orleans, the goods traveled to East Coast markets.

Spain controlled the area west of the Mississippi, including New Orleans. Spain allowed Americans to use the Mississippi and the port of New Orleans for their trade.

In 1802, Spain suddenly stopped letting settlers trade in New Orleans. President Jefferson learned that France and Spain had a secret agreement. France was going to gain control of the Louisiana Territory. He worried that this French control of the Mississippi would hurt U.S. trade.

Robert Livingston represented the U.S. government in France. Congress gave Livingston permission to buy New Orleans and West Florida from France.

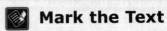 **Visualize It**

1. On the map, color and label the Louisiana Territory.

 **Mark the Text**

2. Underline two things that settlers needed. Why did they need these things?

_____

_____

Identifying

3. Who controlled the Mississippi River?

_____

Explaining

4. Why did settlers need to be able to use the Mississippi River?

_____

✔ **Reading Check**

5. Why was Jefferson worried about French control of the Louisiana Territory?

_____

_____

_____

_____

130

Lesson 2 The Louisiana Purchase, *Continued*

FOLDABLES®

Analyzing

6. Place a three-tab Foldable along the dotted line under the title "An Expanding Nation." Write the title *Louisiana Purchase* on the anchor tab. Label the three tabs *What?, What Cost?,* and *What Result?* On the tabs, describe how the United States acquired the Louisiana Territory from France.

Explaining

7. Why was Napoleon willing to sell Louisiana?

_____

✓ Reading Check

8. List two reasons the Louisiana Purchase was important for the United States.

_____

_____

Mark the Text

9. Circle the goals of the Lewis and Clark Expedition.

Napoleon Bonaparte, the French leader, wanted to rule much of Europe and North America. Napoleon wanted to use the Caribbean island of Santo Domingo as a naval base. It was important to his plan to rule in North America.

Napoleon's plan did not work. Enslaved Africans and other workers in Santo Domingo revolted and claimed independence. By 1804, the French had been forced out of Santo Domingo.

An Expanding Nation

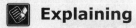

Without Santo Domingo, Napoleon did not want Louisiana. Also, he needed money to pay for his war against Britain. To get money, he decided to sell the Louisiana Territory.

Robert Livingston and James Monroe wanted to buy New Orleans and West Florida. A French official said they could buy all of the Louisiana Territory. They worried they did not have the power to make that decision. In spite of their worry, Livingston and Monroe decided it was too good a chance to miss. They agreed to pay $15 million for the land.

Even Jefferson was not sure he had the authority to buy the Louisiana Territory. The Constitution did not say anything about buying new land. Jefferson decided his right to make treaties allowed him to buy the land. The Senate okayed the purchase in October 1803. The new land doubled the size of the United States.

Having this new territory was good because

- it provided a large amount of new land for farmers.

- it protected shipping on the Mississippi River.

Americans did not know much about the new territory. Jefferson wanted to learn more about it. Congress agreed to send a group to explore the new land.

The group had several goals. They were supposed to

- collect information about the land.

- learn about plants and animals.

- suggest sites for forts.

- find a Northwest Passage, or a water route across North America to Asia.

Jefferson chose Meriwether Lewis to lead the expedition. Lewis's co-leader was William Clark. Both men were interested in science and had done business with Native Americans.

The Jefferson Era

Lesson 2 The Louisiana Purchase, *Continued*

Other Members of the Lewis and Clark Expedition	
sailors	cook
gun makers	Native American–French interpreters
carpenters	York, an African American
scouts	Sacagawea, a Shoshone guide

The group left St. Louis in spring 1804. They traveled about 4,000 miles to the Pacific, and returned in 1806. They brought back a lot of information about the people, plants, animals, and geography of the West. What they found encouraged people to want to move westward.

Zebulon Pike led two expeditions. He brought back information about the Great Plains and the Rocky Mountains. He also mapped part of the Rio Grande and explored what is now northern Mexico and southern Texas.

Federalists in the northeast worried about the country growing in the west. They were afraid they would lose power. One group of Federalists planned to **secede,** or leave, the nation. They decided they needed New York in order to be successful. They asked Aaron Burr to help them, and he agreed.

Alexander Hamilton heard Burr had agreed to help the Federalists secede. He accused Burr of treason. Burr said Hamilton's accusation hurt Burr's political career. To get even, he challenged Hamilton to a duel. Burr shot Hamilton, and Hamilton died the next day. Burr ran away so he would not be arrested.

/ / / / / / / / / / / Glue Foldable here / / / / / / / / / / / /

Check for Understanding

How did Spain play a role in Americans moving west? How did France play a role?

1. _____

2. _____

List two reasons people moved westward after the Louisiana Purchase.

1. _____

2. _____

? Making Connections

10. Why do you think it was important that Lewis and Clark were interested in science and had done business with Native Americans?

_____

_____

👁 Visualize It

11. Make a chart that shows how the Federalists' plan to secede led to Hamilton's death.

FOLDABLES®

12. Place a one-tab Foldable along the dotted line to cover Check for Understanding. Write *Moving West* on the anchor tab. Create a memory map by writing *Exploring New Land* in the middle of the tab and drawing four arrows around the title. List four things you recall about exploration during this time. Use the Foldable to help answer Check for Understanding.

The Jefferson Era

Lesson 3 A Time of Conflict

ESSENTIAL QUESTION
Why does conflict develop?

GUIDING QUESTIONS

1. **How did the United States become involved in a conflict with Tripoli?**
2. **What issues challenged James Madison during his presidency?**

Terms to Know

tribute money paid to a leader or state for protection

neutral rights privileges or freedoms given to countries that don't take sides in a war

embargo blocking of trade with another country

nationalism loyalty or dedication to one's country

Where in the world?

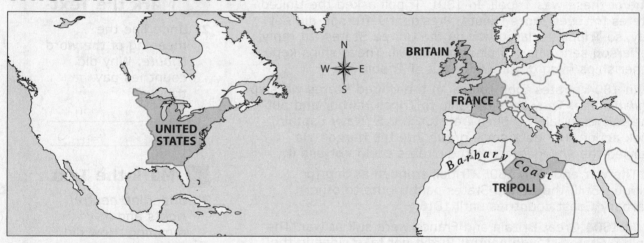

When did it happen?

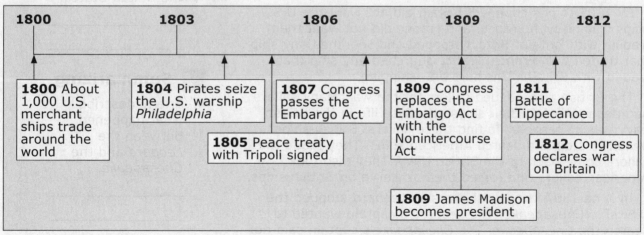

1800 About 1,000 U.S. merchant ships trade around the world

1804 Pirates seize the U.S. warship *Philadelphia*

1805 Peace treaty with Tripoli signed

1807 Congress passes the Embargo Act

1809 Congress replaces the Embargo Act with the Nonintercourse Act

1809 James Madison becomes president

1811 Battle of Tippecanoe

1812 Congress declares war on Britain

The Jefferson Era

Lesson 3 A Time of Conflict, *Continued*

American Ships on the High Seas

U.S. shipping grew in the late 1700s. People sailed to China and other parts of the world, hoping to make money. At the same time, France and Britain were at war. Their merchant ships stayed home so they would not be captured. This gave American merchants less competition.

Along the North African coast, there were pirates. The countries along this coast—the Barbary States—demanded **tribute**—money paid for protection. Many countries paid tribute, because it cost less than war with the pirates.

The United States paid tribute to the Barbary States. One of these was Tripoli. In 1801, Tripoli asked the United States for even more tribute. President Jefferson did not pay, so Tripoli declared war on the United States. In reply, Jefferson sent ships to blockade Tripoli. These ships kept other ships from getting in or out of Tripoli.

In 1804 pirates took control of the United States warship *Philadelphia*. They took the ship to Tripoli Harbor and put the sailors in jail. Stephen Decatur, a U.S. Navy captain, took action. He led a small group into the harbor. He burned the *Philadelphia* so the pirates could not use it.

The war ended in 1805. Tripoli stopped asking for tribute. Still, the United States paid tribute to other Barbary Coast countries until 1816.

In 1804 Great Britain and France were still at war. The United States stayed neutral. It did not take sides in the war. American ships had **neutral rights.** They could sail the seas freely and trade with both Britain and France.

By 1805 things changed. Britain did not want the U.S. ships trading with France, and France did not want them trading with Britain. Britain stopped and searched any ship that traded with France. France searched any ship that traded with Britain. This hurt U.S. shipping.

The British also needed sailors for the war. Many sailors had deserted—left their ships—because life in the British navy was so terrible. To find these sailors, British ships began to stop and search American ships. They made the sailors come back to the British Navy. They also took American sailors and forced them to serve on British ships.

In June 1807, the British warship *Leopard* stopped the U.S. ship *Chesapeake*. The *Leopard*'s captain wanted to search the *Chesapeake*. The *Chesapeake*'s captain said no. The British ship shot at the U.S. ship, killing three sailors.

Americans were very angry. Even though many Americans wanted war with Britain, Jefferson did not.

? Critical Thinking

1. Why did many British and French ships stay home in the mid-1790s?

   _____

   _____

Mark the Text

2. Underline the meaning of the word *tribute*. Why did countries pay tribute?

   _____

   _____

Mark the Text

3. Underline *neutral rights* and its meaning. How did Britain go against the neutral rights of the United States?

   _____

   _____

Summarizing

4. Briefly describe what happened between the *Leopard* and the *Chesapeake*.

   _____

   _____

   _____

netw⊙rks

The Jefferson Era

Lesson 3 A Time of Conflict, *Continued*

? Contrasting

5. What was the difference between the Embargo Act and the Nonintercourse Act?

_____

_____

✓ Reading Check

6. Did the Embargo Act work? Why?

_____

_____

✎ Identifying

7. List three problems Madison faced when he became president.

_____

_____

_____

✎ Mark the Text

8. Underline the reason tensions grew with Native Americans in the West.

? Analyzing

9. Did Madison think France or Britain was the bigger enemy?

_____

After the attack on the *Chesapeake*, Jefferson asked Congress to pass the Embargo Act. Congress passed this law in December 1807. The **embargo** stopped U.S. ships from trading with any other countries.

The Embargo Act failed. People who worked in shipping lost their jobs, and farmers lost markets for their crops. Congress ended the Embargo Act in 1809 and replaced it with the Nonintercourse Act. The new law only stopped trade with Britain and France. It also failed.

Like Washington before him, Jefferson did not run for a third term. In 1808, the candidates were:

Party	Candidate
Republicans	James Madison
Federalists	Charles Pinckney

People were angry about the embargo. Federalists hoped this anger would make people vote for Pinckney. Still, Madison easily won the election.

War at Home and Abroad

When James Madison became president, he faced three big problems:

- The embargo hurt the economy, so people were angry.
- Britain kept stopping American ships.
- In the West, tension with Native Americans grew.

In 1810, Congress said it would stop the embargo with the country that lifted its trade ban. Napoleon said France would allow open trade with the United States.

Even though trade started again, the French kept taking American ships. The French sold the ships and kept the money. The United States was about to go to war. Was the enemy Britain or France? Madison thought Britain was more dangerous to the United States.

Madison also had problems in the western United States. White settlers wanted more land. The land they wanted had been given to Native Americans. Tensions grew.

Native Americans tried two things:

- They talked to the British in Canada about working together.
- They joined with other Native American groups.

The Jefferson Era

Lesson 3 A Time of Conflict, *Continued*

Tecumseh was a Shawnee chief who got several Native American groups to work together to protect their land rights. He also wanted Native Americans to work with the British. He thought that together they could stop settlers from moving into Native American lands.

Tecumseh's brother, the Prophet, told Native Americans to go back to their old ways. He founded Prophetstown in Indiana near the Tippecanoe and Wabash Rivers.

William Henry Harrison was governor of the Indiana Territory. He worried about the power of Tecumseh and the Prophet. He was afraid they would join forces with the British. Harrison attacked Prophetstown and won. This was called the Battle of Tippecanoe

Americans claimed the Battle of Tippecanoe as a great victory. It was also bad news for the Americans, though. It convinced Tecumseh to join forces with the British.

A group of young Republicans called the War Hawks wanted war with Britain. They wanted the United States to be more powerful. Many Americans liked the War Hawks' **nationalism,** or loyalty to their country. There were two groups in the War Hawks:

- Southern Republicans who wanted Florida
- Western Republicans who wanted lands in Canada

Federalists in the Northeast were against war.

On June 1, 1812, Madison asked Congress to declare war on Britain. In the meantime, the British had decided to stop searching American ships. By the time American leaders learned of the change, it was too late. The United States had already declared war on Britain.

//////////////// Glue Foldable here ////////////////

Check for Understanding

Why did Tripoli declare war on the United States?

_____

_____

Madison faced several challenges as president. List one challenge inside the country and one challenge from outside the country.

1. _____

2. _____

Listing

10. List two things Tecumseh thought Native Americans should do to protect their land.

_____

_____

Mark the Text

11. Underline a negative result of the victory at Tippecanoe.

✓ Reading Check

12. List the three things that led to war with Britain.

_____

_____

FOLDABLES®

13. Place a two-tab Foldable along the dotted line to cover Check for Understanding. Write *Challenges of the Madison Presidency* on the anchor tab. Label the tabs *Shipping* and *Tippecanoe*. List two facts that you remember about each challenge. Use the Foldable to help answer Check for Understanding.

The Jefferson Era

Lesson 4 The War of 1812

ESSENTIAL QUESTION
Why does conflict develop?

GUIDING QUESTIONS
1. *In what ways was the United States unprepared for war with Britain?*
2. *Why were Americans instilled with national pride after the battle of New Orleans?*

> **Term to Know**
> **frigate** fast, medium-sized warship

Where in the world?

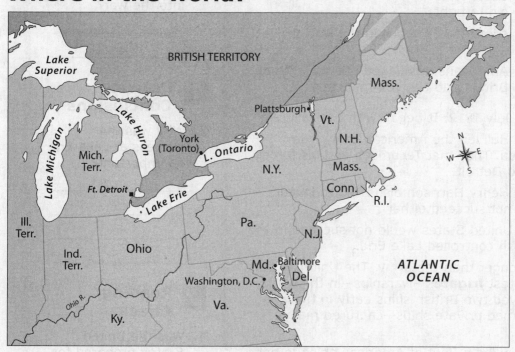

When did it happen?

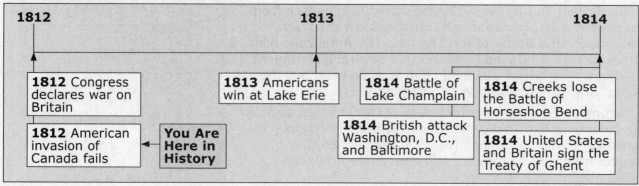

1812	1813	1814

1812 Congress declares war on Britain

1812 American invasion of Canada fails

You Are Here in History

1813 Americans win at Lake Erie

1814 Battle of Lake Champlain

1814 British attack Washington, D.C., and Baltimore

1814 Creeks lose the Battle of Horseshoe Bend

1814 United States and Britain sign the Treaty of Ghent

137

The Jefferson Era

Lesson 4 The War of 1812, *Continued*

Defeats and Victories

The War Hawks thought the United States would defeat Britain quickly, but America was not ready for war.

Reasons the United States Was Unprepared for War	
Troops	• fewer than 12,000 soldiers • 50,000–100,000 poorly trained state militia soldiers
Leaders	experienced leaders were too old to fight
Public opinion	some states opposed the war
Enemy strength	Americans misjudged the strength of Britain and Native Americans.

The war began in July 1812. It began with two failures:

• General William Hull led the American army from Detroit to Canada. They met Tecumseh and his forces. Hull surrendered Detroit.

• General William Henry Harrison also tried to invade Canada. He did not succeed either.

Harrison said the United States would not succeed in the north while the British controlled Lake Erie.

The navy was stronger than the army. The United States had three of the fastest **frigates**—warships—in the world. One of them destroyed two British ships early in the war. U.S. privateers—armed private ships—captured many British ships.

Oliver Hazard Perry led a fleet of American ships to get control of Lake Erie. On September 10, 1813, his ships destroyed the British fleet. Americans controlled Lake Erie.

The British and Native Americans tried to pull back from the Detroit area. Harrison and his troops cut them off. They fought the Battle of the Thames. The Americans also attacked York, in Canada, and burned several government buildings. The British still held control of Canada, but the United States had won several victories.

Tecumseh was killed in the Battle of the Thames. Before the battle, he had asked the Creeks in the Mississippi Territory to join his confederation. After he died, the confederation never formed, and the Native American alliance with the British ended.

138

🖊 Mark the Text

1. Underline the definition of *frigate*.

🖊 Identifying

2. What was one strength of the United States going into the war?

_____

_____

❓ Drawing Conclusions

3. Why was the success at Lake Erie so important?

_____

_____

_____

_____

✓ Reading Check

4. Was the United States prepared for war? Why?

_____

_____

_____

_____

The Jefferson Era

Lesson 4 The War of 1812, *Continued*

📝 Explaining

5. Why were the British able to send more troops to fight the United States in 1814?

_____

_____

❓ Contrasting

6. What happened when the British attacked Washington, D.C.?

_____

How was the battle in Baltimore different?

_____

❓ Sequencing

7. Number these events to show the order in which they happened:

Americans win Battle of New Orleans.

British defeat France.

British lose Battle of Lake Champlain.

U.S. and Britain sign Treaty of Ghent.

British attack Washington, D. C.

In March 1814, Andrew Jackson attacked the Creeks. He and his forces killed more than 550 Creek people in the Battle of Horseshoe Bend. After this defeat, the Creeks gave up most of their land.

The British Offensive

When the War of 1812 started, the British were still at war with France. In 1814, they won that war. This made it possible for them to send more troops to fight in America.

In August 1814, the British arrived in Washington, D.C. They quickly defeated the American militia. They burned and wrecked much of the city. Americans were surprised when the British did not try to hold the city.

Instead they left Washington, D.C., and headed to Baltimore. They attacked Baltimore in September 1814. Baltimore was ready. Fort McHenry in Baltimore harbor helped defend the city and kept the British out.

Francis Scott Key watched the bombs exploding over Fort McHenry on September 13. The next morning he saw the American flag still flying over the fort. It inspired him to write the poem "The Star-Spangled Banner." In 1931, this became the national anthem.

In the meantime, General Prevost was leading 10,000 British troops from Canada into New York. He wanted to capture Plattsburgh, an important city on Lake Champlain. In September 1814, an American naval force defeated the British fleet on Lake Champlain. Afraid the Americans would surround his troops, Prevost turned them around and went back to Canada.

After the Battle of Lake Champlain, the British decided to stop fighting. The war cost too much, and there was little to gain from it.

In December 1814, representatives from the United States and Britain signed a peace treaty in Ghent, Belgium. The Treaty of Ghent ended the war, but it did not:

• change borders.

• end impressment of sailors.

• mention neutral rights.

On January 8, 1815, before people in the United States knew about the treaty, British troops moved to attack New Orleans. Andrew Jackson and his troops were ready for them. The Americans hid behind cotton bales. The bales protected them from bullets. The unprotected redcoats were easy targets. Hundreds of British soldiers died.

139

The Jefferson Era

Lesson 4 The War of 1812, *Continued*

The Battle of New Orleans was a clear victory for the Americans. Andrew Jackson became a famous hero. His fame helped him become president in the election of 1828.

Federalists in New England were against the war from the start. They met in Hartford in December 1814. A few wanted to secede. Most wanted to stay in the United States. They made a list of changes they wanted made to the Constitution.

Pride in America grew with the success in the war. After the war, many people thought the Federalist complaints were unpatriotic. They lost respect for the Federalists, and the party grew weaker.

As the Federalists grew weaker, the War Hawks grew stronger. The War Hawks took control of the Republican Party. They wanted five things:

- trade
- more settlement in the West
- fast growth of the economy
- a strong national government
- a strong army and navy

After the war of 1812, Americans had great pride in their country. Other countries had more respect for the United States, too.

///////////// Glue Foldable here ///////////////

Check for Understanding

List four ways the United States was unprepared for war in 1812.

1. _____

2. _____

3. _____

4. _____

What happened to the Federalists and the Republicans after the War of 1812?

_____

_____

Explaining

8. What were the results of the Battle of New Orleans?

_____

_____

_____

Reading Check

9. List three things that happened as a result of the War of 1812.

_____

_____

_____

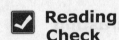

10. Place a two-tab Foldable along the dotted line to cover Check for Understanding. Write the title *War of 1812* on the anchor tab. Label the tabs *Federalists* and *Republicans*. Recall and list ways the War of 1812 affected each group. Use the Foldable to help answer Check for Understanding.

Growth and Expansion

Lesson 1 A Growing Economy

ESSENTIAL QUESTION
How does geography influence the way people live?

GUIDING QUESTIONS

1. ***How did new technology affect the way things were made?***

2. ***Why did agriculture remain the leading occupation of Americans in the 1800s?***

3. ***How did the growth of factories and trade affect cities?***

Terms to Know

cotton gin a machine that removes the seeds from cotton fiber

interchangeable part a part of a machine or device that can be replaced by another part just like it

patent legal rights to an invention and its profits

capitalism economic system in which people and companies control production

capital money or other resources used to create wealth

free enterprise a type of economy in which people are free to buy, sell, and produce whatever they want

Where in the world?

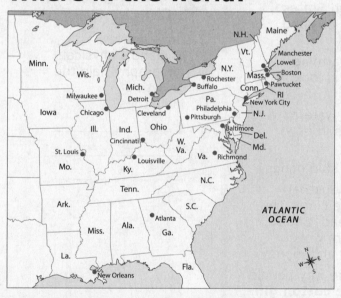

When did it happen?

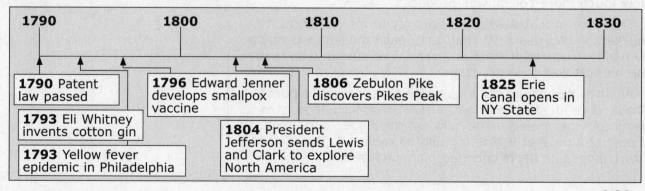

| 1790 | 1800 | 1810 | 1820 | 1830 |

1790 Patent law passed

1793 Eli Whitney invents cotton gin

1793 Yellow fever epidemic in Philadelphia

1796 Edward Jenner develops smallpox vaccine

1804 President Jefferson sends Lewis and Clark to explore North America

1806 Zebulon Pike discovers Pikes Peak

1825 Erie Canal opens in NY State

141

Growth and Expansion

Lesson 1 A Growing Economy, *Continued*

Industrial Growth

Most Americans lived and worked on farms in colonial times. People used simple tools to make goods by hand. They made household items, furniture, and farm equipment.

In the mid-1700s, the way goods were made began to change. The changes began in Great Britain. The British began using machines. For example, they used a machine to make cloth. They built textile mills along rivers. The water from the river powered their machines.

People stopped working only in their homes or on their farms. They moved to cities to work in the mills and earn money. This big change in how people worked and how things were made is known as the Industrial Revolution.

The Industrial Revolution came to the United States around 1800. The changes began first in New England. There were three main reasons.

1. New England did not have good soil for farming. People were willing to give up farming and look for other kinds of work.

2. New England had rivers and streams for waterpower. People used waterpower to run machines in new factories.

3. New England had many ports that could ship goods.

Technology was an important part of the Industrial Revolution. There were new machines to make cloth. The water frame and the spinning jenny spun thread. Before, people had to do this by hand. The power loom wove thread into cloth. These machines saved time and money.

The invention of new machines changed the way people made goods. In 1793 Eli Whitney invented the **cotton gin**. The word *gin* is from the word "engine." The cotton gin made it easy and fast to remove the seeds from cotton. Now much more cotton was produced.

The government wanted Eli Whitney to make 10,000 muskets in two years. At that time, each musket was made by hand. It was made one at a time. The person who made the musket was carefully trained.

Whitney developed the idea of **interchangeable parts**. These were identical musket parts. Workers could put the parts together quickly. They did not need special training. If part of a musket broke, it could be replaced. The idea of interchangeable parts changed manufacturing.

⮂ Mark the Text

1. Underline the text that describes interchangeable parts. How did they help the economy?

_____

_____

✓ Reading Check

2. How did New England's physical geography help the growth of industries?

_____

_____

_____

Growth and Expansion

Lesson 1 A Growing Economy, *Continued*

In 1790, the U.S. Congress passed a **patent** law. A patent gives the inventor the sole right to make money from his or her invention for a certain period of time.

The British, too, tried to protect their inventions. Textile workers could not leave the country. They could not tell others about British machines. Still, some people in Britan brought the information to the United States.

Samuel Slater was one of these people. In Britain, he memorized how to make the machines that made cotton thread. In the 1790s Slater built copies of those machines in the United States. Francis Cabot Lowell made Slater's idea even better. All the steps of making cloth, or textiles, were done in one factory. When all the manufacturing steps are done in one place, it is called a factory system.

The economic system of the United States encourages industrial growth. It is called **capitalism.** People put their **capital,** or money, into a business. They hope the business will make a profit.

The American economy is a **free enterprise** economy.

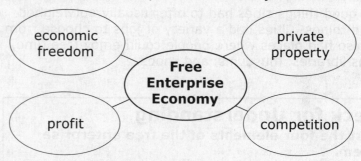

Agriculture Grows

Many people went to work in factories. Still, agriculture (farming) was the main economic activity in the United States in the 1800s. In the Northeast, farms were small. Families did all the work. They sold their products locally.

There were many farmers in the West. They raised such crops as corn and wheat. They produced pork.

The growth of textile industries increased the demand for cotton. Cotton was grown in the South. The cotton gin made it faster to process cotton. Southern farmers moved west to find new land to grow cotton. To grow more cotton, Southern farmers needed more enslaved workers. In 1790 there were 700,000 enslaved Africans in the United States. By 1810, there were 1.2 million.

Abc Defining

3. What is a patent?

_____

_____

✔ Reading Check

4. Why did the number of enslaved people grow quickly between 1790 and 1810?

_____

_____

Growth and Expansion

Lesson 1 A Growing Economy, *Continued*

Economic Independence

Small investors began to invest money in new businesses. They hoped to make money in return. Large businesses called corporations were formed. Corporations are companies owned by many people. The corporations sold stock, or shares of ownership in a company. This helped to pay for industrialization.

The growth of factories and trade led to the growth of cities. Many cities grew up near rivers because factories could use water to power their machines. People could ship their goods to markets more easily. Older cities, such as New York and Boston, grew as centers of shipping and trade. In the West, towns such as Cincinnati and Pittsburgh were located on major rivers. These towns grew rapidly as farmers shipped their products by river.

Cities at that time had no sewers to carry away waste. Diseases such as cholera and yellow fever sometimes killed many people. Many buildings were made of wood, and few cities had fire departments. Fires spread quickly.

The good things cities had to offer usually outweighed the bad things. Cities had a variety of jobs to choose from. They also had places where people could enjoy free time, such as libraries, museums, and shops.

/ / / / / / / / / / / / / Glue Foldable here / / / / / / / / / / / /

Check for Understanding

List the four elements of the free enterprise system.

_____

_____

_____

_____

List two examples of new technology that helped drive the industrial revolution.

_____

_____

? Analyzing

5. Why did many cities grow along major rivers?

_____

_____

✓ Reading Check

6. Why were cities attractive to people?

_____

_____

FOLDABLES®

7. Place a three-tab Venn diagram Foldable along the dotted line to cover Check for Understanding. Write the title *Capitalism* on the anchor tab. Label the tabs *Industrial Revolution*, *Both*, and *Free Enterprise System*. Recall information about each and list facts to determine what they have in common. Use the Foldable to help answer Check for Understanding.

Growth and Expansion

Lesson 2 Moving West

ESSENTIAL QUESTION

How does geography influence the way people live?

GUIDING QUESTIONS

1. **What helped increase the movement of people and goods?**

2. **Why did Americans tend to settle near rivers?**

Terms to Know

census the official count of the population

turnpike a road on which tolls are collected

canal waterway made by people

lock a separate compartment in which water levels rise and fall in order to raise or lower boats on a canal

Where in the world?

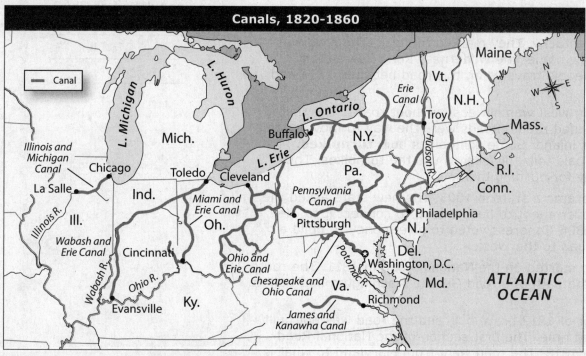

Canals, 1820-1860

When did it happen?

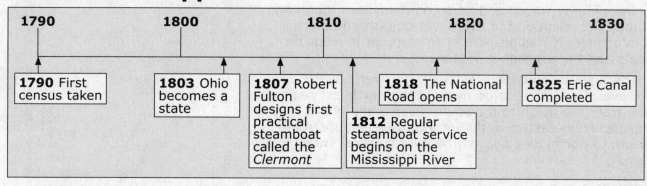

1790	1800	1810	1820	1830

1790 First census taken

1803 Ohio becomes a state

1807 Robert Fulton designs first practical steamboat called the *Clermont*

1812 Regular steamboat service begins on the Mississippi River

1818 The National Road opens

1825 Erie Canal completed

networks

Growth and Expansion

Lesson 2 Moving West, *Continued*

Headed West

In 1790 the first **census** was taken. A census is an official count of the population. The census found that nearly 4 million people lived in the United States. Most Americans lived east of the Appalachian Mountains. That pattern soon changed. More settlers headed west.

Daniel Boone was an explorer. He was one of the early pioneers who went west. In 1769 he explored a Native American trail that crossed the Appalachian Mountains. It was called Warriors' Path. The path went through a break in the mountains called the Cumberland Gap. Beyond the path was the place that is now Kentucky.

Boone got 30 workers. They widened Warrior's Path and cleared rocks from the Cumberland Gap. They cut down trees in Kentucky. They marked the trail. The road was given a new name, the Wilderness Road. More than 100,000 people traveled on this road between 1775 and 1790.

Traveling west was not easy without roads. The United States needed roads. Roads were the way to move people and goods inland. Some companies built **turnpikes.** Travelers paid tolls, or fees, to use the turnpikes. This helped pay for building them.

Ohio became a state in 1803. The new state asked the federal government to build a road to connect it to the East. In 1806 Congress voted to give money to build a national road to the West.

Building started on the National Road in 1811. The route followed the path of a road George Washington had built in 1754.

The War of 1812 broke out, and the road was not built during that time. The first section of the National Road opened in 1818. The road went from Maryland to what is now West Virginia.

Traveling by wagon and horse on roads was rough and bumpy. Traveling on the rivers was quicker and more comfortable. It was also easier to carry large loads on boats and barges than in wagons.

There were some big problems with river travel, however. First, most large rivers in the northeast region flow from the north to the south. People and goods mostly traveled from east to west. Second, traveling upstream (south to north) was against the river current. Travel was slow.

Locating

1. Where did most people in the United States live in 1790?

_____

Predicting

2. How do you think the National Road affected the population of Ohio?

_____

_____

_____

Growth and Expansion

Lesson 2 Moving West, *Continued*

Copyright by The McGraw-Hill Companies.

FOLDABLES®

📝 Describing

3. Place a one-tab Foldable along the dotted line to cover the text that begins with "Thousands of workers built the Erie Canal." Write the title *Locks and Canals* on the anchor tab. Define *lock* and define *canal*. Use the back of the tab to describe how the building of locks and canals affected the growth and economy of the United States.

✔️ Reading Check

4. Which regions were connected by the Erie Canal?

_____

_____

Travel by land	Travel by river
• Roads were rough and bumpy • It was hard to carry large loads	• Travel was more comfortable • More goods could be carried on a boat • Rivers could not move people east to west • Traveling against the river current was hard and slow

Robert Fulton developed a steamship with a powerful engine. He called it the *Clermont*. It could travel upstream. In 1807 the *Clermont* traveled north on the Hudson River. It traveled from New York City to the city of Albany in 32 hours. That was a 150-mile trip (241 km). A ship using only sails would have taken four days to make the trip.

The use of steamboats changed river travel. Steamboats made transportation easier and more comfortable. Shipping goods by steamboat became cheaper and faster. Steamboats also helped river cities, such as St. Louis and Cincinnati, grow. By 1850 there were 700 steamboats carrying goods and passengers.

Steamboats improved river transportation. However, steamboats could not link the eastern and western parts of the country. De Witt Clinton and other officials made a plan to link New York City with the Great Lakes region. They would build a **canal** across the state of New York. A canal is a waterway built by people.

///////////// Glue Foldable here ////////////

Thousands of workers built the Erie Canal. Many were Irish immigrants. They built a series of **locks** along the canal. Locks are a way to raise or lower water levels.

The Erie Canal opened in 1825. The governor of New York boarded a barge in Buffalo, New York. He traveled eastward on the canal to Albany. Then he sailed down the Hudson River to New York City. Crowds cheered as officials poured water from Lake Erie into the Atlantic Ocean.

At first, there were no steamboats allowed on the Erie Canal. Their powerful engines could damage the canal. In the 1840s, canals were made stronger to allow steamboats to travel on them. Many other canals were built. By 1850, the United States had more than 3,600 miles (5,794 km) of canals. Canals lowered the cost of shipping goods. They

147

Growth and Expansion

Lesson 2 Moving West, *Continued*

linked parts of the United States. They helped towns and cities along their routes grow larger.

The Move West Continues

The United States added four new states between 1791 and 1803. The states were Vermont, Kentucky, Tennessee and Ohio.

Between 1816 and 1821, Indiana, Illinois, Mississippi, Alabama, and Missouri became states. By 1820 there were 2.4 million people west of the Appalachian Mountains.

Pioneers moved west to find a better life. Most pioneer families settled along the big rivers and canals. They could more easily ship their crops and goods to markets. People usually settled with others from their original home state.

/ / / / / / / / / / / Glue Foldable here / / / / / / / / / / / /

Check for Understanding

List three people who helped make travel to the West easier. Explain what they did.

_____

_____

_____

Explain how America in 1790 was different from America in 1820.

_____

_____

☑ **Reading Check**

5. How did improved transportation affect the economy and the growth of cities?

_____

_____

☑ **Reading Check**

6. How did rivers and canals affect where settlers lived?

_____

FOLDABLES

7. Place a two-tab Foldable to cover Check for Understanding. Write *Moving West* on the anchor tab. Label the right tab *East* and the left tab *West*. Draw an arrow across the tabs from right to left. List why people might have wanted to leave the East and list ways they traveled to the West. Use the Foldable to help answer Check for Understanding.

Growth and Expansion

Lesson 3 Unity and Sectionalism

ESSENTIAL QUESTION

Why does conflict develop?

GUIDING QUESTIONS

1. **How did the country change after the War of 1812?**
2. **How did the United States define its role in the Americas?**

Terms to Know

sectionalism rivalry based on the special interests of different areas

interstate commerce economic activity taking place between two or more states

monopoly a market where there is only one seller

cede to transfer control of something

Where in the world?

The Missouri Compromise, 1820

CANADA

Unorganized Territory

Michigan Territory

NEW SPAIN

Mo. *slave state in 1821*

Missouri Compromise Line

36°30'N

Arkansas Terr.

Ill. Ind. Ohio

Ky.

Tenn.

Miss. Ala. Ga.

La.

Fla.

Vt. N.H.

Maine *free state in 1820*

N.Y. Mass.

R.I. Conn.

Pa. N.J.

Del.

Md.

Va.

N.C.

S.C.

ATLANTIC OCEAN

Gulf of Mexico

Free state/territory

Closed to slavery by the Missouri Compromise

Slave state/territory

Territory opened to slavery by the Missouri Compromise

When did it happen?

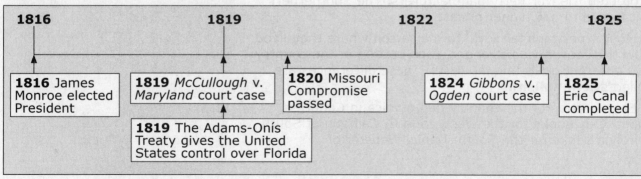

1816　　1819　　1822　　1825

1816 James Monroe elected President

1819 *McCullough* v. *Maryland* court case

1820 Missouri Compromise passed

1824 *Gibbons* v. *Ogden* court case

1825 Erie Canal completed

1819 The Adams-Onís Treaty gives the United States control over Florida

149

Growth and Expansion

Lesson 3 Unity and Sectionalism, *Continued*

National Unity

A feeling of national unity grew in the United States after the War of 1812. James Monroe, a Republican, easily won the election of 1816 because the Federalist Party had become weak.

A Boston newspaper called these years the Era of Good Feelings. President Monroe was a symbol of these good feelings. Other feelings at the time were those of loyalty to the nation, or nationalism. The Republicans wanted a strong federal government.

Henry Clay of Kentucky was a leader in the House of Representatives. Clay proposed the American System to help the economy in each section of the country, and also to increase the power of the federal government. Clay's system called for higher tariffs, a new national bank, and internal improvements such as new roads, bridges, and canals.

The First Bank of the United States ended in 1811. In 1816, Congress created the Second Bank of the United States. After the First Bank closed, many state banks made poor business decisions. They made too many loans. There was too much money around. This caused prices to rise. The Second Bank of the United States controlled how much money was available. It helped American businesses grow.

After the War of 1812, many people purchased goods from British factories. The British goods were better than American goods. They cost less, too. Britain hoped they could keep Americans from competing with them. They sent a lot of their products to America.

American manufacturers wanted to protect growing industries. They wanted high tariffs. The Republicans passed a protective tariff in 1816. This encouraged people to buy American-made goods.

Southerners did not like the tariffs. They felt the tariffs protected the Northern manufacturers. The Southerners felt forced to pay higher prices.

Most Americans felt loyal to the region where they lived. Now this feeling was stronger. Each section of the country had different goals and interests. These differences are called **sectionalism.**

Each section of the country had a voice in Congress. Henry Clay spoke for the West. John C. Calhoun of South Carolina spoke for the South. Daniel Webster of

 Describing

1. What was the mood of the country after the War of 1812?

_____

_____

 Explaining

2. Why was it necessary to create a Second Bank of the United States in 1816?

_____

_____

Mark the Text

3. Underline the text that describes Southerners' feelings about tariffs. Why did they feel this way?

_____

_____

Growth and Expansion

Lesson 3 Unity and Sectionalism, *Continued*

🔤 Defining

4. Underline the text that defines *monopoly*. What did the Supreme Court decide about interstate commerce?

_____

_____

✓ Reading Check

5. What problem did the Missouri Compromise try to resolve?

_____

_____

_____

Massachusetts spoke for the North. Each leader tried to protect the interests of his own section of the country.

The Supreme Court made decisions that backed the power of the national government. In *Fletcher* v. *Peck* (1810), the Court decided that courts could overrule decisions of a state's government if the decisions went against the Constitution. In *McCulloch* v. *Maryland* (1819) , the Court ruled that a state could not tax property of the national government. In *Gibbons* v. *Ogden*, the Court ruled that only Congress could make laws governing **interstate commerce**, or trade between states. In this case, the state of New York had granted a **monopoly** to a steamship operator. He was running ships between New Jersey and New York. A monopoly is sole control over an industry. People who supported states' rights did not agree with the Court's rulings.

In 1819 there was a clash between the North and the South. Missouri wanted to enter the Union as a slave state. Congress disagreed. Henry Clay came up with a plan to solve this disagreement over slavery. The Missouri Compromise called for Missouri to be admitted as a slave state. Another new state, Maine, would be a free state. This meant that there would still be an equal number of slave and free states. This kept a balance of power in the Senate. Neither side could change the laws governing slavery.

The Missouri Compromise also dealt with slavery in the rest of the Louisiana Territory. The land south of Missouri could allow slavery, and the land north of it could not.

Foreign Affairs

Americans had a lot of pride in their country following the War of 1812.

In 1817, Britain and the United States made an agreement called the Rush-Bagot Agreement. It called for each country to limit the number of war ships on the Great Lakes.

The Convention of 1818 was an agreement between the United States and Britain. It set the boundary of the Louisiana Purchase between the United States and Canada at the 49th parallel. It made a secure border without armed forces. Americans got the right to settle in the Oregon Country

The United States had a dispute with Spain over parts of Florida. Spain controlled Florida. The United States claimed

Growth and Expansion

Lesson 3 Unity and Sectionalism, *Continued*

that West Florida was part of the Louisiana Purchase. They argued that it belonged to the United States.

In 1810 and 1812, Americans took control of West Florida to Louisiana and Mississippi. Spain took no action. In 1818 General Andrew Jackson was ordered to stop Native American raids from East Florida. He invaded West Florida and continued into East Florida. He captured several Spanish forts. The Spanish realized they were not strong enough to hold on to Florida. The Adams-Onís Treaty was signed in 1819. In the treaty, Spain **ceded,** or gave up, Florida. At the same time, Spain was losing power in Mexico. In 1821 Mexico finally gained its independence.

Simón Bolívar won independence from Spain for the present-day countries of Venezuela, Colombia, Panama, Bolivia, and Ecuador. José de San Martín won freedom from Spain for Chile and Peru. By 1824, Spain had lost control of most of South America.

In 1822 several European countries talked about a plan to help Spain take back its American colonies. President Monroe did not want more European involvement in North America. In 1823 he issued the Monroe Doctrine. It said that European powers could no longer set up colonies in North America and South America.

///////////////// Glue Foldable here //////////////////

Check for Understanding

List the three parts of Henry Clay's American system.

_____

_____

_____

What helped bring about feelings of sectionalism in the United States?

_____

_____

_____

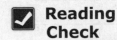

Describing

6. What was the result of the Adams-Onís Treaty?

_____

_____

✓ **Reading Check**

7. Why did President Monroe issue the Monroe Doctrine?

_____

_____

FOLDABLES®

8. Place a two-tab Foldable to cover Check for Understanding. Write the title *After the War* on the anchor tab. Label the two tabs *American System* and *Foreign Affairs*. List two things you recall about each. Use the Foldable to help answer Check for Understanding.

The Jackson Era

Lesson 1 Jacksonian Democracy

ESSENTIAL QUESTION
What are the characteristics of a leader?

GUIDING QUESTIONS

1. *What new ways of campaigning appeared during the elections of 1824 and 1828?*

2. *How did Andrew Jackson make the American political system more democratic?*

3. *How did a fight over tariffs become a debate about states' rights versus federal rights?*

Terms to Know

favorite son a candidate for national office who has support mostly from his home state

plurality the largest number of something, but less than a majority

majority greater than half of a total number of something

mudslinging a method in election campaigns that uses gossip and lies to make an opponent look bad

bureaucracy a system of government in which specialized tasks are carried out by appointed officials rather than by elected ones

spoils system practice of handing out government jobs to supporters; replacing government employees with the winning candidate's supporters

nominating convention a meeting in which representative members of a political party choose candidates to run for important elected offices

When did it happen?

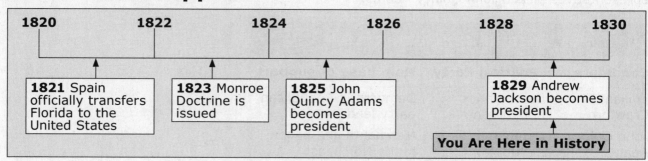

1820	1822	1824	1826	1828	1830

1821 Spain officially transfers Florida to the United States

1823 Monroe Doctrine is issued

1825 John Quincy Adams becomes president

1829 Andrew Jackson becomes president

You Are Here in History

What do you know?

In the first column, answer the questions based on what you know before you study. After this lesson, complete the last column.

Now...		Later...
	How many strong political parties were there in the 1824 presidential election?	
	What area of the country favored higher tariffs and what area opposed them?	

153

The Jackson Era

Lesson 1 Jacksonian Democracy, *Continued*

New Parties Emerge

Early political groups became political parties. The parties and their views changed over time. From 1816 to 1824, the Democratic-Republican party was the only major political party.

The four candidates for president in the election of 1824 were all members of the same party. Party leaders supported William Crawford. The other three were **favorite sons** who got most of their support from their home states. Each favored the interests of his state.

Support for John Quincy Adams of Massachusetts came from merchants and business owners in the Northeast. Henry Clay of Kentucky was supported by his state on the frontier. Andrew Jackson of Tennessee was a war hero. He was well-known and popular. He came from a poor family and wanted ordinary people to have a voice in politics.

The vote was split among the four candidates. Jackson won a **plurality**, or more votes than any of the other candidates. No candidate had a **majority**, or more than half, of the electoral votes. The Constitution stated that if a candidate does not win a majority of the electoral votes, the House of Representatives must decide the winner. The representatives picked John Quincy Adams.

Presidential candidates, 1824		
Candidate	**Political Party**	**Main base of support**
William Crawford	Democratic-Republican	Democratic-Republican party leaders
John Quincy Adams	Democratic-Republican	Merchants and people in the Northeast
Henry Clay	Democratic-Republican	People in Kentucky and on the frontier
Andrew Jackson	Democratic-Republican	People in Tennessee and the West; people who felt left out of politics

Like many in the Northeast, Adams wanted a strong federal government. Others did not agree, especially those on the frontier. The Democratic-Republicans split into two parties before the election in 1828. The Republicans backed Adams and a strong central government. The Democrats supported Jackson and states' rights.

Identifying

1. Who won the election of 1824, and how was the winner determined?

_____

_____

Assessing

2. What did Crawford's failure to win the 1824 election say about the strength of the party leaders?

_____

_____

_____

Lesson 1 Jacksonian Democracy, Continued

✔ **Contrasting**

3. What were two major differences between the Democrats and the National Republicans in 1828?

_____

_____

	Democrats	National Republicans
Idea of government	favored states' rights	wanted strong federal government
National bank	opposed national bank	supported national bank
Base of support	workers, farmers, immigrants	wealthy voters, merchants
Candidate	Andrew Jackson	John Quincy Adams

In the election of 1828, Jackson faced Adams. Their ideas and supporters were very different. Adams and the National Republicans wanted a strong federal government and a national bank to help the economy. Many National Republicans were wealthy business owners. Many of the Democrats were workers, farmers, or immigrants.

? **Drawing Inferences**

4. What changes taking place in the country contributed to Jackson's victory?

_____

_____

_____

_____

The campaign grew ugly. Both parties used **mudslinging,** or insults meant to make candidates look bad. The candidates also came up with slogans, handed out printed flyers, and held rallies and barbecues to try to win voters' support. Jackson's popularity gave him an easy victory in the 1828 election.

Jackson as President

Jackson thought more people should be involved in government. By 1828, most people no longer had to own property to be able to vote. Many states had changed their constitutions so that voters selected the presidential electors in their states. Jackson also thought that the federal **bureaucracy** was not democratic. Many workers were not elected officials. He used the **spoils system** to fire many workers and replace them with people who had supported his election.

✔ **Reading Check**

5. What campaign practices of the 1828 election are still used today?

_____

_____

_____

_____

The caucus system was replaced by special state meetings called **nominating conventions**. At these meetings, elected representatives voted for party candidates.

The Tariff Debate

Americans were also split on their views about **tariffs,** or taxes, on goods from other countries. Merchants in the

155

The Jackson Era

Lesson 1 Jacksonian Democracy, *Continued*

Northeast wanted higher tariffs so that European goods would cost more than American goods. Southerners, however, liked buying cheaper goods from Europe. They also worried that Europeans might tax the U.S. cotton sold in Europe, meaning Southerners would lose business.

Jackson's vice president, John C. Calhoun of South Carolina, was a strong supporter of states' rights. However, his views were different from those of Jackson. When Congress raised tariffs, Calhoun did not think it was good for his state. He felt that a state could and should nullify, or cancel, federal laws that were not good for that state.

When Congress again raised tariffs in 1832, South Carolina passed a law saying that the state would not pay them. It also threatened to secede from, or leave, the United States if the federal government tried to enforce the tariff law. Jackson did not agree with his vice president. He did not believe the states had the right to nullify federal laws or to secede from the Union.

Jackson did not think the federal government should support projects that helped only one state. He thought the federal government should support projects that helped the entire nation. These included tariff laws which involved international trade.

Jackson tried to calm angry Southerners by working to lower the tariffs. But to keep the union together and strong, he also supported the Force Act. This act would allow him to enforce federal laws by using the military if necessary. South Carolina was happy to have the tariffs lowered. Still, the state nullified the Force Act.

/ / / / / / / / / / / Glue Foldable here / / / / / / / / / / /

Check for Understanding

List two ways in which the country became more democratic in the 1820s.

1. _____

2. _____

What was Jackson's opinion when it came to states nullifying a federal law and seceding from the United States?

_____

_____

Reading Check

6. How would Northeastern factory owners react to a high tariff?

_____

_____

_____

FOLDABLES®

7. Place a two-tab Foldable along the dotted line to cover the Check for Understanding. Write the title *Jackson Presidency* on the anchor tab. Label the two tabs *Federal Government* and *States' Rights*. Recall information about each and list facts to compare the candidates and the outcome of the election. Use the Foldable to help answer Check for Understanding.

The Jackson Era

Lesson 2 Conflicts over Land

ESSENTIAL QUESTION

What are the consequences when cultures interact?

GUIDING QUESTIONS

1. **Why were Native Americans forced to abandon their land and move west?**

2. **Why did some Native Americans resist resettlement?**

> **Term to Know**
> **relocate** to move to another place

Where in the world?

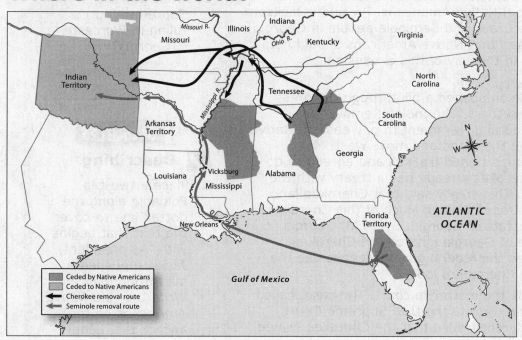

When did it happen?

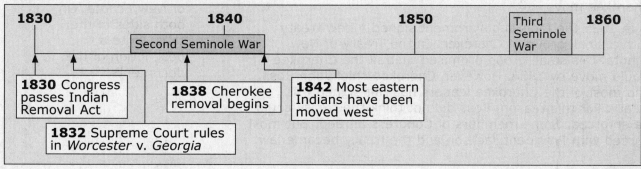

Copyright by The McGraw-Hill Companies.

157

The Jackson Era

Lesson 2 Conflicts over Land, *Continued*

Removing Native Americans

In the early 1800s, American settlers were moving both west and south. The country had to decide what to do about Native Americans who lived on this land. The Cherokee, Creek, Seminole, Chickasaw, and Choctaw peoples lived in Georgia, Alabama, Mississippi, and Florida. These Native American groups were farmers. Their communities were much like many other American communities. As a result, other Americans called these groups the "Five Civilized Tribes."

As settlers moved farther south and west, many people wanted the federal government to force the Five Civilized Tribes to **relocate**. Settlers needed more land. They wanted to take it from Native Americans. President Jackson had once fought the Creek and Seminole people in Georgia and Florida. He agreed that Native Americans should not be allowed to stand in the way of this expansion.

/ / / / / / / / / / / Glue Foldable here / / / / / / / / / / / /

As president, Jackson pushed a bill through Congress that would help the settlers. The Indian Removal Act of 1830 allowed the federal government to pay eastern Native Americans to give up their land and move west. Most Native American groups signed treaties and agreed to do so. However, the Cherokee already had a treaty with the federal government. That treaty said that Cherokee land was not part of the United States. Much of this Cherokee land was inside the state of Georgia. By 1830, Georgia wanted it. The state of Georgia ignored the Cherokee treaty. Georgia asked the federal government to use the new law to take the Cherokee's land.

The Cherokee took the matter to court. The case, called *Worcester* v. *Georgia*, went to the U.S. Supreme Court. Chief Justice John Marshall ruled that the Cherokee owned the land. He said that the state of Georgia could not take control of it. President Jackson disagreed with the Court's ruling. He refused to prevent Georgia from making the Cherokee move.

In 1835 the federal government signed a new treaty with a small group of Cherokee. In the Treaty of New Echota, this small group promised that all the Cherokee would move by 1838. However, Cherokee chief John Ross and most of the Cherokee leaders had not signed this treaty. For this reason, Ross did not think the treaty could be enforced. Some members of Congress agreed. But most agreed with President Jackson and the treaty became law.

 Locating

1. In which states did most of the "Five Civilized Tribes" live?

_____

_____

_____

 Explaining

2. What was the Supreme Court's ruling in *Worcester* v. *Georgia*?

_____

_____

_____

☑ **Describing**

3. Place a two-tab Foldable along the dotted line to cover the text that begins with "As president, Jackson pushed a bill through . . ." Write the title *Native Americans* on the anchor tab. Label the two tabs *The Indian Removal Act of 1830* and *Treaty of New Echota*. On both sides of the tabs, write a description of the documents.

The Jackson Era

Lesson 2 Conflicts over Land, *Continued*

Abc Marking the Text

4. Underline the sentence that explains the meaning of *guerrilla tactics*.

✓ Identifying

5. Who were the Black Seminoles?

_____

_____

? Making Connections

6. Why were Black Seminoles willing to support the Seminole fight to stay in Florida?

_____

_____

🖌 Summarizing

7. What finally happened to the Seminoles?

_____

_____

Most Cherokee did not want to relocate. In 1838 President Van Buren sent the army to enforce the treaty. The army forced the Cherokee off their land and into a new territory west of the Mississippi River. It was called the Indian Territory because Congress had created it to be the new home of many eastern Native Americans. Most of this territory is the present-day state of Oklahoma. The other Five Civilized Tribes and other Native Americans were also forced to move to the Indian Territory.

The Cherokee had to travel from their homes in Georgia to the Indian Territory. Losing their homes and taking this long and difficult journey greatly saddened the Native Americans. Many died waiting for the journey to begin. Many more died along the way. Their journey was later called the Trail of Tears.

Resistance and Removal

Most of the Five Civilized Tribes did not want to sell their lands. Osceola, a leader of the Seminoles in Florida, refused to move. Instead, he and his followers decided to stay and fight. This began a long and bloody fight called the Seminole Wars. The Seminoles were skilled at fighting in Florida's swamps and marshlands. Small groups surprised and attacked army troops and then ran away into the swamps. This method of fighting is called guerilla tactics. It was successful, at least for a while. The Seminoles were greatly outnumbered, but they kept the army from a quick victory.

In their fight, Seminoles were joined by Black Seminoles. Black Seminoles were escaped slaves who ran away to Florida. Because Florida was not a state yet, they thought they would be safe there. Some of the runaway slaves built their own homes. Others lived with the Seminole people. When war broke out, Black Seminoles fought alongside the Native Americans. They were afraid that the army might return them to slavery.

The fighting continued, on and off, for more than 20 years, from 1832 to 1858. Neither side was able to defeat the other. Eventually, most of the Seminoles either died or moved to the Indian Territory. Some, however, stayed in Florida, where their descendants still live today.

By the end of the Seminole Wars, very few Native American groups were still living in the eastern United States. Most had been removed to the Indian Territory. They shared the land with other Native American groups

159

The Jackson Era

Lesson 2 Conflicts over Land, *Continued*

already living there. In later years, American settlers would look to expand into the Indian Territory, too. Many of the same problems would be repeated years later.

//////////// Glue Foldable here //////////////

Check for Understanding

Besides the Cherokee, name three other Native American groups who were forced to relocate.

1. _____

2. _____

3. _____

Identify two ways that Native Americans resisted being relocated.

1. _____

2. _____

FOLDABLES

8. Place a one-tab Foldable along the dotted line to cover Check for Understanding. Write the title *Trail of Tears* on the anchor tab. Label the right side of the tab *Northeast* and the left side *Oklahoma*. List two things you remember about why Native Americans were forced to leave their land and go west. Use the Foldable to help answer Check for Understanding.

The Jackson Era

Lesson 3 Jackson and the Bank

ESSENTIAL QUESTION

How do governments change?

GUIDING QUESTIONS

1. What events occurred when President Jackson forced the National Bank to close?

2. What events occurred during the 1840s that led to the weakening of the Whig Party?

Term to Know

veto to reject a bill and prevent it from becoming law

When did it happen?

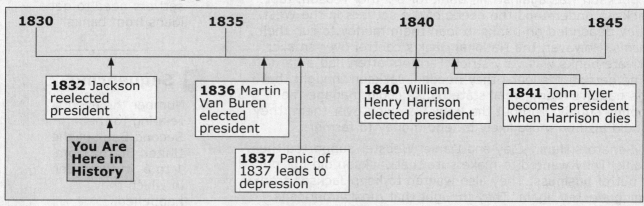

1830   1835   1840   1845

1832 Jackson reelected president

You Are Here in History

1836 Martin Van Buren elected president

1837 Panic of 1837 leads to depression

1840 William Henry Harrison elected president

1841 John Tyler becomes president when Harrison dies

What do you know?

In the first column, answer the questions based on what you know before you study. After this lesson, complete the last column.

Now...		Later...
	Why was the Second Bank of the United States important to the economy?	
	Why did President Jackson oppose the National Bank?	
	Why did the Whigs think they could win the presidential election in 1840?	
	How did President Harrison's death affect the Whigs' plans for the country?	

161

Jackson's War Against the Bank

Congress created the Second Bank of the United States to hold the federal government's money. Its job was to control the nation's money supply. However, the Bank was not run by government officials. Instead it was run by Eastern bankers. Most of these bankers had wealth and a good education.

President Andrew Jackson had neither of these. He was a pioneer from the West. He had worked hard and became president. He did not like the wealthy bankers who ran the Bank.

Jackson was against the Bank for another reason, too. Jackson understood the needs of the settlers in the West. They depended on banks to loan them money to run their farms. However, the National Bank's control over smaller private banks was very strict. Farmers often had a hard time getting the loans they needed. Jackson thought that the nation's many small state banks could manage the money supply. Without the Bank watching over them, they would also be more likely to lend money to farmers.

Senators Henry Clay and Daniel Webster supported the Bank. They wanted to make sure that Jackson did not put it out of business. They also wanted to keep Jackson from being elected again. They thought that most Americans liked the Bank, and if Jackson tried to close it, he would lose votes in the next election.

Years earlier, Congress had given the Bank a charter for 20 years. A charter is a legal document that gives an organization permission to do its work. Clay and Webster helped the Bank get a new charter from Congress before the old charter ran out. They thought Jackson would not dare to **veto** the new charter, or prevent it from becoming a law. They thought he would not veto it because it was an election year and he might lose votes. Jackson vetoed it anyway. This meant that the Bank would be forced to go out of business in a few years. Most people supported Jackson's veto. It actually helped him get reelected.

After the election, Jackson took the federal government's money out of the Bank and put it into smaller state banks. When the Bank's charter ended, the Second Bank of the United States closed.

Martin Van Buren, Jackson's vice president, ran for president in 1836. Jackson was still very popular. Jackson's support helped Van Buren win. Soon after the election,

Marking the Text

1. Underline the text that describes the role of the Second Bank of the United States.

Explaining

2. Why did Western settlers need to get loans from banks?

_____

Sequencing

3. Number the events relating to the Second Bank of the United States from 1 to 6, in the order in which they happened.

____ government's money put in state banks

____ Congress passes new charter for Bank

____ Second Bank of United States closes

____ Jackson vetoes new charter

____ Bank's charter expires

____ Jackson removes government's money from Bank

The Jackson Era

Lesson 3 Jackson and the Bank, *Continued*

 Reading Check

4. After the Bank closed, what kind of payment did the government require from people who wanted to buy public land?

_____

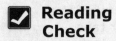 **Explaining**

5. What was President Van Buren's response to the Panic of 1837?

_____

✓ **Reading Check**

6. What was the purpose of the new treasury system?

_____

✓ **Explaining**

7. Why did the Whigs think they had a chance to win the presidency in 1840?

_____

_____

though, the country was in trouble. Jackson's actions toward the Bank had led to an economic panic.

When the Bank's charter expired and it closed, there was no national bank to control the state banks. They began printing more banknotes. Federal officials became concerned that these notes had little value. As a result, the federal government decided to require gold and silver as payment for public land. It would not accept the banknotes.

People who had banknotes feared their notes might become worthless. This fear set off an economic panic, called the Panic of 1837. Many people lost their jobs and their land. Thousands of businesses had to close.

President Van Buren believed that the government should not do anything to help the nation during the depression. He did, however, work with Congress to create a federal treasury where the federal government would keep its money. The government, not private bankers, would own and run the treasury. Leaders hoped that this new treasury would prevent future panics.

The Whigs in Power

Van Buren ran for reelection in 1840. With the country still in the depths of a depression, the Whigs thought they had a chance to win the presidency. The Whigs ran William Henry Harrison against Van Buren.

Like Andrew Jackson, Harrison became a hero during the War of 1812. He fought at the Battle of Tippecanoe. His running mate was John Tyler, a planter from Virginia. Their campaign slogan was "Tippecanoe and Tyler Too."

Harrison had to gain the support of the workers and farmers who had voted for Jackson. He was wealthy and from Ohio, but his campaign painted him as a simple frontiersman like Jackson. The Democrats responded to this false picture. They said all Harrison was good for was sitting in front of a log cabin and collecting his military pension. The Whigs turned the attack around. They adopted the simple frontier log cabin as the symbol of their campaign.

At the same time, the Whigs painted Van Buren as a wealthy snob with perfume-scented whiskers. They blamed him for the depression. They accused him of spending money on fancy furniture for the White House. The Whigs' plan worked. A record number of voters elected Harrison by a wide margin.

The Jackson Era

Lesson 3 Jackson and the Bank, *Continued*

Harrison gave his long inaugural speech in the bitter cold without a hat or coat. He died of pneumonia 32 days later. He served the shortest term of any president. John Tyler became the first vice president to become president because the elected president died in office.

Tyler had been elected as a Whig. He had once been a Democrat and did not support many Whig policies. Whig Party leaders thought he would attract voters in the South. Webster and Clay believed that they would be able to get Harrison to agree to their plans for the country. Harrison's death spoiled their plan.

Tyler vetoed several Whig bills. His lack of party loyalty angered many Whigs. Finally, they threw him out of the party. He became a president without a party. Tyler's biggest success was the Webster-Ashburton Treaty, which was signed by the United States and Great Britain. The treaty ended the disagreement over the border between Maine and Canada. It also settled the location of the long U.S.-Canadian border from Maine to Minnesota.

Unfortunately, the Whigs could not agree on goals for their party. They did agree on their dislike for President Tyler, however. The Whigs continued to vote more and more according to sectional ties—North, South, and West—and not party ties. It is likely that Whig presidential candidate Henry Clay lost the election of 1844 because of this division. James Polk, a Democrat, became the new president.

/ / / / / / / / / / / / / / Glue Foldable here / / / / / / / / / / / / /

Check for Understanding

List two reasons that President Jackson shut down the Second Bank of the United States.

1. _____

2. _____

Why was John Tyler not an effective president?

_____

_____

✓ Reading Check

8. How did the Whigs lose power in the election of 1844?

_____

_____

9. Place a two-tab Foldable along the dotted line to cover Check for Understanding. Cut the tabs in half to form four tabs. Write the title *Changes* on the anchor tab. Label the four tabs *Andrew Jackson*, *Martin Van Buren*, *William Henry Harrison*, and *John Tyler*. List two things you remember about each president. Use the Foldable to help answer Check for Understanding.

Manifest Destiny

Lesson 1 The Oregon Country

ESSENTIAL QUESTION
How does geography influence the way people live?

GUIDING QUESTIONS
1. **Why did Americans want to control the Oregon Country?**
2. **What is Manifest Destiny?**

Terms to Know

joint occupation people from two countries living in the same region

mountain man person who lived in the Rocky Mountains and made his living by trapping animals for their fur

emigrants people who leave their country

prairie schooner cloth-covered wagon that was used by pioneers to travel West in the mid-1800s

Manifest Destiny the idea that the United States was meant to spread freedom from the Atlantic Ocean to the Pacific Ocean

Where in the world?

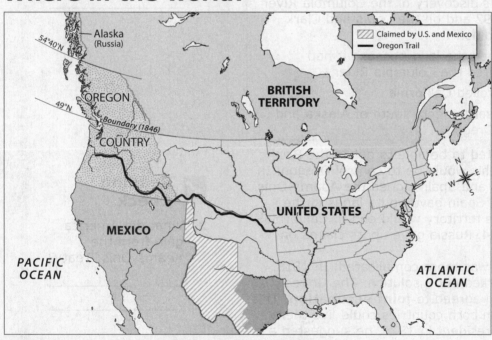

When did it happen?

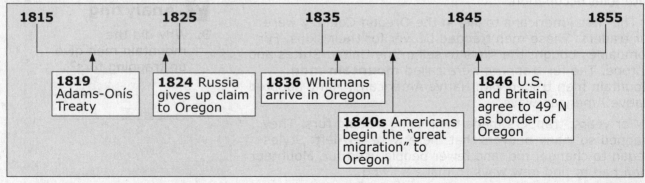

1819 Adams-Onís Treaty

1824 Russia gives up claim to Oregon

1836 Whitmans arrive in Oregon

1840s Americans begin the "great migration" to Oregon

1846 U.S. and Britain agree to 49°N as border of Oregon

networks

Manifest Destiny

Lesson 1 The Oregon Country, *Continued*

Rivalry in the Northwest

The Oregon Country covered much more land than today's state of Oregon. Oregon, Washington, Idaho and parts of Montana and Wyoming were all a part of it.

In the early 1800s, four countries claimed the Oregon Country. They were the United States, Great Britain, Spain and Russia.

Claims in the Oregon Country	
Country	**Reason for Claim**
United States	Claimed the land based on Robert Gray's discovery of the Columbia River in 1792 and on the Lewis and Clark expedition
Great Britain	Claimed the land because it had explored the Columbia River
Spain	Controlled California
Russia	Had settlements south of Alaska and into Oregon

Many Americans wanted to be able to get to the Pacific Ocean. One way to do this would be to control Oregon. In 1819, the United States and Spain signed the Adams-Onís Treaty. With this treaty, Spain gave up its lands in the Oregon Country. Spain's territory would end at California's northern border. In 1824, Russia gave up its claims on lands south of Alaska.

The deal with Britain was more complicated. In 1818, John Quincy Adams worked out a solution. The United States and Great Britain agreed to **joint occupation.** This meant that settlers from both countries could live there. When Adams became president in 1825, he suggested a plan for Britain and the United States to divide the land. Britain said no to the plan, so both countries continued on with joint occupation.

The first Americans to live in the Oregon Country were fur traders. These men trapped beaver for their skins. Fur companies bought the skins to sell in the United States and Europe. The fur trappers were called **mountain men.** Mountain men traded with Native Americans. Many adopted Native American ways.

For years, trappers made their living trading furs. They trapped so many beavers that there were few left. Styles began to change, too, and fewer people used fur. Mountain men had to find new ways to make a living.

Copyright by The McGraw-Hill Companies.

 Mark the Text

1. Underline the definition of *joint occupation*. Which two countries agreed to joint occupation of Oregon?

_____

_____

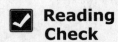 **Reading Check**

2. What did America gain from the Adams-Onís Treaty?

_____

_____

? **Analyzing**

3. Why did the mountain men give up trapping furs?

_____

_____

Manifest Destiny

Lesson 1 The Oregon Country, *Continued*

Making Inferences

4. Why were the Whitmans killed?

_____

_____

Defining

5. What is an *emigrant*?

_____

_____

Some became farmers. Others used their knowledge of the region and became guides. Jim Bridger and Kit Carson were two mountain men who became guides.

Guides helped settlers who were moving west to the Oregon Country. They created new routes that led from the east to the west. The best-known route was the Oregon Trail. Guides created other important routes. One was the California Trail and another was the Santa Fe trail.

Oregon and Manifest Destiny

Americans began to settle all over the Oregon country in the 1830s.

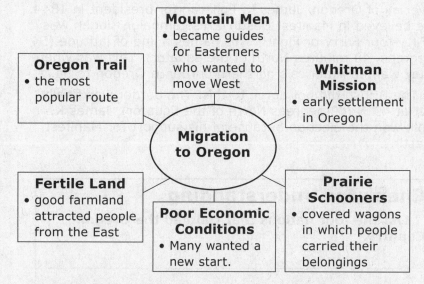

Oregon Trail
• the most popular route

Mountain Men
• became guides for Easterners who wanted to move West

Whitman Mission
• early settlement in Oregon

Migration to Oregon

Fertile Land
• good farmland attracted people from the East

Poor Economic Conditions
• Many wanted a new start.

Prairie Schooners
• covered wagons in which people carried their belongings

Dr. Marcus Whitman and his wife Narcissa were among the first settlers. They built a mission among the Cayuse people in 1836. The Cayuse are Native Americans who lived near what is now Walla Walla, Washington. The Whitmans wanted to convert the Cayuse to Christianity. They also wanted to provide medical care.

New settlers came to the mission. They did not know it, but they carried the disease, measles. The Cayuse had no defenses against measles, and the disease spread. Many children died of measles. The Cayuse blamed the Whitmans for the deaths. In November 1847, the Cayuse attacked the mission. They killed the Whitmans and 11 others.

Settlers kept coming to Oregon. Reports of fertile land attracted many of them. Others faced economic hard times and wanted a fresh start. These pioneers were called **emigrants.** Emigrants are people who leave their home

167

Manifest Destiny

Lesson 1 The Oregon Country, *Continued*

country for another place. To reach Oregon, they had to travel about 2,000 difficult miles. They packed everything they owned in covered wagons. These wagons were called **prairie schooners.** From a distance, they looked like a ship called a schooner. Even though it was a very hard trip, thousands of people started for Oregon.

In the early 1800s, many Americans thought the nation had a special role to play in the world. Many Americans thought they should spread freedom by settling the whole country, all the way to the Pacific Ocean. In the 1840s, newspaper editor John O'Sullivan called this mission **"Manifest Destiny."**

Many Americans thought the United States should take over all of Oregon. James K. Polk ran for president in 1844. He believed in Manifest Destiny. His campaign slogan was "Fifty-four Forty or Fight!" This names a line of latitude (54 degrees, 40 minutes North of the equator). This was where they wanted America's northern border in Oregon to be.

The British did not agree to this. The border was finally set at 49°N (49 degrees North of the Equator). James K. Polk won the election because of his support for Manifest Destiny.

/ / / / / / / / / / / Glue Foldable here / / / / / / / / / / / / /

Check for Understanding

List the four nations that claimed the Oregon Country.

_____

_____

_____

_____

List three reasons Americans moved to Oregon.

_____

_____

_____

 Describing

6. "Manifest Destiny" was America's special mission. Describe it.

_____

_____

✓ **Reading Check**

7. What views did Polk present in the 1844 election campaign?

_____

_____

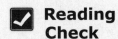

8. Place a two-tab Foldable along the dotted line to cover Check for Understanding. Write *Migration to Oregon* on the anchor tab. Label the left tab *West: Oregon Country* and the right tab *East: Manifest Destiny*. Draw an arrow from east to west across both tabs. Write what you remember about each and the migration to Oregon. Use the Foldable to help answer Check for Understanding.

Lesson 2 Statehood for Florida and Texas

ESSENTIAL QUESTION
Why does conflict develop?

GUIDING QUESTIONS
1. *How did Florida become a state?*
2. *How did Texas become a state?*

> **Terms to Know**
> **Tejano** a Texan of Hispanic, and often Mexican, descent
> **decree** official order
> **barricade** block off
> **annex** take control of

Where in the world?

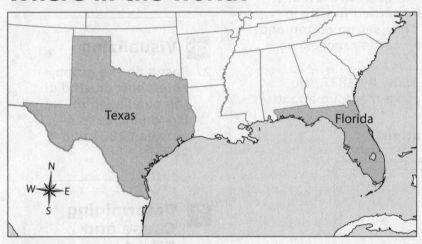

When did it happen?

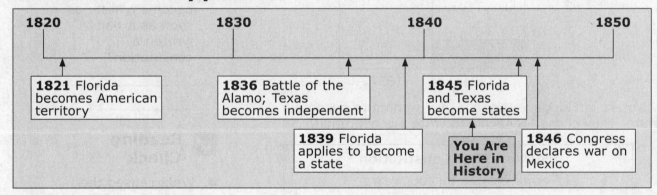

1820   **1830**   **1840**   **1850**

1821 Florida becomes American territory

1836 Battle of the Alamo; Texas becomes independent

1845 Florida and Texas become states

1839 Florida applies to become a state

You Are Here in History

1846 Congress declares war on Mexico

169

networks

Manifest Destiny

Lesson 2 Statehood for Florida and Texas, *Continued*

Florida

Florida belonged to Spain until 1821. In that year, Spain transferred Florida to the United States. Tallahassee was made the capital of the territory in 1824. It was located between two major cities, St. Augustine and Pensacola.

Thousands of new settlers came to Florida from the United States. Many came because of the fertile soil. Among these were planters from Virginia, Georgia, and the Carolinas. The soil in those states had been overused. It did not grow crops well. The planters settled mostly in western and northwestern Florida. They set up cotton and tobacco plantations. Small farms and cattle ranches were started in central Florida.

The population began to grow quickly. By 1837, the population was 48,000. Enslaved people made up about half of the population.

Florida Population

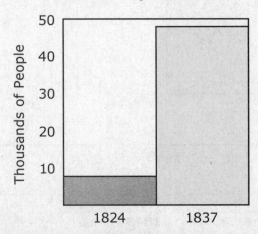

Voters in Florida voted that they wanted to become a state. They chose 56 people to write a constitution.

Florida's First Constitution
• Governor elected for four years
• An elected General Assembly, or legislature
• Public schools to be set up
• Slavery allowed

In 1839, the constitution was submitted to the U.S. Congress for approval. The question of allowing slavery created a problem. Congress wanted to keep the number

Explaining

1. Why did planters move to Florida from Virginia, Georgia, and the Carolinas?

_____

_____

Visualizing

2. Based on the graph, about how much did the population of Florida increase between 1824 and 1837?

_____

Determining Cause and Effect

3. Why didn't Florida become a state as soon as it had written a constitution?

_____

_____

Reading Check

4. What caused the population of Florida to grow?

_____

_____

170

Manifest Destiny

Lesson 2 Statehood for Florida and Texas, *Continued*

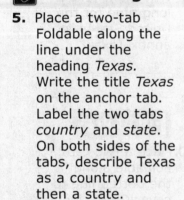

Describing

5. Place a two-tab Foldable along the line under the heading *Texas.* Write the title *Texas* on the anchor tab. Label the two tabs *country* and *state.* On both sides of the tabs, describe Texas as a country and then a state.

Mark the Text

6. Circle the definition of *decree.* Then underline what the Mexicans decreed.

Identifying

7. Who was Santa Anna?

_____

Analyzing

8. What happened to Texas after the battle of San Jacinto?

_____

_____

of slave states and the number of free states equal. Admitting Florida as a slave state would make the number uneven. Six years later, in 1845, Iowa joined the Union as a free state and Florida joined as a slave state.

Texas

/ / / / / / / / / / / Glue Foldable here / / / / / / / / / /

In 1821, Mexico won its freedom from Spain. Mexico owned Texas. Mexican citizens who lived there were called **Tejanos** (teh • HAH • nohs). Mexico wanted more people to settle in Texas. They encouraged Americans to come and live there. Stephen F. Austin brought 300 American families to Texas and became their leader.

Americans did not want to follow the rules that Mexico made for those living in Texas. The rules included learning Spanish and becoming Catholic. Mexico made a **decree,** or official order, that no more Americans could come to Texas. American leaders Stephen Austin and Sam Houston tried to reach an agreement with Mexico, but could not. They decided to break away from Mexico so that they could form their own government.

In 1835, Mexican general Santa Anna led an army into Texas to stop the Americans. The Mexicans had many more soldiers. Still, the Texans captured the city of San Antonio.

Santa Anna did not give up. In 1835, his army marched to San Antonio. It found a group of American soldiers **barricaded,** or blocked off, in a mission building called the Alamo. Santa Anna attacked. The defenders of the Alamo fought long and hard for 13 days. In the end Santa Anna killed all the American soldiers. The general was sure the Texans were beaten. The bravery of the defenders inspired other Texans. "Remember the Alamo!," Texans would cry.

In 1836 while fighting was going on at the Alamo, Texan leaders met. They announced that they were independent of Mexico. Sam Houston gathered an army and supplies. The Texan army made a surprise attack near San Jacinto (san hah • SIHN • toh). They beat the Mexican army and captured General Santa Anna. Santa Anna signed a treaty agreeing that Texas was independent of Mexico.

Texas was now a country. It was named the Lone Star Republic. In September 1836, voters elected Sam Houston president. He asked the United States to annex, or take control of, Texas. Again the problem of balancing slave and free states came up. Adding Texas as a slave state would upset the balance in Congress.

171

Manifest Destiny

Lesson 2 Statehood for Florida and Texas, *Continued*

Southerners wanted to annex Texas. Northerners were against adding another slave state. By 1844, the mood of the country had changed. Manifest Destiny had become a very popular idea. James K. Polk was elected president. He strongly supported expanding the country in Oregon and in Texas. In 1845 Texas entered the Union.

/ / / / / / / / / / / Glue Foldable here / / / / / / / / / / / /

Check for Understanding

Where in Florida did each of the following develop?

cattle ranches _____

cotton plantations _____

tobacco plantations _____

small farms _____

Write one thing each of the following men did in Texas:

Sam Houston _____

Santa Anna _____

Stephen Austin _____

☑ **Reading Check**

9. Why did it take a long time for the United States to annex Texas?

_____

_____

FOLDABLES®

10. Place a two-tab Foldable along the dotted line to cover Check for Understanding. Write the title *New States* on the anchor tab. Label the two tabs *Texas* and *Florida*. List two things you recall about each. Use the Foldable to help answer Check for Understanding.

Manifest Destiny

Lesson 3 War With Mexico

ESSENTIAL QUESTION
Why does conflict develop?

GUIDING QUESTIONS

1. **How did the Santa Fe Trail benefit the New Mexico Territory?**

2. **How did the culture of California develop?**

3. **Why did war break out between the United States and Mexico?**

Terms to Know
rancho ranch, especially the large estates set up by Mexicans in the American West
ranchero rancher, owner of a rancho

Where in the world?

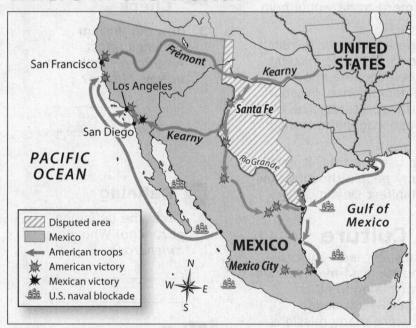

When did it happen?

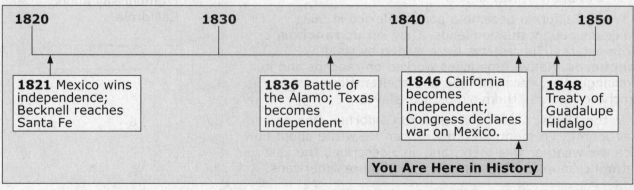

1820 **1830** **1840** **1850**

1821 Mexico wins independence; Becknell reaches Santa Fe

1836 Battle of the Alamo; Texas becomes independent

1846 California becomes independent; Congress declares war on Mexico.

1848 Treaty of Guadalupe Hidalgo

You Are Here in History

Lesson 3 War With Mexico, *Continued*

The New Mexico Territory

The New Mexico Territory included all of present-day New Mexico, Arizona, Nevada, Utah, and parts of Colorado and Wyoming. Mexico and the United States fought a war over this land.

Native Americans had lived in the area for thousands of years. Then Spanish explorers claimed it for Spain. They started a settlement at Santa Fe. In 1821, Mexico won its independence. New Mexico then became part of Mexico.

The Spanish did not want Americans to live in Santa Fe. They were afraid the Americans would take the land away from them. However, the new government of Mexico welcomed Americans. They hoped more trade would help the economy.

William Becknell was the first American trader to reach Santa Fe in New Mexico. He arrived in 1821. He brought many goods to sell. The route he took became known as the Santa Fe Trail. It began near Independence, Missouri. That was the western edge of the United States. The trail was mostly flat, so Becknell could use wagons to transport his goods.

Other American traders began to use the trail. It became a busy route. Settlers followed. Many people thought New Mexico was part of the country's Manifest Destiny.

California's Spanish Culture

The Spanish were the first Europeans to reach California. In the 1700s, Spanish explorers and Mexican missionaries settled there. Captain Gaspar de Portolá and Father Junipero Serra (hoo•NIP•uh•roh SEHR•uh) began building missions. Over time, there were many missions built between San Diego and Sonoma. Missions were built to convert Native Americans to Christianity and to teach them the Spanish way of life.

When California became a part of Mexico in 1821, Mexicans bought mission lands. They set up **ranchos,** or large estates. The estates were owned by wealthy **rancheros**. Native Americans worked on ranchos and in exchange, they received food and shelter. However, rancheros treated them almost like slaves.

In the 1840s, Americans came to California. One person was John C. Frémont, an army officer. He wrote about how nice the weather was there, and also described the vast natural resources. This attracted even more Americans.

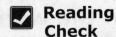

Identifying

1. Who claimed New Mexico before 1821?

_____

2. Who claimed it after 1821?

_____

✓ Reading Check

3. How did William Becknell affect American settlement in New Mexico?

_____

_____

A^bc Defining

4. Circle the definition of *rancho*. Who were *rancheros*?

_____

_____

Summarizing

5. What did John C. Frémont say about California?

_____

_____

174

Manifest Destiny

Lesson 3 War With Mexico, *Continued*

✓ Reading Check

6. Why did Americans want to add California to the United States?

_____

_____

⇄ Identifying

7. Where did the United States say the border between Texas and Mexico was? What did Mexico say?

_____

_____

Americans began to talk about adding California to the United States. If California became a state, the nation's western border would be the Pacific Ocean. Americans would not have to worry about sharing a western border with any other country. Shippers also wanted to build seaports on the coast. From there, they could trade with countries in Asia.

Conflict Begins

President Polk wanted to get both New Mexico and California from Mexico. He offered to buy the land, but Mexico would not sell it. Polk planned to get the land by going to war with Mexico. He hoped to get Mexico to start the fighting.

Mexico and the United States disagreed about where the border was between Texas and Mexico. The United States said it was the Rio Grande, the river to the south. Mexico said the border was the Nueces (nu•AY•sehs) River. It was 150 miles (241 km) farther north. Polk sent General Zachary Taylor to march his army into the area between the two rivers. He hoped that Mexican soldiers would fire first. On April 25, 1846, they did. On May 13, Congress voted to go to war with Mexico.

Polk had three goals to win the war.

U.S. Goals for War With Mexico
1. Push Mexican forces out of Texas
2. Take control of New Mexico and California
3. Capture Mexico City

General Taylor accomplished the first goal in Texas by 1847. General Stephen Kearney led American troops down the Santa Fe trail and captured Santa Fe, New Mexico's capital. Then Kearney headed toward California.

Meanwhile, General John C. Frémont was leading a revolt against Mexico in California. Frémont won. The rebels declared California independent of Mexico.

They named California the Bear Flag Republic. However, the Bear Flag Republic did not stay independent for long. American navy ships sailed into the ports of both San Francisco and San Diego. The Navy claimed California for the United States.

Mexico did not give up, however. Since Mexico had not given up yet, American soldiers were sent to Mexico.

175

Manifest Destiny

Lesson 3 War With Mexico, *Continued*

Finally, General Winfield Scott and his troops captured Mexico City.

In 1848, the Mexicans stopped fighting. The treaty, or agreement, that ended the war was called the Treaty of Guadalupe Hidalgo (GWAH•duh•loop he•DAHL•goh). Mexico gave up California and the New Mexico Territory. It also agreed that the Rio Grande was the border between Mexico and Texas. Mexico gave more than 500,000 square miles (1,295,000 sq. km) of land to the United States. The United States paid Mexico $15 million dollars for the land. They also took on $3.25 million in debts that Mexico owed to American citizens. The dream of Manifest Destiny had become a reality.

////////////// Glue Foldable here ///////////////

Check for Understanding

What did the Mexican War have to do with the idea of Manifest Destiny?

_____

_____

List three results of the Mexican War.

_____

_____

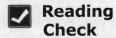

Reading Check

8. What did America gain from the Mexican War?

_____

_____

FOLDABLES

9. Place a three-tab Venn diagram Foldable along the dotted line to cover Check for Understanding. Write *Compare* on the anchor tab. Label the three tabs *New Mexico Territory*, *Both*, and *California*. List two things you recall about each and what they had in common. Use the Foldable to help answer Check for Understanding.

Manifest Destiny

Lesson 4 California and Utah

ESSENTIAL QUESTION

How do new ideas change the way people live?

GUIDING QUESTIONS

1. How did the discovery of gold help California?
2. Why did the Mormons settle in Utah?

Terms to Know

forty-niner person who came to California to find gold in 1849
boomtown a fast-growing community
vigilante person who takes it on himself to bring law and order to a place

Where in the world?

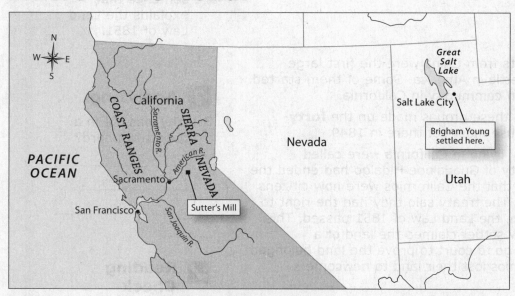

When did it happen?

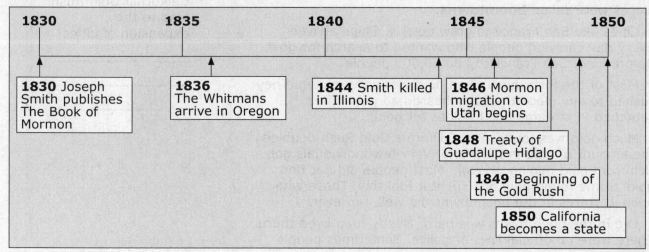

1830 Joseph Smith publishes The Book of Mormon

1836 The Whitmans arrive in Oregon

1844 Smith killed in Illinois

1846 Mormon migration to Utah begins

1848 Treaty of Guadalupe Hidalgo

1849 Beginning of the Gold Rush

1850 California becomes a state

Manifest Destiny

Lesson 4 California and Utah, *Continued*

California Gold Rush

Gold was discovered at Sutter's Mill in California in 1848. The news traveled fast. Soon many people came to California to see if they could get rich.

Where did they come from?

- About 80 percent of these people were American.

Others were from:

- Mexico
- South America
- Europe
- Australia
- China

The 300 immigrants from China were the first large group of Asians to settle in America. Some of them started the Chinese American community in California.

Taken together, all these groups made up the **forty-niners.** That is because most got there in 1849.

The people already living in California were called Californios. The Treaty of Guadalupe Hidalgo had ended the Mexican War. It said that the Californios were now citizens of the United States. The treaty said they had the right to keep their land. Then, the Land Law of 1851 passed. This law said that if a new settler claimed the land of a Californio, he had to go to court to prove the land belonged to him. Many Californios lost their land to newcomers because of this law.

When miners rushed to new areas to look for gold, they built new villages. These grew quickly into cities. Such places were called **boomtowns.**

Cities like San Francisco grew quickly. Ships arrived every day carrying people who wanted to search for gold. Before long, San Francisco had 20,000 people.

Most of the forty-niners had no experience mining. They rushed to any place that they heard had gold. They searched in streams and hillsides for gold.

Much gold was found. The California Gold Rush doubled the amount of gold in the world. Very few individuals got rich from gold mining, though. Most people did not find gold. Some found gold and spent it foolishly. Those who opened stores in the boomtowns did well, however.

Life in the boomtowns was hard. Mostly men lived there. There were no official laws or police. Sometimes people

Defining

1. Why were miners called *forty-niners*?

_____

_____

Mark the Text

2. Underline the sentence that explains the Land Law of 1851.

Analyzing

3. Why was life in a boomtown hard?

_____

_____

_____

Reading Check

4. How did the California Gold Rush lead to the expansion of cities?

_____

_____

_____

Manifest Destiny

Lesson 4 California and Utah, *Continued*

📝 Identifying

5. Who was Joseph Smith?

_____

6. What happened to him in Illinois?

_____

❓ Reading Check

7. Why did the Mormons have to keep moving from one place to another?

_____

_____

formed groups of **vigilantes** to protect themselves. Vigilantes took the law into their own hands. They acted as police, judge, and jury.

The Gold Rush had many lasting effects:

*   Agriculture, shipping, and trade grew
*   Many people who came to look for gold stayed
*   Those who stayed went into farming or business
*   In 1849 California asked to become a state

Californians wrote a new constitution. The new constitution banned slavery. Southern states did not want California to join the Union. Congress wanted an equal number of slave states and free states. In 1850 a compromise was reached. California became a state.

A Religious Refuge in Utah

While the Gold Rush was taking place in California, change was also taking place in Utah. Mormons were building a new community there.

Joseph Smith founded the Mormon religion. He founded it during the religious awakenings that took place during the 1830s and 1840s.

Smith said he had visions that led him to build a church. He called it the Church of Jesus Christ of Latter-day Saints. The religion is also known as the Mormon religion.

Smith began to preach his ideas in 1830. He published *The Book of Mormon* that year as well.

Smith wanted to build an ideal community. Mormons believed in hard work. They also believed that a man could have more than one wife. This belief made them unpopular wherever they went. They created a prosperous community named Nauvoo in Illinois. Then, in 1844, Joseph Smith was killed by an angry mob.

Brigham Young took over as leader of the Mormons. He decided that the Mormons should move again to find religious freedom. He led them westward to the Great Salt Lake. The territory was in present-day Utah. It was part of Mexico at the time. However, no Mexicans lived there. The land was dry and harsh.

The Mormons built a successful community through hard work. They:

*   planned their towns,
*   built irrigation canals,

Manifest Destiny

Lesson 4 California and Utah, *Continued*

- taxed property,
- regulated natural resources,
- founded industries, and
- sold supplies to forty-niners who were on their way to California.

In 1850 Congress set up the Utah Territory. Brigham Young was named governor.

The Mormons often had conflicts with the U.S. government. Utah did not become a state until 1896.

/ / / / / / / / / / / /Glue Foldable here/ / / / / / / / / / / /

Check for Understanding

Read each statement. Write *T* if it is true. If it is false, write *F*.

____ Mormons worked hard to grow crops in Utah.

____ Utah became a state soon after it was settled.

In what ways did the Gold Rush affect California?

_____

_____

_____

FOLDABLES®

8. Place a two-tab Foldable along the dotted line to cover Check for Understanding. Write the title *Go West* on the anchor tab. Label the left tab *Gold Rush: California* and the right tab *Religious Refuge: Utah*. List what you remember about each and the movement west. Use the Foldable to help answer Check for Understanding.

North and South

Lesson 1 The Industrial North

ESSENTIAL QUESTION

How does technology change the way people live?

GUIDING QUESTIONS

1. How did technology and industry change during the 1800s?
2. What changes made agriculture more profitable in the 1830s?

Terms to Know

clipper ship ship with sleek hulls and tall sails that "clipped" time from long journeys

Morse code a system of dots and dashes that represent the alphabet

telegraph a device that used electric signals to send messages

When did it happen?

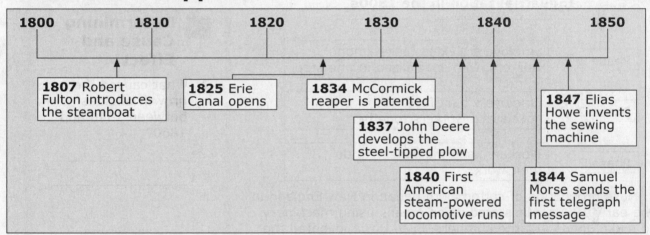

1800	1810	1820	1830	1840	1850

1807 Robert Fulton introduces the steamboat

1825 Erie Canal opens

1834 McCormick reaper is patented

1837 John Deere develops the steel-tipped plow

1840 First American steam-powered locomotive runs

1844 Samuel Morse sends the first telegraph message

1847 Elias Howe invents the sewing machine

What do you know?

In the first column, answer the questions based on what you know before you study.
After this lesson, complete the last column.

Now...		Later...
	What was one change as a result of the Erie Canal?	
	In which part of the country was there more industry?	
	What was the telegraph?	

Lesson 1 The Industrial North, *Continued*

Technology and Industry

The early 1800s saw many **innovations** in industry, or the production of goods. Innovations are improved ways of doing things. There were new machines and new ways to use them. The ways in which Americans worked, traveled, and communicated with each other changed as well. Much of this took place in the North.

At the start of the 1800s, most products were made one at a time. A worker would make a product from start to finish. Innovations in industry changed that way of working.

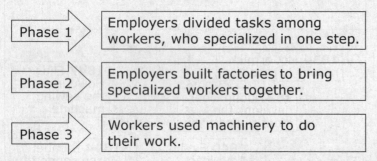

Industrialization in the 1800s

Phase 1 → Employers divided tasks among workers, who specialized in one step.

Phase 2 → Employers built factories to bring specialized workers together.

Phase 3 → Workers used machinery to do their work.

Mass production of cotton cloth began in New England in the early 1800s. Mass production means using machinery to make goods in large numbers. Elias Howe invented the sewing machine in 1846. These changes **transformed,** or changed, the clothing industry. Workers could now make more clothing faster. Other changes transformed other industries. By 1860, the Northeast's factories made at least two-thirds of the country's manufactured goods.

Transportation improved. Between 1800 and 1850, crews built thousands of miles of roads and canals. The canals connected lakes and rivers to make new shipping routes. In 1807, Robert Fulton introduced the steamboat. Steamboats carried goods and people cheaply and quickly.

By 1860 about 3,000 steamboats traveled major rivers and canals, as well as the Great Lakes. Cincinnati, Buffalo, and Chicago grew because they were on major shipping routes.

Sailing was still an important way to travel. A new, faster ship was developed in the 1840s. Called **clipper ships,** they could sail as fast as most steamships at that time.

The railroad was developed. The first steam-powered railroad engine began running in Britain in 1829.

Explaining

1. List three changes in the way goods were made during the early 1800s.

_____

_____

_____

Determining Cause and Effect

2. What caused the growth of cities between 1840 and 1860?

_____

_____

North and South

Lesson 1 The Industrial North, Continued

Determining Cause and Effect

3. What were some effects of the railroad on the country?

_____

_____

Reading Check

4. What effect did canals and railways have on transportation from the East to the Midwest?

_____

_____

Peter Cooper built the first American steam-powered railroad engine in 1830. By 1860, there were about 31,000 miles (19,220 km) of track. These tracks were mostly in the North and Midwest. Rail lines connected many cities. They united the Midwest and the East.

Growth of Railroads in 1800s

1830	**1840**	**1860**
steam-powered railroad engine in America	3,000 miles of railroad track	31,000 miles of track connects many cities

The Erie Canal opened in 1825. With the railroads and the canal, farm products could be moved directly from the Midwest to the East. Farmers and manufacturers could move goods faster and more cheaply. As a result, people could buy them at lower prices than in the past.

The railroads also played an important role in the settlement of the Midwest and the growth of business there. People moved to Ohio, Indiana, and Illinois. New cities and industries developed in the area.

The growth of industry and the speed of travel created a need for faster ways to send messages great distances. Samuel Morse invented the **telegraph**—a machine that uses electric signals to send messages. In 1844 Morse sent his first message.

Telegraph companies formed. Their operators used **Morse code** to send messages. Telegraph lines were put up across the country. By 1852, there were about 23,000 miles (37,015 km) of telegraph lines in the United States.

Farming Innovations

In the early 1800s, few farmers were willing to settle in the West. They were worried that they would not be able to plow on the Great Plains or the prairie. They worried that the soil would not be good enough to grow crops.

183

North and South

Lesson 1 The Industrial North, *Continued*

/ / / / / / / / / / / ,Glue Foldable here / / / / / / / / / / /

Three inventions of the 1830s helped farmers overcome these difficulties in farming the land. Because of this, more people moved to the Midwest.

One of these inventions was the steel-tipped plow developed by John Deere in 1837. This plow easily cut through the hard prairie ground. Also important were the reaper and the thresher, invented by Cyrus McCormick. The reaper sped up the harvesting, or gathering, of wheat. The thresher quickly separated the grain from the stalk, or stem, of the wheat.

McCormick's reaper greatly increased the amount of grain a farmer could harvest. Because farmers could harvest more, they could plant more. Growing wheat brought more money than before. Raising wheat became the main economic activity on the Midwestern prairie.

Because of the new machines and the railroads, farmers could plant more crops. Midwestern farmers grew wheat and shipped it east by train and canal barge. Northeast and Middle Atlantic farmers grew more fruits and vegetables.

Despite improvements in farming, the North turned away from farming and toward industry. The number of people working in factories continued to rise.

/ / / / / / / / / / / ,Glue Foldable here / / / / / / / / / / /

Check for Understanding

List two inventions that transformed the way goods and people were moved in the 1800s.

_____

_____

What are two reasons that farmers were able to make more money growing wheat?

_____

_____

FOLDABLES®

Describing

5. Place a three-tab Foldable along the dotted line. Title the anchor tab *Three Inventions*. Label tabs: *Steel-tipped Plow*, *Mechanical Reaper*, *Thresher*. On the tabs, describe how the inventions helped farmers.

✓ Reading Check

6. What sped up the harvest of wheat?

_____

_____

FOLDABLES®

7. Place a one-tab Foldable along the dotted line. Create a memory map. Write *Technology Changed Lives in the 1800s* in the middle. Draw four arrows around the titles. Write words or phrases about the changes industrialization brought. Use this Foldable to help you complete the Check for Understanding.

North and South

Lesson 2 People of the North

ESSENTIAL QUESTION

Why do people adapt to their environment?

GUIDING QUESTIONS

1. *Why did many Americans push for reform in the workplace during this era?*
2. *What challenges did European immigrants face in Northern cities?*

Terms to Know

trade union group of workers with the same trade, or skill

strike a refusal to work in order to force an employer to make changes

prejudice an unfair opinion not based on facts

discrimination unfair treatment

emigrant person who leaves his or her homeland to move elsewhere

famine an extreme shortage of food

nativist person opposed to immigration

Where in the world?

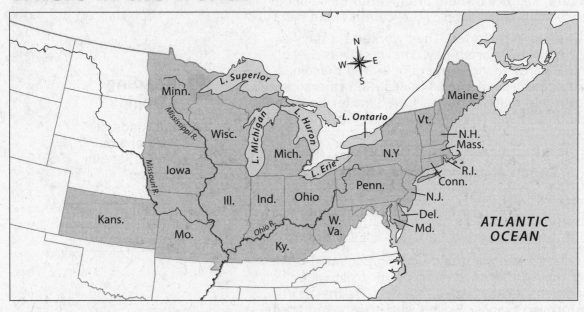

When did it happen?

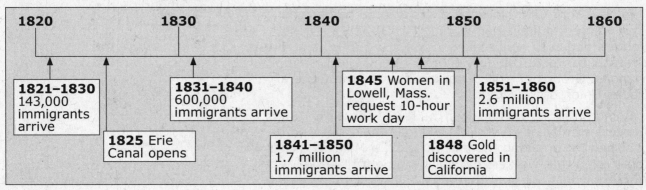

185

Lesson 2 People of the North, *Continued*

The Factories of the North

By the mid-1800s, more and more things were made by machine. Clothing, shoes, watches, guns, and farming machines were made by machine. Conditions for factory workers were bad. By 1840, the average workday was 11.4 hours. Workers became very tired and more likely to have work accidents. Many factory machines had rapidly moving parts. Workers, especially children, were often hurt by the machines.

Factories had no cooling or heating systems. In the summer, they were very hot. In the winter, workers were often cold.

There were no laws to control working conditions or protect workers. Factory owners often cared more about making money than about employees' comfort and safety.

Children worked in factories. They worked six days a week and 12 hours or more a day. The work was dangerous and hard. Young workers operated machines. They worked underground in coal mines. Reformers called for laws that would make factories have shorter hours and better conditions. It was many years before such laws were passed.

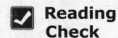

Child Labor In the Mid-1800s		
long hours	dangerous work	no laws to protect children

Workers tried to improve their working conditions. They thought that they would have more power to change working conditions if they joined together. By the 1830s, they began forming unions. Skilled workers started **trade unions**. All the workers in these groups had the same trade, or skill.

In New York City, skilled workers wanted higher pay. They wanted to limit their workday to 10 hours. These workers began to hold strikes in the mid-1830s. A **strike** is a refusal to work. The goal is to force employers to make changes. Groups of skilled workers formed the General Trades Union of New York.

Going on strike was against the law in the early 1800s. Workers who went on strike could lose their jobs and be punished for breaking the law. In 1842, a Massachusetts court ruled that workers did have the right to strike. Workers would not get other legal rights for many years.

186

Determining Cause and Effect

1. What were three changes that workers hoped to make by forming trade unions?

_____

_____

_____

✓ Reading Check

2. What kinds of conditions did workers face in factories?

_____

_____

_____

Aᵇᶜ Mark the Text

3. Underline the meaning of *strike*.

North and South

Lesson 2 People of the North, *Continued*

Mark the Text

4. Underline the meanings of *prejudice* and *discrimination*.

Explaining

5. What change was the Female Labor Reform Organization trying to make?

_____

_____

6. How successful were they?

_____

_____

In the North, slavery was mostly ended by the 1830s. However, racial **prejudice**—an unfair opinion of a group—and **discrimination**—unfair treatment of a group—continued. For example, white men in New York could vote even if they did not own property. Few African Americans had the right to vote, however. Rhode Island and Pennsylvania even passed laws to keep them from voting.

Most **communities** in the North did not allow African Americans to go to public schools. African Americans often had to go to lower-quality schools. They had to go to hospitals that were just for them.

A few African Americans did well in business. In 1845, Macon B. Allen became the first African American **licensed**, or given the official right, to practice law in the United States. Most African Americans were poor in the mid-1800s.

```
        Discrimination against
         African Americans
        ┌────────┴────────┐
  not allowed        not allowed to go to good
   to vote           public schools or hospitals
```

Women also faced discrimination. They were paid less than men. Men stopped women from joining unions. Men wanted to keep women out of the workplace.

In the 1830s and 1840s, some female workers tried to organize for better working conditions. Sarah G. Bagley was a weaver from Massachusetts. She started the Lowell Female Labor Reform Organization. In 1845, her group asked the state legislature for a 10-hour workday. Because most of the workers were women, the legislature ignored the request.

The Growth of Cities

Industrialization caused big changes in cities. Factories were usually in cities. Because factories attracted workers, Northern cities became much bigger in the early 1800s. Industrialization caused small Western cities to grow.

Between 1820 and 1840, some Midwestern towns grew into major cities. These towns were located along rivers. St. Louis was one. It is located on the Mississippi River, just south of the Illinois and Missouri rivers. By the mid-1800s, many steamboats stopped at St. Louis. Pittsburgh, Cincinnati, and Louisville also were located on waterways.

187

North and South

Lesson 2 People of the North, *Continued*

These cities became centers of trade. They linked farmers in the Midwest with cities in the Northeast.

Between 1840 and 1860, immigration to the United States increased greatly. Immigration means to enter a new country in order to live there. The greatest number of immigrants came from Ireland. About 1.5 million people came. They left because there was **famine,** or an extreme shortage of food. Over a million people had died in Ireland.

The second-largest group of immigrants came from Germany. Some wanted work and opportunity. Others left to escape political problems.

European immigrants brought their languages, customs, religions, and traditions to the United States.

In the 1830s and 1840s, some Americans were against immigration. These Americans were called **nativists.** They believed that immigrants would make life hard for "native," or American-born, citizens. They said immigrants would take jobs from "real" Americans. They said immigrants brought crime and disease.

In 1849, nativists formed a new political party. Their members often answered questions about their group by saying, "I know nothing." That is why they were known as the Know-Nothing Party. The Know-Nothings wanted laws that would make it harder to become a citizen. In 1854 the Know-Nothings became known as the American Party.

/ / / / / / / / / / / Glue Foldable here / / / / / / / / / / / /

Check for Understanding

Give three reasons that many Americans wanted reform in the workplace.

_____

_____

_____

How did Americans feel about immigrants?

_____

_____

Mark the Text

7. Circle what nativists believed.

✓ Reading Check

8. Which two nations did most immigrants come from in the mid-1800s?

_____

_____

FOLDABLES®

9. Place a Venn-diagram Foldable along the dotted line to cover Check for Understanding. Label the anchor tab *Dealing with Difficulties.* Label the left tab *Workers,* the middle tab *Both,* and the right tab *Immigrants.* Write what you remember about difficulties faced by each group and determine what they had in common. Use the Foldable to answer Check for Understanding.

North and South

Lesson 3 Southern Cotton Kingdom

ESSENTIAL QUESTION

Why do people make economic choices?

GUIDING QUESTIONS

1. **How were the economies of the South and North different?**

2. **Why did industry develop slowly in the South?**

Terms to Know

productivity a measure of how much a worker can produce with a given amount of time and effort

domestic slave trade the trade of enslaved people within the United States

Where in the world?

Major cotton-producing areas 1820

When did it happen?

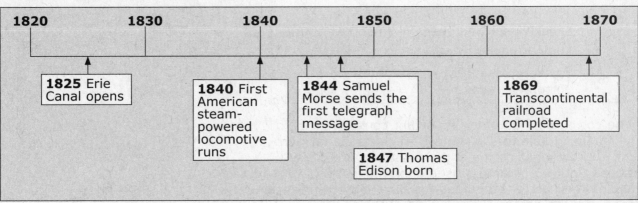

1825 Erie Canal opens

1840 First American steam-powered locomotive runs

1844 Samuel Morse sends the first telegraph message

1847 Thomas Edison born

1869 Transcontinental railroad completed

North and South

Lesson 3 Southern Cotton Kingdom, *Continued*

Rise of the Cotton Kingdom

In the early years of the United States, the South's economy was based mostly on farming. Most Southerners lived in an area called the Upper South. The Upper South was the Atlantic coast of Maryland, Virginia, and North Carolina. Fewer people settled in Georgia and South Carolina.

By 1850, the South had changed. People had moved away from the coast. They now lived in the Deep South. The Deep South included Georgia, South Carolina, Alabama, Mississippi, Louisiana, and Texas.

The economy of the South was very strong. That economy depended, however, on enslaved workers. Slavery was growing in the South, even though it had almost ended in the North.

In colonial times, Southern planters grew mostly rice and tobacco. After the American Revolution, there was less demand for these crops. There was more demand for cotton. Factories in Europe wanted Southern cotton.

It took a lot of time and work to grow and process cotton. After the cotton was picked, workers had to carefully remove the plant's sticky seeds.

Eli Whitney solved this problem. In 1793, he invented a machine called the cotton gin. Whitney's machine quickly removed seeds from cotton fibers. Using the cotton gin, **productivity** went up. Productivity is the amount of anything that a worker can make, or produce, in a given time. Workers could **process** 50 times more cotton using the cotton gin than they used to process by hand.

> **Fact Sheet: The Cotton Gin**
> - Invented by Eli Whitney in 1793
> - Quickly removed seeds from cotton fibers
> - Made it easier to raise a cotton crop
> - Workers could process 50 times more cotton each day

The cotton gin had other important consequences, or effects. Being able to use the cotton gin made farmers want to grow more cotton and grow it in more places. Because Southern planters used enslaved workers to plant and pick their cotton, the need for slave labor increased. Slavery spread across a larger area of the South.

Explaining
1. On what two things did the economy of the South depend in the early years of the United States?

_____

_____

Mark the Text
2. Underline the definition of the word *productivity*.

Making Connections
3. Why did the need for slave labor increase in the South?

_____

_____

Lesson 3 Southern Cotton Kingdom, *Continued*

Explaining

4. What was the domestic slave trade?

_____

_____

_____

Effects of Cotton Gin on Slavery

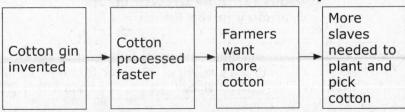

Cotton gin invented → Cotton processed faster → Farmers want more cotton → More slaves needed to plant and pick cotton

By 1860, the Deep South and Upper South grew different crops. The Upper South produced:

- tobacco
- hemp
- wheat
- vegetables

The Deep South produced:

- rice
- sugarcane
- cotton

Many enslaved workers were needed to produce the cotton and sugar crops. As a result, the sale of enslaved Africans was a big business. The Upper South became the place where most of the sales took place. This kind of slave trade took place within the United States, so it was known as the **domestic slave trade.** *Domestic* means "local."

Reading Check

5. List three effects that the cotton gin had on the South's economy.

_____

_____

_____

Southern Industry

Industry did not grow as quickly in the South as it did in the North. One reason was cotton. Cotton brought great profits. Another reason was the cost of building new industries. To raise the money to build factories, planters would have had to sell enslaved people or land. White Southerners made plenty of money growing cotton, rice, sugar, and tobacco. They also made money selling slaves. They did not feel the need to earn money from industry.

There was not much market, or demand, for factory-made products in the South. Many people in the South were enslaved people. They had no money to buy goods. No market for goods stopped industries from growing.

For these reasons, it is not surprising that some white Southerners just did not want industry.

North and South

Lesson 3 Southern Cotton Kingdom, *Continued*

```
          Reasons for Slow Growth of
             Industry in the South
```

Growing cotton was very profitable	Building new industry is very expensive	Limited market for factory goods

Some Southern leaders did want industry in the region. They thought the South depended too much on the North for factory goods. These leaders also thought that factories would improve the economy of the Upper South. A few men opened factories.

Transportation systems in the South were different from those in the North. In the South, farmers and the few factory owners moved their goods on natural waterways. Most towns were located on coasts or along rivers. There were few canals, and roads were poor.

The South had fewer railroads than the North. Southern rail lines were not long, and they were not linked together. Poor railroad systems are another reason Southern cities grew more slowly. By 1860, only about one-third of the nation's rail lines lay within the South. This rail shortage would hurt the South in the years to come.

```
               Problems with
          Transportation in the South
```

few canals	poor roads	few rail lines

/ / / / / / / / / / / / Glue Foldable here / / / / / / / / / / /

Check for Understanding

List two ways that the South's economy was different from the North's economy.

_____

_____

Why did industry develop so slowly in the South?

_____

_____

Contrasting

6. How were Southern railroads different from Northern railroads?

_____

_____

☑ Reading Check

7. How did slavery affect the growth of the South's economy?

_____

_____

FOLDABLES®

8. Place a Venn-diagram Foldable along the dotted line to cover Check for Understanding. Label the left tab *Northern Economy*, the middle tab *Both*, and the right tab *Southern Economy*. Write what you remember about each region and determine what they had in common. Use the Foldable to help answer Check for Understanding.

netw⬤rks

North and South

Lesson 4 People of the South

ESSENTIAL QUESTION

How do people adapt to their environment?

GUIDING QUESTIONS

1. **How were Southern farms different from Southern plantations?**
2. **How did enslaved African Americans try to cope with their lack of freedom?**
3. **What changes did urbanization introduce in the South by the mid-1800s?**

Terms to Know

yeomen farmers who owned small farms
overseer plantation manager
spiritual African American religious song
slave codes laws in Southern states that controlled enslaved people
Underground Railroad a system to aid the escape of enslaved people
literacy the ability to read and write

When did it happen?

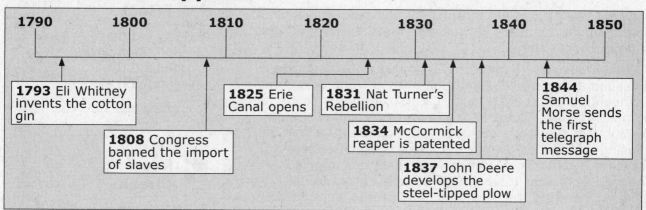

| 1790 | 1800 | 1810 | 1820 | 1830 | 1840 | 1850 |

1793 Eli Whitney invents the cotton gin

1808 Congress banned the import of slaves

1825 Erie Canal opens

1831 Nat Turner's Rebellion

1834 McCormick reaper is patented

1837 John Deere develops the steel-tipped plow

1844 Samuel Morse sends the first telegraph message

What do you know?

In the first column, answer the questions based on what you know before you study. After this lesson, complete the last column.

Now...		Later...
	What were Southern farms like in the 1800s?	
	What kind of family life did enslaved African Americans have?	

193

North and South

Lesson 4 People of the South, *Continued*

Southern Agriculture

Slavery was at the center of the Southern economy. That does not mean that every white person owned large numbers of enslaved people. There were four main groups of white society. There were yeomen, tenant farmers, the rural poor, and plantation owners.

Most white people in the South were **yeomen** farmers. Yeomen farmers owned small farms. These farms were in the Upper South and in hilly parts of the Deep South. Yeomen farmers owned only a few slaves. Some owned no slaves. They grew crops for themselves and to trade for things they needed.

Tenant farmers did not own their land. They rented the land that they farmed. Yeomen farmers and tenant farmers were most of the white farmers in the south.

A few free African Americans kept enslaved workers. Some bought members of their own families. They did this in order to free them.

Plantations were large farms. They could be several thousand acres in size. Plantation owners wanted to earn as much money as they could. Large plantations cost a lot of money to run. There were fixed costs. Fixed costs are the costs of running a business. For example, the cost of housing and feeding workers is a fixed cost. Fixed costs stayed the same from year to year. The price of cotton changed from year to year. Owners sold cotton to earn money. Therefore, their earnings and profits were different from year to year.

The owners were usually men. Owners traveled often on business. Their wives ran the households. They managed the enslaved workers. They kept the financial records.

Enslaved people did many different jobs on the plantation. They cleaned the house, cooked, did laundry and sewing, and served meals. They were blacksmiths, carpenters, shoemakers, or weavers. They took care of the or animals. Most enslaved African Americans worked in the fields. They worked from sunrise to sunset. An **overseer**, or plantation manager, was their boss in the fields.

The Lives of Enslaved People

Life was hard for most enslaved African Americans. They worked hard, earned no money, and had little hope of ever being free. They feared that an owner could sell them or members of their family. Even with all this, enslaved

◻ Listing

1. List the four groups of white society in the South in the 1800s.

   _____

   _____

   _____

   _____

☑ Determining Cause and Effect

2. Why did many plantation wives manage the plantation alone?

   _____

   _____

☑ Reading Check

3. Which group made up the largest number of whites in the South?

   _____

Lesson 4 People of the South, *Continued*

Specifying

4. What kind of work did most enslaved African Americans do?

_____

_____

_____

Explaining

5. Why did enslaved people need extended families?

_____

_____

Reading Check

6. How did African American spirituals develop?

_____

_____

African Americans kept up their family lives as best they could. They developed a culture, or way of life. It blended African and American elements.

Enslaved people married and raised families. Still, there were no laws that could stop a slave owner from selling a family member. This broke the family apart.

If an owner sold an enslaved father or mother, then a relative or a close friend took care of the children left behind. Large, close-knit families became an important part of African American culture.

In 1808, Congress stopped new slaves from being brought into the United States. Slavery was still legal, however. By 1860, almost all the enslaved people in the South had been born there.

Enslaved people kept old African customs. They told traditional African folk stories to their children. They performed African music and dance.

Enslaved people created their own kind of music. They used their African music styles for the music. The beat of the music set the pace for their work in the fields.

Many enslaved African Americans followed traditional African religious practices. Others accepted Christianity. Enslaved people expressed their beliefs through **spirituals.** These are African American religious folk songs.

The **slave codes** were laws in the Southern states. Slaves codes controlled enslaved people. One purpose of the slave codes was to prevent slaves from rebelling. Slave codes prevented enslaved people from meeting in large groups. They needed a written pass to leave the slaveowner's property. It was a crime to teach enslaved people to read or write.

White people had reasons to fear slave rebellion. Enslaved African Americans did sometimes openly rebel.

Nat Turner was a popular religious leader among enslaved people. Turner had taught himself to read and write. In 1831, he led a group of followers on a brief, violent rebellion in Virginia.

Effects of Nat Turner's Rebellion

Turner's group kills at least 55 whites.	→	White mobs kill more than 100 African Americans.	→	Whites pass even stricter slave codes.

Enslaved people also resisted by running away. They ran away to find family members on other plantations. They ran away to escape punishment. Sometimes, enslaved

195

North and South

Lesson 4 People of the South, *Continued*

African Americans ran North to freedom. Harriet Tubman and Frederick Douglass were two such people. They became important African American leaders.

A runaway might receive aid from the **Underground Railroad.** This was a network of "safe houses" owned by people who were against slavery. The Underground Railroad helped enslaved people escape slavery.

Southern Cities

By the mid-1800s, the South had several large cities. Two cities were Baltimore and New Orleans. The ten largest Southern cities were seaports or river ports. Chattanooga, Montgomery, and Atlanta were cities that formed near railroads.

Free African Americans formed communities. They worked. They set up churches and other institutions. They were not equal to whites in economic and political ways, though. They could not move freely from state to state.

In the early 1800s, there were no statewide public school systems in the South. There was less **literacy,** or the ability to read and write, in the South than in other parts of the country. People who had enough money sent their children to private schools. By the mid-1800s, North Carolina and Kentucky set up and ran public schools.

Reasons for Low Literacy in the South		
People were spread out over a wide area.	People could not send their children so far away.	Many in the South did not believe in public education.

Check for Understanding

List two differences between Southern farms and plantations.

_____

_____

List two things enslaved African Americans did to help themselves cope with a lack of freedom.

_____

_____

Glue Foldable here / / / / / / / / / / / / / /

✓ Reading Check

7. What led to the growth of Southern cities?

_____

_____

FOLDABLES®

8. Place a one-tab Foldable along the dotted line to cover Check for Understanding. Create a memory map. Write: *How did enslaved people cope with their lack of freedom?* in the middle of the tab, and draw four arrows around the title. Use both sides of the tab to write words or phrases you remember about ways enslaved people adjusted their lives to survive. Use the Foldable to help answer Check for Understanding.

The Spirit of Reform

Lesson 1 Social Reform

ESSENTIAL QUESTION

Why do societies change?

GUIDING QUESTIONS

1. **What was the effect of the Second Great Awakening?**
2. **What type of American literature emerged in the 1820s?**

Terms to Know

revival religious meeting

utopia community based on a vision of the perfect society

temperance drinking little or no alcohol

normal school state-supported school for training high-school graduates to become teachers

civil disobedience refusing to obey laws considered unjust

Where in the world?

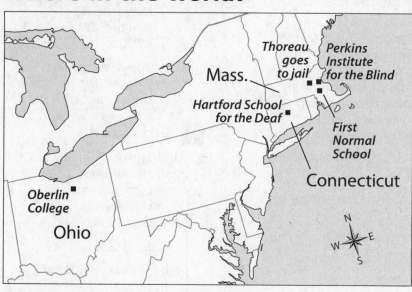

When did it happen?

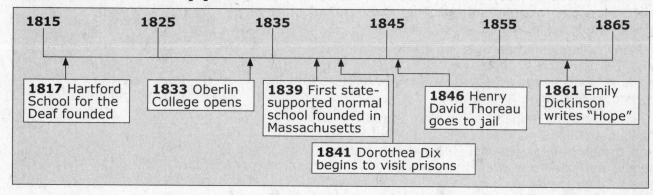

| 1815 | 1825 | 1835 | 1845 | 1855 | 1865 |

1817 Hartford School for the Deaf founded

1833 Oberlin College opens

1839 First state-supported normal school founded in Massachusetts

1841 Dorothea Dix begins to visit prisons

1846 Henry David Thoreau goes to jail

1861 Emily Dickinson writes "Hope"

The Spirit of Reform

Lesson 1 Social Reform, *Continued*

Religion and Reform

Religious meetings, called **revivals**, were popular in the early 1800s. People traveled far to hear certain preachers. It was a time of great interest in religion. It was known as the Second Great Awakening. The first Great Awakening had been in the mid-1700s.

People thought of ways to reform, or improve, society as a result of attending revival meetings. Some thought that they should set up **utopias** (yu•TOH•pee•uhs). These were communities based on their idea of a perfect society. Most utopias did not last. One of the groups that did last, however, was the Mormons.

Several social reform movements came about in the 1800s. Some reformers called for **temperance**. Lyman Beecher was one such reformer. Temperance means to drink little or no alcohol. Reformers used **lectures** and booklets to warn people about the dangers of drinking alcohol. Some laws were passed to prevent people from drinking. Most of the laws were later repealed, or canceled.

Reformers wanted to fix some problems with education.

- Many teachers were not well-trained.

- Many people did not believe children had to go to school.

- Girls were often kept from going to school.

- Many schools refused to allow African American students to attend.

Horace Mann was a lawyer in Massachusetts. He believed education was the key to getting ahead. Thanks to his work, in 1839, Massachusetts founded the nation's first state-supported **normal school**. This was a school in which people were trained to be teachers.

Many colleges and universities started during this time. Most of them only accepted students who were white and male. A few colleges accepted students who were female or who were African American.

Some reforms helped people with disabilities. Thomas Gallaudet (GA•luh•DEHT) created a way to teach people who could not hear. Samuel Gridley Howe helped teach people who could not see. He made books with large raised letters. People could "read" the books with their fingers. Dorothea Dix told people about the bad conditions in prisons.

Finding the Main Idea

1. Place a checkmark next to the best statement of the main idea of this passage.

____ Several social reform movements started in the 1800s.

____ Some reformers worked for temperance.

Evaluating

2. Which reformer do you think made the most important contribution to American society?

_____

Why do you think so?

_____

_____

Reading Check

3. How did Samuel Howe help the visually impaired?

_____

The Spirit of Reform

Lesson 1 Social Reform, *Continued*

Person	Contributions
Lyman Beecher	tried to prevent drinking of alcohol
Horace Mann	started first state-supported teacher's college
Thomas Gallaudet	developed a way to teach the deaf
Dorothea Dix	made people aware of bad conditions in prisons

🖊 Identifying

4. Identify the person described in each of the following:

A transcendentalist who supported women's rights in her writings

_____

An American poet who wrote story poems

_____

? Drawing Conclusions

5. How did art in the United States change in the 1800s?

_____

_____

_____

✓ Reading Check

6. How did the spirit of reform influence American authors?

_____

_____

_____

Culture Changes

The changes that were taking place in American society affected art and literature. American artists developed their own style. Their art showed American places and ways of life.

Reform also had an effect on literature. A movement began called Transcendentalism. Its members were called transcendentalists. These thinkers and writers showed more of a connection between people and nature. They wrote that a person's conscience, or sense of right and wrong, was important.

Margaret Fuller wrote about women's rights. Ralph Waldo Emerson was also a writer in that movement. He wanted people to think about right and wrong. He wanted people to treat others fairly.

Henry David Thoreau practiced a form of protest called **civil disobedience** (dihs•uh•BEE•dee•uhns). He would not obey laws he thought were unjust. He went to jail because of this belief. In 1846, he would not pay a tax that supported the Mexican War.

American poets created great works. Henry Wadsworth Longfellow wrote poems that told a story. One of his well-known poems is the *Song of Hiawatha*. In *Leaves of Grass*, a poet named Walt Whitman tried to show the feelings and spirit of America. The poet Emily Dickinson wrote hundreds of poems. They were mostly about her personal feelings. Many of her poems are about nature.

American artists were developing a purely American style. They showed American life and landscapes. One group of painters was called the Hudson River School. They painted scenes of the Hudson River Valley in New York. Two well-known artists were Currier and Ives. They made prints of Americans celebrating holidays or enjoying themselves in other ways.

The Spirit of Reform

Lesson 1 Social Reform, *Continued*

Fuller: supported women's rights	Thoreau: practiced civil disobedience	Longfellow: wrote story poems

Transcendentalist Thinkers
- humans and nature
- importance of individual conscience

Emerson: wrote about the importance of conscience	Dickinson: wrote personal poems	Whitman: wrote about the new American spirit

/ / / / / / / / / / / / Glue Foldable here / / / / / / / / / / / / /

Check for Understanding

List four areas of reform in the 1800s.

_____

_____

_____

_____

List three transcendentalists.

_____

_____

FOLDABLES®

7. Place a one-tab Foldable along the dotted line to cover Check for Understanding. Write *Reform and Change* on the anchor tab. Create a memory map by writing the title *American Society* in the middle of the Foldable tab. Draw five arrows around the title and write words or phrases that explain how society changed due to reforms during the 1800s. Use the Foldable to help complete Check for Understanding.

The Spirit of Reform

Lesson 2 The Abolitionists

ESSENTIAL QUESTION
What motivates people to act?

GUIDING QUESTIONS

1. **How did Americans' attitudes toward slavery change?**

2. **Why did the reform movement gain momentum?**

3. **Who opposed the abolition of slavery?**

Term to Know
abolitionists reformers who worked to abolish, or end, slavery in the early 1800s in the United States

When did it happen?

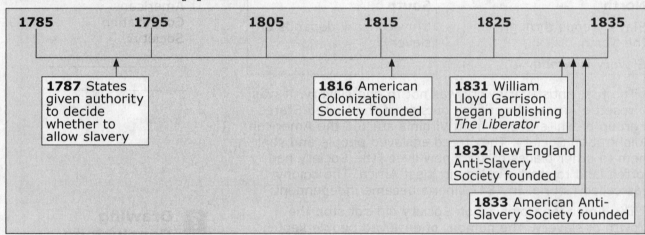

| 1785 | 1795 | 1805 | 1815 | 1825 | 1835 |

1787 States given authority to decide whether to allow slavery

1816 American Colonization Society founded

1831 William Lloyd Garrison began publishing *The Liberator*

1832 New England Anti-Slavery Society founded

1833 American Anti-Slavery Society founded

What do you know?

In the first column, write what you know about each person before you study. After the lesson, fill in the last column.

Now...	Who was...	Later...
	William Lloyd Garrison	
	Frederick Douglass	
	Harriet Tubman	

201

networks

Lesson 2 The Abolitionists, *Continued*

The Start of the Abolition Movement

The early 1800s was a time of reform. One type of reform was the work of abolitionists. **Abolitionists** were people who worked to abolish, or end, slavery. By the early 1800s, Northern states had ended slavery. Slavery was still an important part of the South's economy, however. By the mid-1800s, more and more Americans came to believe that slavery was wrong. The conflict over slavery grew.

Different Attitudes	
North Slavery ends throughout the North. Slavery is wrong.	**South** Our economy depends on slavery.

The first antislavery work was not to end slavery. It was to resettle African Americans outside of the United States. A group of white people from Virginia started the American Colonization Society. They freed enslaved people and sent them to other places to start new lives. The Society had gotten land to start a colony in West Africa. The colony was called Liberia. In 1847 Liberia became independent.

The American Colonization Society did not stop the growth of slavery. The number of enslaved people kept growing. The society could send only a small number of people to Africa. Besides, most African Americans did not want to go to Africa. Their families had lived in America for many years. They just wanted to be free.

The Movement Builds Strength

Around 1830, slavery became the most important issue for reformers. William Lloyd Garrison had a great effect on the antislavery movement. He started a newspaper called *The Liberator*. He also started the American Anti-Slavery Society. He was one of the first to call for an immediate end to slavery.

Two sisters, Sarah and Angelina Grimké, spoke and wrote against slavery. They used their money to free several of the family's enslaved workers. Their book, *American Slavery As It Is,* was one of the strongest works against slavery at that time.

Defining

1. Who were the abolitionists?

_____

_____

Reading Check

2. What was the purpose of the American Colonization Society?

_____

_____

Drawing Conclusions

3. How did William Lloyd Garrison influence the abolition movement?

_____

_____

networks

The Spirit of Reform

Lesson 2 The Abolitionists, *Continued*

 Mark the Text

4. Underline the ways that Samuel Cornish, John Russwurm, and David Walker worked for abolition.

✓ **Reading Check**

5. What were Underground Railroad "stations"?

_____

_____

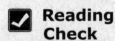 **Describing**

6. Place a two-tab Foldable along the dotted line to cover the graphic organizer. Label the two tabs *Free African American Abolitionists* and *Underground Railroad.* On both sides of the tabs, record information about key free African American abolitionists and describe the network of escape routes.

Free African Americans also played an important role in the abolitionist movement. They helped set up and run the American Anti-Slavery Society. Samuel Cornish and John Russwurm began the first African American newspaper. It was called *Freedom's Journal*. David Walker was a writer who urged African Americans to rise up against slavery. In 1830, free African American leaders held an important meeting in Philadelphia.

Frederick Douglass was the best-known African American abolitionist. Douglass escaped from slavery in Maryland in 1838. He settled in Massachusetts. Later he moved to New York. He was a powerful speaker. He spoke at many meetings in the United States and abroad. Douglass was the editor of an antislavery newspaper called *North Star*.

Sojourner Truth escaped from slavery in 1826. She worked with Frederick Douglass and William Lloyd Garrison to end slavery. She traveled throughout the North. She spoke about her life as an enslaved person. She also worked in the women's rights movement.

Some abolitionists helped African Americans escape from slavery. There was a network of escape routes from the South to the North. It was called the Underground Railroad. Along the routes, whites and African Americans guided the runaway "passengers" to freedom in Northern states or in Canada. They traveled at night. By day they rested at "stations." These were barns, basements, and attics in safe houses. Harriet Tubman became the most famous "conductor" on the Underground Railroad.

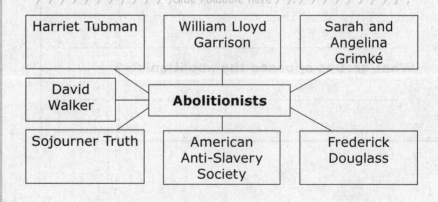

/ / / / / / / / / / / Glue Foldable here / / / / / / / / / / /

| Harriet Tubman | William Lloyd Garrison | Sarah and Angelina Grimké |

| David Walker | **Abolitionists** |

| Sojourner Truth | American Anti-Slavery Society | Frederick Douglass |

203

The Spirit of Reform

Lesson 2 The Abolitionists, *Continued*

Reaction to the Abolitionists

Only a small number of Northerners were abolitionists. Many Northerners believed that freed African Americans could never fully be a part of American society.

Some Northerners were afraid that the abolitionists would start a war between the North and South. Other Northerners feared that freed African Americans would take their jobs.

Opposition toward abolitionists was cruel at times. An angry white mob destroyed Elijah Lovejoy's antislavery newspaper offices three times. The fourth time, the mob set fire to the building and killed Lovejoy.

Many Southerners said abolition threatened their way of life. Southerners defended slavery. They thought it was a necessary part of the Southern economy. Southerners said they treated enslaved people well. They said they gave enslaved people food and medical care. Some of their beliefs were based on racism. Many whites believed African Americans could not take care of themselves and were better off under the care of white people.

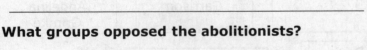

```
//////////////Glue Foldable here///////////
```

+--+
| **Check for Understanding** |
| |
| List three ways that abolitionists tried to end|
| slavery in America. |
| |
| _____ |
| |
| _____ |
| |
| _____ |
| |
| **What groups opposed the abolitionists?** |
| |
| _____ |
| |
| _____ |
+--+

 Listing

7. List two reasons Northerners opposed abolition.

_____

_____

Reading Check

8. How did Southerners defend the idea of slavery?

_____

_____

FOLDABLES®

9. Place a two-tab Foldable along the dotted line to cover Check for Understanding. Label the tabs: *What motivated the abolitionists?* and *What motivated those who were against the abolitionists?* Recall why each group felt strongly about slavery. Write the reasons for their beliefs. Use the Foldable to help answer Check for Understanding.

The Spirit of Reform

Lesson 3 The Women's Movement

ESSENTIAL QUESTION
How do new ideas change the way people live?

GUIDING QUESTIONS
1. **What did women do to win equal rights?**
2. **In what areas did women make progress in achieving equality?**

Terms to Know
suffrage the right to vote
coeducation the teaching of males and females together

Where in the world?

Wyoming — Woman Suffrage 1890

Seneca Falls Convention — NY

Mount Holyoke Female Seminary

Troy Female Seminary

Mass.

Oberlin College — Ohio

When did it happen?

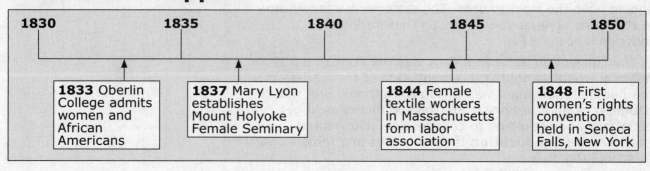

1830	1835	1840	1845	1850

1833 Oberlin College admits women and African Americans

1837 Mary Lyon establishes Mount Holyoke Female Seminary

1844 Female textile workers in Massachusetts form labor association

1848 First women's rights convention held in Seneca Falls, New York

The Spirit of Reform

Lesson 3 The Women's Movement, *Continued*

Reform for Women

Many women abolitionists also worked for women's rights. In July 1848, Lucretia Mott and Elizabeth Cady Stanton held the first women's rights convention. It was in Seneca Falls, New York. The Seneca Falls Convention laid the foundation for the women's rights movement.

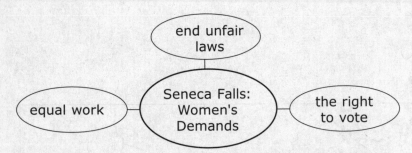

The convention put out a statement. The statement demanded an end to laws that were unfair to women. It said women should be allowed to work in jobs and businesses where the workers were mostly men.

People at the convention also talked about **suffrage,** or the right to vote. Elizabeth Cady Stanton wanted the statement to say that women must have the right to vote. Lucretia Mott thought that idea was too extreme.

The abolitionist, Frederick Douglass, agreed with Stanton. He made powerful arguments about why women should be able to vote.

In the end, the convention did demand that women should have the right to vote. The statement was written in the same style as the American Declaration of Independence of 1776.

The convention at Seneca Falls was the start of a national women's rights movement. One of the leaders of the national movement was Susan B. Anthony. She was the daughter of an abolitionist. She said women should get equal pay and should go to college. She also wanted coeducation. **Coeducation** is when males and females go to school together.

Anthony also started the country's first women's temperance organization. Anthony and Stanton met at a temperance meeting in 1851. They became friends, and they joined together to work for women's rights.

Opportunities for women increased. Women got the right to vote in Wyoming in 1890. Other states followed.

Copyright by The McGraw-Hill Companies.

Mark the Text

1. Underline the text that explains the debate at the Seneca Falls Convention over women voting.

Making Connections

2. Do most schools offer coeducation today? Does yours?

_____

_____

Reading Check

3. What is *suffrage*?

_____

_____

The Spirit of Reform

Lesson 3 The Women's Movement, *Continued*

Individual → **Contribution**

| Lucretia Mott | → | at Seneca Convention |

| Elizabeth Cady Stanton | → | at Seneca Convention; worked with Anthony on suffrage and temperance. |

| Susan B. Anthony | → | national leader, worked with Stanton on temperance and suffrage. |

📝 Categorizing

4. Match the education reformer with her school.

_____ Catherine Beecher

_____ Emma Willard

_____ Mary Lyon

a. Troy Female Seminary

b. Milwaukee College for Women

c. Mount Holyoke Female Seminary

🔤 Mark the Text

5. Underline the text to show the progress of women in the middle to late 1800s in marriage and property laws.

✅ Reading Check

6. What gains did women make in education?

_____

_____

Women Make Gains

Some people wanted better education for women. Catherine Beecher thought that women should be trained for traditional roles. The Milwaukee College for Women used Beecher's ideas. At that college, women learned to be successful wives, mothers, and homemakers.

Other people thought that women would make good teachers. Still others thought women should be trained to be leaders and have a career.

Emma Willard was one of these women. She taught herself science and mathematics. In 1821, she set up the Troy Female Seminary in New York State. There, young women learned math, history, geography, and physics. They also learned homemaking subjects.

Mary Lyon worked as a teacher for 20 years. Then she began to raise money to open a college for women. She started Mount Holyoke Female Seminary in 1837, in Massachusetts.

Before the mid-1800s, women did not have many rights. Anything a woman owned belonged to her husband when they got married.

In the mid- to late 1800s, women got some rights. Some states recognized the right of a woman to own her own property even after she married. Some states passed laws that gave rights to divorced women. These laws had to do with who raised the children. Several states decided to allow a woman to get a divorce if her husband drank alcohol too often.

Many careers were closed to women, however. They had to struggle to work in some professions. Two examples were medicine and the ministry. In the 1800s, women began to break through these barriers.

The Spirit of Reform

Lesson 3 The Women's Movement, *Continued*

Elizabeth Blackwell tried many times to get into medical school. Many schools said no. Finally, she was accepted to Geneva College in New York State. Blackwell graduated first in her class. She became a famous doctor.

Maria Mitchell also broke down walls for herself and for women after her. Maria Mitchell had been taught by her father.

- In 1847, she became the first person to discover a comet with a telescope.
- The next year, she was the first woman elected to the American Academy of Arts and Sciences.
- In 1865, Mitchell became a teacher at Vassar College.

Women had made many gains during the 1800s. There were many limits to what they could do, however. The struggle for equality continued.

Education for Women	Marriage and Family	Career
• better training for traditional roles • can be good teachers • Troy Female Seminary teaches math, history, science	• women gain right to own property • divorced women gain rights in raising children • women gain right to divorce husbands who abuse alcohol	• Elizabeth Blackwell breaks the barrier to women in medicine

/ / / / / / / / / / / Glue Foldable here / / / / / / / / / / / /

Check for Understanding

List three demands made at the Seneca Falls Convention in 1848.

_____

_____

_____

List two gains that women made in the field of education.

_____

_____

FOLDABLES®

7. Place a two-tab Foldable along the dotted line to cover Check for Understanding. Write the title *Seneca Falls 1848* on the anchor tab. Label the tabs *Cause* and *Effect*. Recall and record the reasons for the convention in 1848, and how it changed lives of women. Use the Foldable to help answer Check for Understanding.

Toward Civil War

Lesson 1 The Search for Compromise

ESSENTIAL QUESTION
Why does conflict develop?

GUIDING QUESTIONS
1. **What political compromises were made because of slavery?**
2. **What is the Kansas-Nebraska Act?**

Terms to Know
fugitive person who runs away from the law
secede leave
border ruffian armed pro-slavery supporter who crossed the border from Missouri to vote in Kansas
civil war fighting between citizens of the same country

Where in the world?

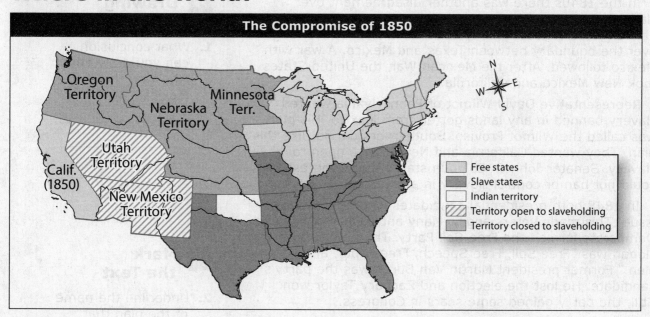

The Compromise of 1850

Oregon Territory
Nebraska Territory
Minnesota Terr.
Utah Territory
Calif. (1850)
New Mexico Territory

Free states
Slave states
Indian territory
Territory open to slaveholding
Territory closed to slaveholding

When did it happen?

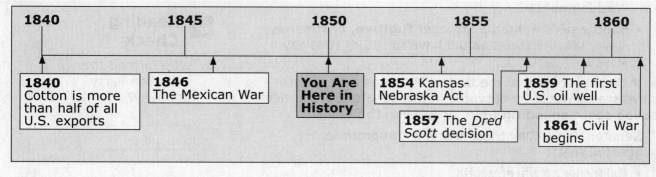

1840	1845	1850	1855	1860

1840 Cotton is more than half of all U.S. exports

1846 The Mexican War

You Are Here in History

1854 Kansas-Nebraska Act

1857 The *Dred Scott* decision

1859 The first U.S. oil well

1861 Civil War begins

209

Toward Civil War

Lesson 1 The Search for Compromise, *Continued*

Political Conflict Over Slavery

The question of slavery divided Americans. Many Northerners wanted to ban it. Most Southerners wanted Northerners to stay out of the South's business. Each time there was a debate over slavery, the nation's leaders came up with a compromise. For example, Congress passed the Missouri Compromise in 1820. This kept a balance of power in the Senate between slave states and free states. It also stopped the debate over slavery for a little while.

In the 1840s there was another disagreement over slavery in new territories. Texas became a state in 1845. This angered Mexico. The United States and Mexico fought over the boundary between Texas and Mexico. A war with Mexico followed. After the Mexican War, the United States took New Mexico and California.

Representative David Wilmot of Pennsylvania wanted slavery banned in any lands gotten from Mexico. His plan was called the Wilmot Proviso. Southerners did not like this plan. They wanted California and New Mexico open to slavery. Senator John C. Calhoun stated that Congress could not ban or control slavery in any territory.

In 1848 both presidential candidates ignored the slavery issue. This made voters angry. Many antislavery Whigs and Democrats formed the Free-Soil Party. The new party's slogan was "Free Soil, Free Speech, Free Labor, and Free Men." Former president Martin Van Buren was the party's candidate. He lost the election and Zachary Taylor won. Still, the party gained some seats in Congress.

The debate over slavery came up again in 1849 because:

- California wanted to become a state as a free state;

- antislavery groups wanted to ban slavery in Washington, D.C.;

- Southerners wanted a stronger **fugitive,** or runaway slave, law. All states would have to return runaway slaves.

If California entered the United States as a free state, slave states would be outvoted in the Senate. Southerners talked about **seceding** from, or leaving, the Union.

Senator Henry Clay tried to find a compromise. He suggested that:

- California be a free state.

- slavery would be allowed in new territories.

? Drawing Conclusions

1. What conclusion can you draw about who won the Mexican War?

_____

_____

Mark the Text

2. Underline the name of the plan that would ban slavery from any lands taken from Mexico.

✓ Reading Check

3. Who formed the Free-Soil Party and why?

_____

_____

Toward Civil War

Lesson 1 The Search for Compromise, Continued

? Critical Thinking

4. How do you think Clay's proposal for Washington, D.C., pleased both the North and the South?

_____

_____

Abc Vocabulary

5. Who were the border ruffians?

_____

_____

• the slave trade would be illegal in Washington, D.C., but slavery itself would be allowed.

• there would be a stronger fugitive slave law.

Congress discussed the ideas and argued about them. Senator Stephen A. Douglas of Illinois solved the problem. He divided Clay's plan into parts. Congress voted on each part separately. In this way, Congress passed five laws. Together, they are called the Compromise of 1850.

Compromise of 1850	Major Ideas
Senator Henry Clay had the ideas.	1. Stronger Fugitive Slave Law
Senator Stephen A. Douglas made the plan.	2. California to be a free state
Five separate laws were passed.	3. Other new territories could have slavery
	4. Okay to have slaves in Washington, D.C.
	5. However, no slave trade in Washington, D.C.

The Kansas-Nebraska Act

In 1854 Senator Douglas suggested making the lands west of Missouri into two territories. They would be called Kansas and Nebraska. They were north of the line that limited slavery, so the two states would be free states. Douglas knew the South would object. He suggested that Congress repeal the Missouri Compromise. Instead, settlers in those areas would vote on whether to allow slavery. Douglas called this "popular sovereignty." That means the people are allowed to decide.

Many Northerners did not like Douglas' plan. It would allow slavery in places that had been free for years. Southerners liked the plan. They thought Kansas would be settled mostly by slaveholders from Missouri. Since slavery was legal in Missouri, those settlers would vote to make slavery legal in Kansas, too.

Pro-slavery and antislavery groups rushed to Kansas. Thousands of pro-slavery supporters crossed the border from Missouri just for the purpose of voting in Kansas. They traveled in armed groups. They were known as **border ruffians** (BOHR•duhr RUH•fee•uhns).

211

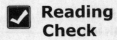
Toward Civil War

Lesson 1 The Search for Compromise, *Continued*

The Kansas-Nebraska Act passed in 1854. The pro-slavery group had won. Kansas passed laws in favor of slavery. People opposed to slavery refused to accept the laws. Instead, they held their own election. They adopted a constitution that banned slavery. By 1856, Kansas had two separate governments.

Both antislavery and pro-slavery groups had weapons. Soon fighting broke out. Pro-slavery supporters attacked a town where many antislavery supporters lived. Then John Brown, an abolitionist, led an attack on a pro-slavery group. Brown's group killed five slavery supporters. Newspapers called the conflict "Bleeding Kansas" and the "Civil War in Kansas." A **civil war** is a war between people of the same country.

////////// Glue Foldable here //////////

```
┌──────────────────────────────────────────────────┐
│                                                    │
│  Check for Understanding                           │
│     Why did Senator Douglas suggest that Congress  │
│  repeal the Missouri Compromise?                   │
│                                                    │
│     _____   │
│                                                    │
│     _____   │
│                                                    │
│     What two groups were involved in a "civil war" │
│  in Kansas?                                         │
│                                                    │
│     _____   │
│                                                    │
│     _____   │
│                                                    │
└──────────────────────────────────────────────────┘
```

✓ Reading Check

6. What events led to "Bleeding Kansas"?

_____

_____

_____

FOLDABLES®

7. Place a two-tab Foldable along the dotted line to cover Check for Understanding. Write the title *Slavery* on the anchor tab. Label the tabs *pro-slavery* and *antislavery*. Write two things you remember about each group. Use the Foldable to help answer Check for Understanding.

networks

Toward Civil War

Lesson 2 Challenges to Slavery

ESSENTIAL QUESTION

Why does conflict develop?

GUIDING QUESTIONS

1. **How did a new political party affect the challenges to slavery?**
2. **Why was the Dred Scott case important?**
3. **How did Abraham Lincoln and Stephen A. Douglas play a role in the challenges to slavery?**

Terms to Know

arsenal a place to store weapons
martyr a person who dies for a cause

Where in the world?

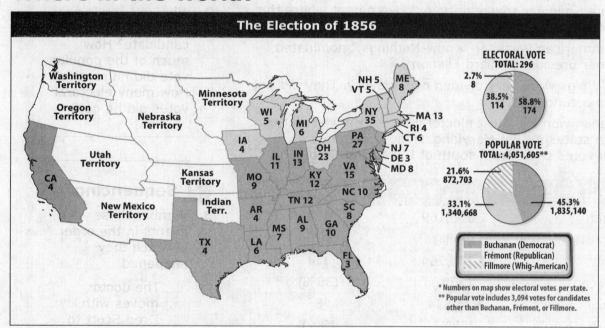

The Election of 1856

NH 5
VT 5
ME 8
WI 5
MI 6
NY 35
MA 13
RI 4
CT 6
IA 4
PA 27
NJ 7
DE 3
MD 8
IL 11
IN 13
OH 23
VA 15
MO 9
KY 12
NC 10
TN 12
SC 8
AR 4
AL 9
GA 10
MS 7
LA 6
FL 3
TX 4
CA 4

Washington Territory
Oregon Territory
Minnesota Territory
Nebraska Territory
Utah Territory
Kansas Territory
New Mexico Territory
Indian Terr.

ELECTORAL VOTE
TOTAL: 296
2.7%
8
38.5%
114
58.8%
174

POPULAR VOTE
TOTAL: 4,051,605*
21.6%
872,703
33.1%
1,340,668
45.3%
1,835,140

Buchanan (Democrat)
Frémont (Republican)
Fillmore (Whig-American)

* Numbers on map show electoral votes per state.
** Popular vote includes 3,094 votes for candidates other than Buchanan, Frémont, or Fillmore.

When did it happen?

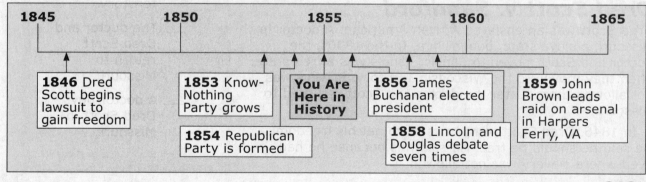

1845 — 1850 — 1855 — 1860 — 1865

1846 Dred Scott begins lawsuit to gain freedom

1853 Know-Nothing Party grows

1854 Republican Party is formed

You Are Here in History

1856 James Buchanan elected president

1858 Lincoln and Douglas debate seven times

1859 John Brown leads raid on arsenal in Harpers Ferry, VA

213

Lesson 2 Challenges to Slavery, *Continued*

Birth of the Republican Party

The Kansas-Nebraska Act drove the North and South further apart. Many Northern Democrats left the party. In 1854, antislavery Whigs and Democrats joined with Free-Soilers. They started the Republican Party. They wanted to ban slavery in new territories. Northerners liked the Republican Party's message. The Republicans won seats in Congress. The Democratic Party became mostly a Southern party.

In the presidential election of 1856:

- the Republicans chose John C. Frémont as their candidate. The party called for free territories.

- the Democrats nominated James Buchanan. The party wanted popular sovereignty, or government where the people are the authority.

- the American Party, or "Know-Nothings," nominated former president Millard Fillmore.

- the Whigs were very divided over slavery. They did not have a candidate.

Buchanan won the most electoral votes. He won all the Southern states except Maryland. None of Frémont's electoral votes came from south of the Mason-Dixon line.

Candidate	Popular Vote	Electoral Vote
Buchanan (Democrat)	1,838,169 (45%)	174 (59%)
Frémont (Republican)	1,341,264 (33%)	114 (38%)
Fillmore ("Know-Nothing")	874,534 (22%)	8 (3%)

Dred Scott v. *Sandford*

Dred Scott was an enslaved African American. A doctor in Missouri, a slave state, bought him. In the 1830s, the doctor and Scott moved to Illinois. Illinois was a free state. Then they moved to the Wisconsin Territory. Slavery was not allowed there. Later the doctor and Scott returned to Missouri.

In 1846, Dred Scott went to court to get his freedom. He said he should be free. He said this because he had lived where slavery was not allowed.

✔ Reading Check

1. Who joined together to form the Republican Party? What was their goal?

_____

_____

👁 Visualize It

2. Who was the "Know-Nothing" Party's candidate? How much of the popular vote did he receive? How many electoral votes did he get?

_____

_____

✍ Sequencing

3. Number these events in the order in which they happened.

____ The doctor moves with Dred Scott to Illinois and then to the Wisconsin territory.

____ The doctor and Dred Scott return to Missouri.

____ A doctor buys Dred Scott in Missouri.

Toward Civil War

Lesson 2 Challenges to Slavery, *Continued*

Explaining

4. Why did Dred Scott think he should be free?

_____

_____

Reading Check

5. In the *Dred Scott* decision, why could voters or Congress *not* ban slavery?

_____

_____

Mark the Text

6. Underline the sentence(s) that tells what people liked about Lincoln.

The case finally came before the Supreme Court in 1857. The case gained a lot of attention. It gave the Court a chance to rule on the question of slavery itself. Justice Roger B. Taney was the head of the Supreme Court. He wrote the Court's decision.

This is what the Supreme Court decided:

- The fact that Scott had lived in areas where slavery was not allowed did not make Scott a free man.
- Dred Scott was not a citizen. Because of this he had no right to go to court.
- Enslaved people were property.
- The Missouri Compromise was not allowed, according to the United States Constitution.
- Popular sovereignty was not allowed, according to the United States Constitution.
- Neither Congress nor voters could ban slavery. That would be like taking away a person's property.

The Court's decision angered Northerners. Southerners believed that now nothing could stop the spread of slavery.

Lincoln and Douglas

In 1858 the Illinois Senate race was the center of attention throughout the country, because of the candidates. Senator Stephen A. Douglas, a Democrat, was running against Abraham Lincoln, a Republican.

Douglas was popular. People thought he might run for president in 1860. Lincoln was not as well known. He challenged Douglas to debate him. A debate is a kind of argument. There are rules for how to state your point.

Lincoln and Douglas debated seven times. Slavery was the main topic each time. All the debates were in Illinois. Thousands of people came to watch. Many newspapers wrote articles about the debates.

Douglas supported popular sovereignty. He believed people could vote to limit slavery. People in the South did not like him after that. Lincoln said that African Americans had rights. He said that slavery was wrong.

Douglas won the election. Even though he lost, Lincoln became popular around the nation. People thought of him as a clear thinker who could state his ideas well.

Southerners felt threatened by Republicans. In 1859 an act of violence added to their fears. Abolitionist John Brown

Lesson 2 Challenges to Slavery, *Continued*

led a raid on Harpers Ferry, Virginia. The target was an **arsenal** (AHRS•nuhl), a place where weapons are stored. Brown hoped to arm enslaved African Americans. He hoped they would revolt against slaveholders.

Local citizens and troops stopped the raid. Brown was convicted of treason and murder. He was hanged. His death divided the North. Some antislavery groups had never approved of Brown's violence. Others saw him as a **martyr**—a person who dies for a great cause.

/ / / / / / / / / / / / Glue Foldable here / / / / / / / / / / /

Check for Understanding

Name the three anti-slavery parties from which people came to start the Republican Party.

_____

_____

List two of the reasons the Supreme Court gave for its decision in the Dred Scott case.

_____

_____

Copyright by The McGraw-Hill Companies.

Reading Check

7. Why did John Brown raid the arsenal at Harpers Ferry?

_____

_____

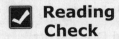

8. Place a Venn diagram Foldable along the dotted line to cover Check for Understanding. Write the title *Opposed to Slavery* on the anchor tab. Label the three tabs *Republican Party*, *Both*, and *Dred Scott*. Write two things you remember about each and one thing they have in common. Use the Foldable to help answer Check for Understanding.

NAME ______________________ DATE ______________ CLASS __________

networks

Toward Civil War

Lesson 3 Secession and War

ESSENTIAL QUESTION

Why does conflict develop?

GUIDING QUESTIONS

1. ***What was the importance of the election of 1860?***
2. ***What did the attack on Fort Sumter signify?***

Where in the world?

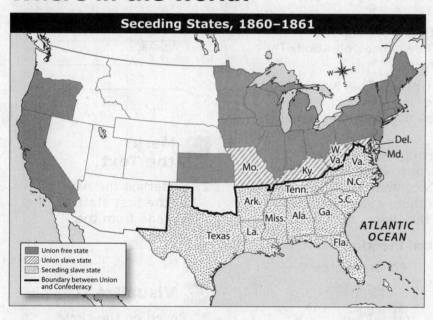

Seceding States, 1860–1861

N
S
E
W
Del.
Md.
W. Va.
Va.
Mo.
Ky.
N.C.
Tenn.
Ark.
S.C.
Miss.
Ala.
Ga.
Texas
La.
Fla.
ATLANTIC OCEAN
Union free state
Union slave state
Seceding slave state
Boundary between Union and Confederacy

Terms to Know

secession withdrawal

states' rights idea that states have the right to control their own affairs, and the federal government does not

When did it happen?

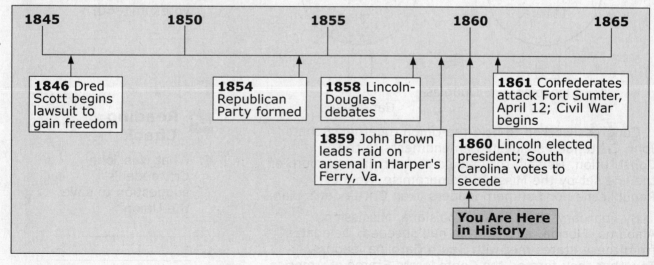

1845 — 1850 — 1855 — 1860 — 1865

- **1846** Dred Scott begins lawsuit to gain freedom
- **1854** Republican Party formed
- **1858** Lincoln-Douglas debates
- **1859** John Brown leads raid on arsenal in Harper's Ferry, Va.
- **1860** Lincoln elected president; South Carolina votes to secede
- **1861** Confederates attack Fort Sumter, April 12; Civil War begins

You Are Here in History

Toward Civil War

Lesson 3 Secession and War, *Continued*

The 1860 Election

The issue of slavery split the Democratic Party in the presidential election of 1860.

- Democrats in the North supported popular sovereignty. They chose Stephen A. Douglas as their candidate.

- Democrats in the South favored slavery. They chose John Breckinridge.

- Moderates in the North and South started the Constitutional Union Party. They chose John Bell. The party took no position on slavery.

- Republicans chose Abraham Lincoln. They wanted to leave slavery where it existed, but ban it in the territories. Lincoln's name was not even on the ballot in most Southern states.

Lincoln won. He won every Northern state. Many Southerners believed the Republicans would try to end slavery wherever it existed. On December 20, 1860, South Carolina left the Union. Other Southern states debated **secession**, or withdrawing from the Union, too.

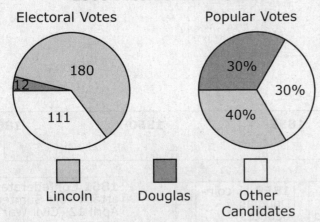

1860 Presidential Election

Electoral Votes — 180, 12, 111
Popular Votes — 30%, 30%, 40%

Lincoln   Douglas   Other Candidates

Congress worked to hold the Union together. Senator John Crittenden suggested amendments to the Constitution. He said they would protect slavery south of the line set by the Missouri Compromise. Neither Republicans nor Southern leaders liked Crittenden's plan.

By February 1861, Texas, Louisiana, Mississippi, Alabama, Florida, and Georgia had seceded. Delegates from these states met with South Carolina leaders. Together they formed the Confederate States of America. They chose Jefferson Davis as their president.

218

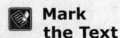

Identifying

1. Name the 1860 political parties and their candidates for president.

_____

_____

_____

_____

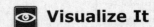

Mark the Text

2. Underline the name of the first state to secede from the Union.

Visualize It

3. Based on the circle graph, who won most of the electoral votes in 1860?

_____

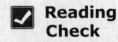

Reading Check

4. What was John Crittenden's suggestion to save the Union?

_____

_____

Toward Civil War

Lesson 3 Secession and War, *Continued*

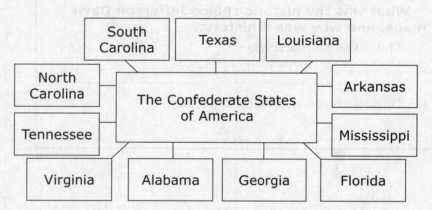

/ / / / / / / / / / Glue Foldable here / / / / / / / / / / /

Southerners used the idea of **states' rights** to explain their decision to secede. They argued that

- each state had joined the Union voluntarily.
- the Constitution was a contract between the federal government and the states.
- the government broke the contract because it did not give Southern states equal rights in the territories.
- therefore, a state had the right to leave the Union.

Not all Southerners believed in secession. Some Northerners were glad to see Southern states leave the Union. Most Northerners, however, thought secession would be bad for the country.

South Carolina | Texas | Louisiana

North Carolina | The Confederate States of America | Arkansas

Tennessee | | Mississippi

Virginia | Alabama | Georgia | Florida

In March 1861, Abraham Lincoln took office as president. He asked the seceding states to rejoin the Union. He pleaded for peace. He also warned that he would enforce federal law in the South.

Fighting at Fort Sumter

The day after Lincoln took office, he received a message. It came from Fort Sumter, a U.S. fort on an island in Charlston Harbor, South Carolina. The fort's commander warned that supplies were low. He said the Confederates were demanding that he surrender. Lincoln sent an unarmed group with supplies. He ordered Union troops at the fort not to fire unless they were fired upon.

Jefferson Davis made a historic choice. He ordered Confederate troops to attack Fort Sumter before the supplies arrived. On April 12, 1861, the Confederates fired on Fort Sumter. Rough, high seas kept Union ships from

FOLDABLES

Describing

5. Place a one-tab Foldable along the dotted line to cover "Southerners used the idea of states' rights ..." Write *Secession* on the anchor tab. Write *State's Rights* in the middle of the tab. Draw three arrows around the title and write three things about secession and states' rights.

Summarizing

6. Describe in your own words the idea of states' rights.

_____

_____

Reading Check

7. Why do you think Lincoln decided not to send armed troops to Fort Sumter?

_____

_____

Toward Civil War

Lesson 3 Secession and War, *Continued*

coming to help. Two days later, Fort Sumter surrendered. The Civil War had begun.

Lincoln issued a call for troops. Volunteers quickly signed up. Meanwhile, Virginia, North Carolina, Tennessee, and Arkansas joined the Confederacy.

/ / / / / / / / / / / / Glue Foldable here / / / / / / / / / / / /

Check for Understanding

Write the name of the new nation formed by the states that seceded and its president.

_____

_____

What was the historic choice Jefferson Davis made, and why was it historic?

The historic choice was

_____

_____.

Davis's choice was historic because

_____.

FOLDABLES®

8. Place a two-tab Foldable along the dotted line to cover Check for Understanding. Cut the tabs in half to form four tabs. Write *Jefferson Davis* on the anchor tab. Label the tabs *who, what, when,* and *where*. List what you remember about Jefferson Davis as you answer each question. Use the Foldable to help answer Check for Understanding.

The Civil War

Lesson 1 The Two Sides

ESSENTIAL QUESTION
Why does conflict develop?

GUIDING QUESTIONS

1. **What were the goals and strategies of the North and South?**

2. **What was war like for the soldiers of the North and the South?**

Terms to Know
border state state on the border between the North and South: Delaware, Maryland, Kentucky, and Missouri
enlist to formally join a military force

Where in the world?

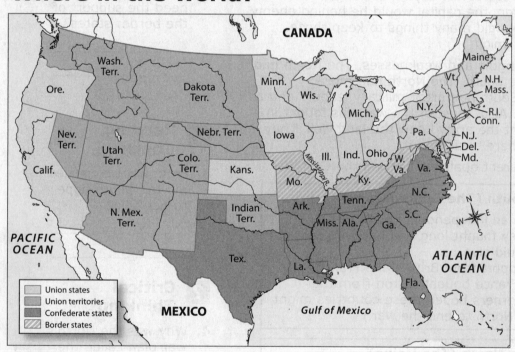

When did it happen?

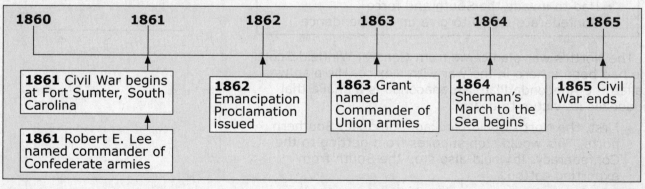

The Civil War

Lesson 1 The Two Sides, *Continued*

Two Very Different Sides

For most states, choosing sides in the Civil War was easy. This was not true for Delaware, Maryland, Kentucky, and Missouri. They were **border states.** They had ties to both the North and the South.

The border states were important to the Union's plans. Missouri could control parts of the Mississippi River. It could control major routes to the West. Kentucky controlled the Ohio River. Delaware was close to Philadelphia. Maryland was close to Richmond, Virginia. Richmond was the Confederate capital. Washington, D.C., was within Maryland. It was the capital of the Union. If Maryland left the Union, the capital would be behind enemy lines. President Lincoln did many things to keep those states as part of the Union.

Each side had strengths and weaknesses. The North had more people than the South. The North had more resources, too. The South had great military leaders and a strong fighting spirit. Also, most of the war was fought in the South. This meant the army knew the land well. They were willing to fight hard to defend it.

Each side had different goals for fighting the Civil War.

The South (The Confederacy)

- Wanted to be an independent country
- Thought if they fought long and hard enough, the North would give up
- Hoped for support from Britain and France (Britain and France bought cotton from the South. Southerners hoped these countries might pressure the North to end the war.)

The North (The Union)

- Wanted to reunite North and South again
- Had to invade the South and force Confederate states to give up independence

---

The North's war plan came from General Winfield Scott. He had been a hero in the war with Mexico. His plan was called the Anaconda Plan. An anaconda is a snake that squeezes its victim to death.

- First, the North would blockade, or close, Southern ports. This would stop supplies from getting to the Confederacy. It would also stop the South from exporting cotton.

Mark the Text

1. Underline the four border states.

Explaining

2. Why did Lincoln need the support of the border states?

_____

_____

Reading Check

3. From what countries did the South hope to get help?

_____

_____

Critical Thinking

4. Why was the North's war plan called the Anaconda plan?

_____

_____

The Civil War

Lesson 1 The Two Sides, *Continued*

- Second, the North would aim to control the Mississippi River. This would split the Confederacy into two parts. It would cut Southern supply lines.

- The North wanted to capture Richmond, Virginia. Richmond was the capital of the Confederacy.

Americans Against Americans

In the Civil War, brother fought brother. Neighbor fought neighbor. Kentucky senator John Crittenden had two sons who became generals. One fought for the Confederacy. The other fought for the Union. Even President Lincoln's wife had relatives in the Confederate army.

Many men left their homes to **enlist** in, or join, the Union or Confederate armies. Each had his own reasons.

Some Reasons for Enlisting
• patriotism
• to avoid being called a coward
• to have an adventure

The average soldier was in his 20s. Many were younger. Some soldiers were younger than 18. Some were younger than 14. To get into the army, many teenagers ran away from home or lied about their age.

At first, the North refused to let free African Americans enlist. Later, they did allow it. The Confederacy did not want to give enslaved people guns. In the last days of the war, they did allow African Americans to fight.

When the war began, each side expected to win quickly. Both sides were mistaken. The war lasted a very long time, and many soldiers died before it ended.

Soldiers came from every part of the country. Most came from farms. Almost half of the Northern soldiers and almost two-thirds of the Southern soldiers had owned or worked on farms before becoming soldiers.

Total Soldiers in Civil War (1861–1865)

Northern Soldiers—2,100,000

Southern Soldiers—900,000

📝 Listing

5. List the three main parts of the Anaconda Plan.

_____

_____

_____

✔️ Reading Check

6. Why weren't African Americans allowed to join the Confederate army until the end of the war?

_____

_____

👁️ Visualize It

7. Which side had more soldiers?

_____

_____

The Civil War

Lesson 1 The Two Sides, *Continued*

Confederate soldiers were sometimes called Rebels. Union soldiers were known as Yankees. Almost 200,000 African Americans served in the Union army. About 10,000 Mexican Americans served in the war.

On both sides, a soldier's life was hard. Soldiers wrote letters to family and friends describing what they saw. Many wrote about their boredom, discomfort, sickness, and fear.

Soldiers lived in army camps. There were some fun times. Often, however, a soldier's life was either dull or dangerous.

Both sides lost many soldiers during the war. There were thousands of wounded soldiers. They did not get good medical care. After the Battle of Shiloh, wounded soldiers lay in the rain for more than 24 hours. They were waiting to be treated. Around them lay dead and dying soldiers.

About 1 of every 11 Union soldiers and 1 of every 8 Confederate soldiers deserted. They left because they were afraid, sick, or hungry.

/ / / / / / / / / / / / Glue Foldable here / / / / / / / / / / / / /

Check for Understanding

What was the battle plan the South made, and why?

_____

_____

How would the Anaconda Plan harm the South?

_____

_____

Drawing Conclusions

8. Why were Confederate soldiers called "Rebels"?

_____

_____

FOLDABLES®

9. Using a two-tab Foldable, cut the tabs in half to make four tabs. Place it along the dotted line to cover Check for Understanding. Write the title *Anaconda Plan* on the anchor tab. Label the tabs *Who*, *What*, *Where*, and *Why*. List the facts that you remember about the Anaconda Plan. Use both sides of the tabs. Use your Foldable to help answer Check for Understanding.

netw🌐rks

The Civil War

Lesson 2 Early Years of the War

ESSENTIAL QUESTION

Why does conflict develop?

GUIDING QUESTIONS

1. **What was the outcome of the first major battle of the war?**
2. **How did the Union respond to important defeats in the East in 1862?**
3. **What was the effect of the Emancipation Proclamation?**

Terms to Know

tributary stream or smaller river that flows into a larger river

ironclad a warship equipped with iron plating for protection

casualty a soldier who is killed, wounded, captured, or missing in battle

Emancipation Proclamation formal announcement from President Lincoln, dated January 1, 1863. It freed enslaved people in parts of the South that were in rebellion.

When did it happen?

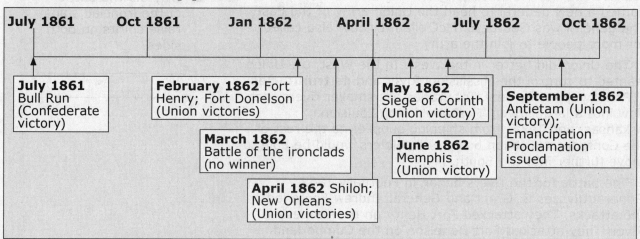

| July 1861 | Oct 1861 | Jan 1862 | April 1862 | July 1862 | Oct 1862 |

July 1861 Bull Run (Confederate victory)

February 1862 Fort Henry; Fort Donelson (Union victories)

March 1862 Battle of the ironclads (no winner)

April 1862 Shiloh; New Orleans (Union victories)

May 1862 Siege of Corinth (Union victory)

June 1862 Memphis (Union victory)

September 1862 Antietam (Union victory); Emancipation Proclamation issued

What do you know?

In the first column, answer the questions based on what you know before you study. After this lesson, complete the last column.

Now...		Later...
	What was important about April 25, 1862?	
	What happened at Antietam?	

War on Land and at Sea

The first big battle of the Civil War took place on July 21, 1861. It happened in northern Virginia near a small river called Bull Run. About 30,000 Union soldiers attacked a smaller Confederate force. People came from nearby Washington, D.C., to watch the battle.

At first, the Yankees pushed the Confederates back. But General Thomas Jackson inspired the rebels to keep fighting. Jackson held his position "like a stone wall," so people called him "Stonewall" Jackson. The Confederates began fighting back hard. They forced Union troops to retreat. The crowd that was watching ran away.

The Battle of Bull Run shocked Northerners. They now realized the war would be long and hard. President Lincoln named a new general to head the Union army of the East. The general was George B. McClellan. Lincoln also called for more people to join the army.

The Union did better in the West. In the West, the Union wanted to control the Mississippi River and its **tributaries** (TRIH•byuh•tehr•eez). Tributaries are smaller rivers that flow into a larger river. This would stop Louisiana, Arkansas, and Texas from shipping supplies to the rest of the Confederacy. Union boats and soldiers would be able to move further into the South.

The battle for the rivers began in February 1862. General Ulysses S. Grant and General Andrew Foote led the attacks. They attacked Fort Henry on the Tennessee River. They attacked Fort Donelson on the Cumberland River. They captured both forts. Grant was now a hero in the North.

The Union had set up a blockade of Confederate ports. Southerners had a secret weapon. It was an old Union warship called the *Merrimack*. The Confederates rebuilt it and covered it with iron to protect it. The **ironclad** ship was renamed the *Virginia*.

On March 8, 1862, the *Virginia* attacked Union ships in Chesapeake Bay. The North fired shells at it, but they just bounced off. Northern leaders were afraid of the *Virginia*. Then, the North got an ironclad ship of its own. It was called the *Monitor*. On March 9, the two ships met in battle. The ships could not sink each other, so neither side won.

In early April 1862, General Grant led about 40,000 soldiers toward Corinth, Mississippi, an important railroad junction. The army stopped 20 miles (32 km) away, near Shiloh Church. More Union soldiers arrived.

Explaining

1. What was surprising about the battle at Bull Run?

_____

_____

Critical Thinking

2. Why did the battle of the ironclad ships raise spirits on both sides?

_____

_____

Lesson 2 Early Years of the War, *Continued*

? Reading Check

3. How did the loss of New Orleans affect the Confederacy?

_____

_____

✓ Reading Check

4. What happened after the Battle of Antietam?

_____

_____

FOLDABLES®

✏ Explaining

5. Use a two-tab Foldable and cut the tabs in half to make four tabs. Place it along the dotted line to cover the heading "The Emancipation Proclamation." Write *Emancipation Proclamation* on the anchor tab. Label the four tabs *What*, *Where*, *When*, and *Why*. Use both sides of the tabs to write information about President Lincoln's proclamation.

The Confederates attacked first. The Battle of Shiloh lasted two days. Both sides lost many soldiers. There were more than 23,000 **casualties** (KA•zhuhl•teez)—people killed, wounded, or captured. In the end, the Union won.

Union soldiers moved on to Corinth. They surrounded it. No food or supplies could reach Corinth. The Confederates withdrew and Union troops entered on May 30. On June 6, they took Memphis, Tennessee. It seemed they would control the Mississippi River soon.

The Union navy also won an important battle. On April 25, the navy captured New Orleans, Louisiana. New Orleans was the largest city in the South. With Louisiana in Union control, the Confederacy could no longer use the Mississippi River to carry its goods to sea. The Union only had to capture Vicksburg, Mississippi, to have full control of the Mississippi River.

War in the Eastern States

In the East, the Union tried hard to capture Richmond, Virginia. That was the Confederate capital. Confederate soldiers fought hard to protect it. The South had good military leaders, such as General Robert E. Lee and General "Stonewall" Jackson. They knew the land well. They inspired their soldiers. They won important battles:

> the Seven Days' Battle (1862)
> the Second Battle of Bull Run (1862)
> Fredericksburg (1862)
> Chancellorsville (1863).

Lee moved his troops into Maryland. He had planned to continue into Pennsylvania. Lee split his army into four parts. He told each part to move in a different direction. He wanted to confuse General McClellan. Lee's plan did not work. A Confederate officer lost his copy of the plan, and it fell into McClellan's hands. On September 17, 1862, the two sides fought the Battle of Antietam near Sharpsburg, Maryland. The Union won this battle.

Antietam was the deadliest single day of fighting in the war. Lee went back to Virginia after the battle. His plan to invade the North had failed.

/ / / / / / / / / / / Glue Foldable here / / / / / / / / / / /

The Emancipation Proclamation

Abolitionists, including Frederick Douglass and Horace Greeley, wanted Lincoln to make the Civil War a fight to

The Civil War

Lesson 2 Early Years of the War, *Continued*

end slavery. They said slavery was wrong. They said it was the reason for the split between North and South. They believed Britain and France would be less willing to support the South if Lincoln said the Civil War was a war to end slavery. The South needed Britain's and France's support.

Lincoln believed that saving the Union was more important than ending slavery.

The Constitution did not give Lincoln power to end slavery. It did give him the power to take property from an enemy during a war, though. Enslaved people were considered to be property. On September 22, 1862, Lincoln said he would issue the **Emancipation Proclamation.** All enslaved people in Rebel-held territory would be freed on January 1, 1863.

The Emancipation Proclamation did not free any enslaved people right away. It was only for places held by the Confederacy. Lincoln had no power there. Also, the proclamation was not for the border states. Still, the proclamation was important. It said that slavery is wrong. If the Union won the war, slavery would end.

/ / / / / / / / / / /Glue Foldable here / / / / / / / / / / /

Check for Understanding

Explain the Northern generals' plan to use the Mississippi River to defeat the South.

_____

_____

_____

How did the Emancipation Proclamation affect slaves in the South?

_____

_____

✓ **Reading Check**

6. How did the Emancipation Proclamation affect the reason for the war?

_____

_____

FOLDABLES

7. Glue a one-tab Foldable along the dotted line to cover Check for Understanding. Draw a large circle on the tab and label it *Civil War*. Draw two smaller circles inside it. Label the small circles *Mississippi River* and *Slavery*. Inside the circles, list facts that show why both were important to the war. Use the reverse side to write additional information. Use your Foldable to help answer Check for Understanding.

The Civil War

Lesson 3 Life During the Civil War

ESSENTIAL QUESTION
Why does conflict develop?

GUIDING QUESTIONS

1. **How did life change during the Civil War?**

2. **What were the new roles for women in the Civil War?**

3. **What were the conditions of hospitals and prison camps during the Civil War?**

4. **What political and economic changes occurred during the Civil War?**

Terms to Know
habeas corpus a legal order that guarantees a prisoner the right to be heard in court.
draft a system of selecting people for required military service
bounty a reward or payment

When did it happen?

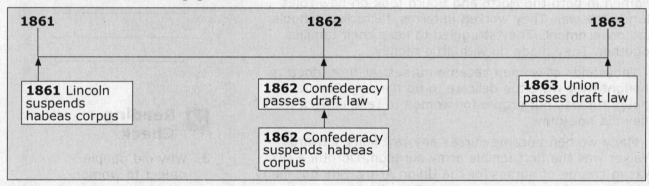

1861	1862	1863

1861 Lincoln suspends habeas corpus

1862 Confederacy passes draft law

1862 Confederacy suspends habeas corpus

1863 Union passes draft law

What do you know?
In the first column, answer the questions based on what you know before you study. After this lesson, complete the last column.

Now...		Later...
	How did the role of nurses change during the Civil War?	
	How did the Union blockade affect life in the South?	

Lesson 3 Life During the Civil War, *Continued*

A Different Way of Life

During the Civil War, life changed for young people. Many teenagers left home to serve in the army. About half of the school-age children did not go to school. Some had to stay home to help their families. Many schools were closed. Some were too close to battle sites. Some schools and churches were used as hospitals.

Most of the battles took place in the South, so people there suffered the most changes. Parts of the South that were in the paths of the armies were destroyed. Many people had to move away. They lost their homes and farms. Also, there was not enough food or other supplies. This made life hard for people everywhere in the South.

New Roles for Women

Women in both the North and South took on new roles during the war. They worked in farms, factories, schools, and government. They struggled to keep their families together. They made do with little money.

Thousands of women became nurses. At first, doctors thought they were too delicate to do nursing. People thought it was not proper for women to take care of men they did not know.

Many women became nurses anyway. Mary Edwards Walker was the first female army surgeon. Dorothea Dix was in charge of nurses for the Union Army. She got many other women to serve as nurses. Clara Barton was a famous nurse on the Union side. Captain Sally Tompkins was the only female officer in the Confederate army.

Some women were spies. Rose O'Neal Greenhow and Belle Boyd gathered information about Union plans and passed it to the Confederacy. Harriet Tubman also served as a spy and scout for the Union. A few women even dressed like men and became soldiers. Loreta Janeta Velázquez fought for the South and became a Confederate spy.

The Captured and the Wounded

Early in the war, the North and the South exchanged soldiers they had captured. Later, they set up prison camps. Prisoners had only a blanket and a cup. Many prisons were very dirty, and there was too little food.

At Andersonville prison in Georgia, prisoners slept on the ground. All they had to eat each day was a teaspoon of

✓ Reading Check

1. Why did many children not go to school during the war?

_____

_____

Listing

2. List three new roles for women during the Civil War.

_____

_____

_____

✓ Reading Check

3. Why did people object to women working as nurses during the war?

_____

_____

✓ Reading Check

4. What happened to soldiers who were captured by the enemy?

_____

_____

The Civil War

Lesson 3 Life During the Civil War, *Continued*

Mark the Text

5. Underline the meaning of *habeas corpus*.

Listing

6. List two ways in which a man could avoid the draft.

_____

_____

Explaining

7. Why did the New York City mobs attack African Americans?

_____

_____

salt, three tablespoons of beans, and a cup of cornmeal. They drank water from a stream that was also a sewer. Thousands of Union prisoners died from disease there.

At the Union prison in Elmira, New York, Confederate prisoners had no blankets or warm clothes, even in winter. They used a pond as a toilet and a garbage dump. A quarter of the prisoners held there died.

Wounded soldiers were treated in field hospitals near the battlefield. Volunteers gave out food to the wounded.

The camps were crowded places, and drinking water was dirty. As many as half the men got sick and died before they ever went into battle.

Political and Economic Change

Both the North and the South faced rebellions. People in the South did not have enough to eat. There were bread riots in Richmond, Virginia, and other cities.

In the North, the War Democrats did not like how Lincoln was running the war. Peace Democrats wanted the war to end right away. Many people thought Peace Democrats were dangerous traitors and called them Copperheads. Copperheads are poisonous snakes.

To deal with people who opposed the war, both President Lincoln (in the North) and President Davis (in the South) suspended **habeas corpus.** Habeas corpus helps protect people against unlawful imprisonment. Thousands who spoke out against the war were jailed without trial.

Soon both sides had trouble recruiting enough soldiers. The Confederate Congress passed a **draft** law in 1862. A draft orders people to serve in the military during a war. In the North, the Union paid a **bounty,** or a sum of money, to encourage volunteers. Then, in March 1863, the Union also passed a draft law. In both the North and the South, a man could avoid the draft by paying a fee or hiring a substitute.

The draft law made people angry. They said that rich people planned the war but only poor people had to fight. Riots occurred in several Northern cities. In July 1863, mobs rioted in New York City. The mobs attacked government and military buildings. They also attacked African Americans. Many workers had opposed the Emancipation Proclamation. They were afraid that freed African Americans would take their jobs. More than 100 people died in the riot.

231

netw⊙rks

The Civil War

Lesson 3 Life During the Civil War, *Continued*

The war was expensive for both sides. The two governments had three ways of paying for the war: They borrowed money, they took in more taxes, and they printed money.

The North's economy did better than the South's. Northern industries made money by producing war supplies. Farms also profited from the war. Still, prices grew faster than wages because goods were in high demand. This increase in prices is called inflation. Inflation made life harder for working people.

The South's economy suffered more. Much of the fighting took place in the South. It destroyed farms and railroad lines. The blockade stopped shipping. Important supplies could not reach the Confederacy. Hungry people rioted because there was not enough food. The riots were in Atlanta, Richmond, and other cities.

The South also suffered worse inflation than the North. After only one year of war, citizens begged Confederate leaders for help.

////////////// Glue Foldable here //////////////

Check for Understanding

List two ways that life changed during the Civil War.

_____

_____

How were prisoners mistreated during the Civil War?

_____

_____

_____

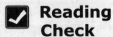

Reading Check

8. How did the war affect the economy in the North and South?

_____

_____

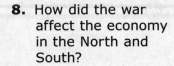

9. Place a three-tab Foldable along the dotted line to cover Check for Understanding. Write the title *War Brings Changes* on the anchor tab. Label the tabs *Women*, *Children*, and *Economy*. Recall how the Civil War affected people on both sides and list the ways that each changed during that time. Use both sides of the tabs. Use your Foldable to help answer Check for Understanding.

netw⊙rks

The Civil War

Lesson 4 The Strain of War

ESSENTIAL QUESTION

Why does conflict develop?

GUIDING QUESTIONS

1. **What factors contributed to the early success of the Confederate forces?**

2. **What role did African Americans play in military efforts?**

3. **How was the battle of Gettysburg a turning point in the war?**

Terms to Know

entrench to place within a trench, or ditch, for defense; to place in a strong defensive position

flank the side or edge of a military formation

When did it happen?

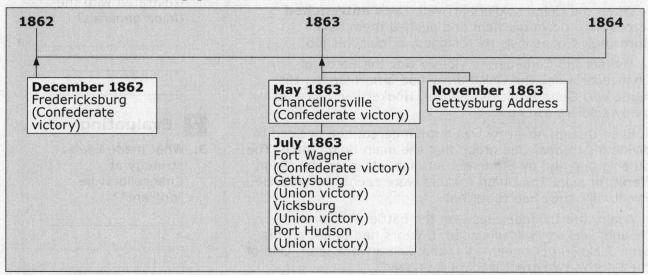

1862	1863	1864

December 1862
Fredericksburg
(Confederate
victory)

May 1863
Chancellorsville
(Confederate victory)

July 1863
Fort Wagner
(Confederate victory)
Gettysburg
(Union victory)
Vicksburg
(Union victory)
Port Hudson
(Union victory)

November 1863
Gettysburg Address

What do you know?

Before reading the text, decide whether these statements are true or false. Write a T or an F in front of each. After reading, check your answers. Were they correct?

_____ 1. The Union had excellent generals throughout the war.

_____ 2. "Stonewall" Jackson was an important Confederate general.

_____ 3. African Americans enlisted in both the Union and the Confederate armies.

_____ 4. The battle at Gettysburg was an important win for the Confederacy.

_____ 5. President Lincoln's famous speech at Gettysburg was very short.

Lesson 4 The Strain of War, *Continued*

Southern Victories

After Antietam, the Confederacy won a number of battles in the East because Generals Robert E. Lee and Stonewall Jackson were so good at their jobs. They knew the land. They knew how to inspire the soldiers. They often defeated the Union armies in battle, even though they had fewer soldiers.

The first victory was the Battle of Fredericksburg. The Union leader, General Ambrose Burnside, began to march toward Richmond, Virginia. Richmond was the capital of the Confederacy. Lee moved his forces to Fredericksburg. They dug trenches in the hills and waited for the Union troops.

When the Union soldiers arrived, Lee's **entrenched** forces fired down on them and pushed them back. Burnside's troops lost. He resigned, or quit, his job.

The second Confederate victory was the Battle of Chancellorsville. The Union army had a new leader. His name was General Joseph Hooker. Hooker had twice as many soldiers as Lee.

Even though his army was outnumbered, Lee decided to divide his troops. One group met the main Union force. The other group, led by Stonewall Jackson, attacked the Union **flank,** or side. The Union soldiers were caught by surprise. Eventually, they had to retreat.

Again, the Confederates won the battle. This time, though, Jackson was wounded. Doctors had to cut off his arm. Jackson got pneumonia, and died a week later. One of the South's two great leaders was dead.

The army leaders in the East frustrated President Lincoln. In less than a year three different generals tried and failed to win the Civil War for the Union. The army's leadership was weak.

- **General McClellan** did not seem to want to do battle. He did not obey Lincoln's order to follow the Confederate troops after the Union's victory at Antietam.

- **General Burnside** lost at Fredericksburg. Lincoln replaced him with General Joseph Hooker.

- **General Hooker** lost at Chancellorsville. Within two months, Hooker resigned, too.

 Explaining

1. What was Lee's strategy at Chancellorsville?

_____

_____

 Reading Check

2. Why was Lincoln frustrated with the Union generals?

_____

_____

_____

? **Evaluating**

3. What made Lee's strategy at Chancellorsville "brilliant"?

_____

_____

_____

The Civil War

Lesson 4 The Strain of War, *Continued*

? Determining Cause

4. Why would African Americans have been eager to enlist and fight for the Union?

_____

✍ Mark the Text

5. In one color, highlight adjectives and phrases that describe what African Americans faced in the military. In another color, highlight phrases that describe African American soldiers' conduct in war.

? Identifying

6 What was the result of Pickett's Charge?

_____

_____

African Americans in the Civil War

The Confederate army never accepted African American soldiers. Confederate officials believed that African Americans might attack their fellow troops or begin a revolt if they were armed.

Still many enslaved African Americans went to war with their white owners. They helped the Confederate army in many ways, like building fortifications.

At first, the Union army did not accept African American soldiers, either. Lincoln feared that allowing them to enlist would anger people in the border states.

By 1862, though, the North needed more soldiers. So Congress created all-black regiments. By the end of the war, about 10 percent of Union soldiers were African American. Some were freed people from the North. Others had run away from enslavement in the South.

It was not easy for African American soldiers in the Union army. Other Union soldiers resented them or thought they could not fight well. In battles, Southern troops, who hated them, fired at them the most.

Despite this, African Americans fought bravely and well. For example, in July 1863, the 54th Massachusetts Regiment served in the front lines of a battle to take Fort Wagner in South Carolina. The regiment suffered nearly 300 casualties. Their sacrifice made the 54th famous for its courage.

The Tide Turns

After the Confederate victory at Chancellorsville, Lee decided to invade the North. He hoped victories there would convince Britain and France to help the Confederacy.

On July 1, 1863, his forces went looking for supplies in Gettysburg, Pennsylvania. There, they encountered, or met, Union troops. Outnumbered, the Union troops fell back to higher ground on Cemetery Ridge.

On July 2, Southern troops tried and failed to force the Union troops from their positions on the hills.

On July 3, Lee ordered an all-out attack. Thousands of Confederate troops, led by General George Pickett, attacked Union forces on Cemetery Ridge. Half of those in Pickett's Charge were wounded or killed.

networks

The Civil War

Lesson 4 The Strain of War, *Continued*

On July 4, Lee retreated. His army had suffered 25,000 casualties. Union troops had suffered almost as many.

Losing at Gettysburg ended Confederate hopes of getting help from Britain and France.

The Confederacy lost two other critical battles in July 1863:

- **Vicksburg** In April, Ulysses S. Grant laid siege to Vicksburg, Mississippi. A siege means surrounding a place to keep it from receiving food or supplies. The siege lasted 47 days. Many soldiers died—not only from wounds, but also from sickness and hunger. Vicksburg finally fell on the same day Lee retreated from Gettysburg.

- **Port Hudson** The Confederacy lost Port Hudson, its last stronghold on the Mississippi River. The Union had cut off Arkansas, Louisiana, and Texas from the rest of the Confederacy.

On November 19, 1863, the Soldiers' National Cemetery opened at Gettysburg, and people gathered there to dedicate it. First, the former governor of Massachusetts gave a two-hour speech. Then President Lincoln spoke for just two minutes. He finished by saying, "[T]hese dead shall not have died in vain. . . . [G]overnment of the people, by the people, for the people shall not perish from the earth." His powerful words became known as the Gettysburg Address.

/ / / / / / / / / / / /Glue Foldable here/ / / / / / / / / / / /

Check for Understanding

Why did Union leaders call for African Americans to be allowed to fight in the Civil War?

_____

_____

Why was the battle of Gettysburg a turning point in the war?

_____

_____

✔ **Reading Check**

7. How did the events at Vicksburg and Port Hudson help change the tide of the war?

_____

_____

FOLDABLES

8. Use a two-tab Foldable and cut the tabs in half to make four tabs. Place it along the dotted line to cover Check for Understanding. Write the title *Turning Points in 1863* on the anchor tab. Label the tabs *African Americans Enter the War*, *Battle of Vicksburg*, *Battle of Port Hudson*, and *Robert E. Lee Retreats*. Use both sides of the tabs to list facts about the people and events of 1863.

The Civil War

Lesson 5 The War's Final Stages

ESSENTIAL QUESTION

Why does conflict develop?

GUIDING QUESTIONS

1. **What events occurred at the end of the war?**

2. **What is total war?**

Terms to Know
resistance refusal to give in
total war a strategy of bringing war to the entire society, not just the military

Where in the World?

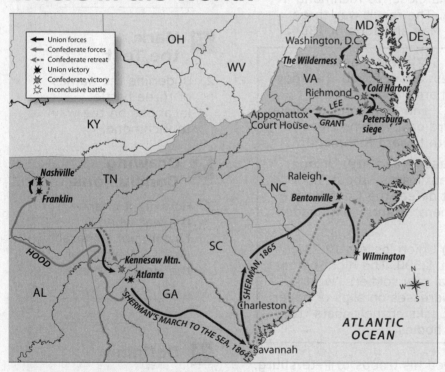

When did it happen?

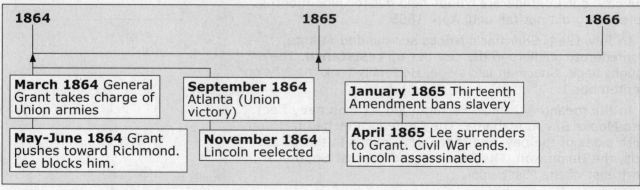

1864	1865	1866

March 1864 General Grant takes charge of Union armies

September 1864 Atlanta (Union victory)

January 1865 Thirteenth Amendment bans slavery

May-June 1864 Grant pushes toward Richmond. Lee blocks him.

November 1864 Lincoln reelected

April 1865 Lee surrenders to Grant. Civil War ends. Lincoln assassinated.

237

The Civil War

Lesson 5 The War's Final Stages, *Continued*

The Union Closes In

By 1864, Union forces had the South surrounded. Union ships blocked Southern ports. The Union controlled the Mississippi River. This cut off supplies to the South.

In March 1864, Lincoln put General Ulysses S. Grant in charge of all Union armies. Grant decided to attack from all sides. His armies would march to Richmond, Virginia, the Confederate capital. At the same time, Union General William Tecumseh Sherman would attack the Deep South.

Grant began moving closer and closer to Richmond in May 1864. Lee tried to stop him. The result was three major battles that took place in May and June of 1864:

- **"The Wilderness"** (May 5–7) Union losses: 17,666; Confederate losses: about 8,000. Two-day battle in a thickly wooded area about halfway between Washington, D.C., and Richmond, Virginia. On the morning of the third day, with no clear winner, Grant headed south toward Richmond.

- **Spotsylvania Court House** (May 8–19) Union losses: 18,399; Confederate losses: about 9,000. The Union army could not defeat the Confederate army. After ten days, General Grant again headed south toward Richmond.

- **Cold Harbor** (June 3–12) Union losses: 12,737; Confederate losses: about 1,500. The night before the battle, a Union general saw soldiers "writing their names and home addresses on slips of paper and pinning them to the backs of their coats" to help people identify their bodies.

After Cold Harbor, Grant moved his troops to Petersburg, Virginia. This city was a railroad center the Confederates needed for moving troops and supplies. Grant laid siege to the city, but Confederate troops held out for nine months. Petersburg did not fall until April 1865.

In July 1864, Sherman's troops surrounded Atlanta. Confederate soldiers in the city put up **resistance.** They fought back. Sherman laid siege. He finally took the city on September 1.

In the meantime, David Farragut led a Union navy fleet into Mobile Bay in Alabama. The Confederates had forts on both sides of the bay, and there were mines in the water. Still, the Union won. The fleet blocked the last Southern port east of the Mississippi.

☑ **Reading Check**

1. Explain Grant's strategy for winning the war.

_____

_____

📝 **Mark the Text**

2. Underline the names of three battle locations on the way to Richmond.

❓ **Drawing Conclusions**

3. How did it change the war when Lincoln put General Grant in charge of the Union armies?

_____

_____

🔤 **Defining**

4. What is a *siege*?

_____

_____

The Civil War

Lesson 5 The War's Final Stages, *Continued*

 Mark the Text

5. Underline the sentence that tells why Sherman's and Farragut's victories were important to the Union.

Identifying

6. What finally ended slavery in the United States?

_____

_____

 Defining

7. What is total war?

_____

_____

_____

So many soldiers were dying in 1864 that people in the North became more unhappy about the war. It looked like they were not going to vote for Lincoln in the November election. If Lincoln lost, the war would likely end. The Confederacy would be recognized as an independent country. This kept hope alive in the South.

Then the Union blocked Mobile Bay and took Atlanta. Northerners began to believe they could win. They reelected Lincoln after all. In the South, people were losing hope.

Union fleet blocks Mobile Bay (August 1864)

↓

Siege of Atlanta ends in Union victory (September 1864)

↓

Lincoln is reelected (November 1864)

Many interpreted Lincoln's victory as a sign that voters wanted to end slavery. Congress passed the Thirteenth Amendment on January 31, 1865. It banned slavery in the United States.

The War Ends

After Sherman took Atlanta, his forces burned the city. Then they marched across Georgia to the Atlantic Coast. As they went, the troops tore up railroad lines. They burned cities and fields and killed livestock. This march across Georgia became known as Sherman's March to the Sea.

In his March to the Sea, Sherman used a strategy called **total war**. Total war is the systematic destruction of an entire land, not just its army. Sherman was not trying to punish the South. He wanted to convince Southerners to stop fighting and end the war.

After reaching the coast, Sherman's troops turned north through the Carolinas to join Grant's forces near Richmond. As they went, thousands of African Americans left their plantations to follow his army. They felt that the army protected them as they marched toward freedom.

On April 2, 1865, Petersburg finally fell to Grant's forces. When President Davis heard that Lee had retreated, he knew that Grant would come to Richmond next. Davis and other Confederate leaders prepared to leave the city. They

239

The Civil War

Lesson 5 The War's Final Stages, *Continued*

ordered weapons and bridges in Richmond burned and then fled.

On April 4, President Lincoln walked around the city with his son, followed by grateful African Americans. When asked what to do with Confederate prisoners of war there, he said to "Let 'em up easy."

The Civil War finally ended on April 9, 1865. On that day, Lee's starving army found themselves surrounded at Appomattox Court House, Virginia. Lee knew it was over. He surrendered to Grant. The terms of the surrender were generous:

- Any soldier with a horse could keep it.
- Lee's officers could keep their small guns.

Grant gave food to the Confederate troops and let them go home.

The Civil War had been terrible. More than 600,000 soldiers died in it—more than in any other American war. Much of the South was destroyed, and it would take years to rebuild.

The North's victory saved the Union and freed millions of African Americans from slavery. Now the United States would have to figure out:

- a way to bring the Southern states back into the Union.
- the status of African Americans in the South.

These were two huge problems that the nation would face in the years following the war—the Reconstruction era.

////////////// Glue Foldable here /////////////

Check for Understanding
Name two important Union victories that helped ensure Lincoln's reelection.

_____

_____

Why did Sherman burn and destroy the South?

_____

_____

✓ **Reading Check**

8. Why did General Lee finally surrender?

_____

_____

_____

❓ **Making Connections**

9. Why would the status of African Americans in the South be a problem after the war?

_____

_____

FOLDABLES®

10. Place a three-tab Foldable along the dotted line to cover Check for Understanding. Write *Final Stages of the Civil War* on the anchor tab. Label the tabs *Mobile Bay*, *Lincoln Reelected*, and *Sherman's March to the Sea*. Use both sides of the tabs to list two facts about each. Use your Foldable to help answer Check for Understanding.

The Reconstruction Era

Lesson 1 Planning Reconstruction

ESSENTIAL QUESTION

How do new ideas change the way people live?

GUIDING QUESTIONS

1. **Why did leaders disagree about the South rejoining the Union?**

2. **How did Lincoln's assassination change the plans for the South rejoining the Union?**

> **Terms to Know**
>
> **Reconstruction** the period of rebuilding the South and readmitting Southern states into the Union
>
> **amnesty** the granting of a pardon to a large number of persons

When did it happen?

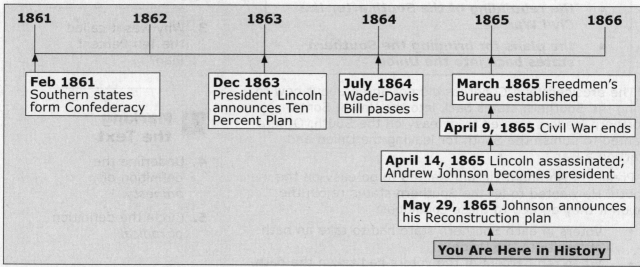

| 1861 | 1862 | 1863 | 1864 | 1865 | 1866 |

Feb 1861 Southern states form Confederacy

Dec 1863 President Lincoln announces Ten Percent Plan

July 1864 Wade-Davis Bill passes

March 1865 Freedmen's Bureau established

April 9, 1865 Civil War ends

April 14, 1865 Lincoln assassinated; Andrew Johnson becomes president

May 29, 1865 Johnson announces his Reconstruction plan

You Are Here in History

What do you know?

In the first column, answer the questions based on what you know before you study. After this lesson, complete the last column.

Now...		Later...
	When did the North begin planning on ways to bring Southern states back into the Union?	
	Who opposed Lincoln's plan?	
	Why was the Thirteenth Amendment to the Constitution important?	

The Reconstruction Era

Lesson 1 Planning Reconstruction, *Continued*

The Reconstruction Debate

The Civil War was fought from 1861 until 1865. The North, or Union, won the war. Now that the war was over, it was time for the country to become whole again. The states in the South needed to rejoin the states in the North. The nation needed to be rebuilt, or reconstructed.

The period of time that followed the Civil War is called **Reconstruction**. Reconstruction also refers to the plans for bringing the Southern states back into the Union. Northern leaders began forming these plans before the war even ended.

RECONSTRUCTION

- *the rebuilding of the South after the Civil War*
- *the plans for bringing the Southern states back into the Union*

The president and Congress did not agree about how to bring the Southern states back into the Union. Some Northern leaders wanted to go easy on the South. Others wanted to punish the South for leaving the Union and starting a war.

President Abraham Lincoln wanted to go easy on the South. He wanted to let the Southern states rejoin the Union if they agreed to these conditions:

- Voters in each Southern state had to take an oath of loyalty to the Union.
- When ten percent of the voters had taken the oath, the state could form a new government.
- The state would have to adopt a new constitution that banned slavery.

Lincoln's plan was called the Ten Percent Plan.

Lincoln went even further. He wanted to give **amnesty** to Southerners who would promise loyalty to the Union. Amnesty means a pardon, or forgiveness. Louisiana, Arkansas, and Tennessee agreed to Lincoln's requirements. However, Congress refused to accept the new states. They also did not allow their senators and representatives in Congress.

There were others who thought the South should be punished. They wanted a more radical, or extreme, approach. This group was called the Radical Republicans, or the Radicals. Thaddeus Stevens, a radical leader, said

Defining

1. What are the two meanings of Reconstruction?

_____

_____

Explaining

2. Who proposed the Ten Percent Plan?

_____

3. Why was it called the Ten Percent Plan?

_____

Marking the Text

4. Underline the definition of *amnesty*.

5. Circle the definition of *radical*.

The Reconstruction Era

Lesson 1 Planning Reconstruction, *Continued*

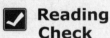 **Explaining**

6. Why did the Wade-Davis Bill not become a law?

_____

_____

 Reading Check

7. What were the three requirements for rejoining the Union stated in the Wade-Davis Bill?

_____

_____

_____

FOLDABLES

 **Describing**

8. Use a two-tab Foldable and cut each tab in half to make four tabs. Place it along the dotted line to cover the text beginning with "Meanwhile, Lincoln and Congress..." Write the title *Freedman's Bureau* on the anchor tab. Label the four tabs *Who*, *What*, *Why*, and *How*. Use both sides of the tabs to write information about the Freedman's Bureau.

that Southern institutions "must be broken up or relaid, or all our blood and treasure will have been spent in vain."

Radical Republicans in Congress passed their plan for Reconstruction in 1864. The Plan was called the Wade-Davis Bill. The Wade-Davis Bill would make it difficult for Southern states to rejoin the Union.

The Wade-Davis Bill required the Southern states to do three things:

- A majority (more than 50 percent) of the state's white male adults had to promise loyalty to the Union.
- Only white males who swore they had not fought against the Union could vote for representatives to a convention to write a new constitution.
- All new states had to ban slavery.

The Wade-Davis Bill was harsher than Lincoln's Ten Percent Plan. The bill passed Congress, but President Lincoln refused to sign it. The bill did not become law. There were still no plans for Reconstruction.

/ / / / / / / / / / Glue Foldable here / / / / / / / / / / /

Meanwhile, Lincoln and Congress worked together to create a new government department called the Freedman's Bureau. The Freedmen's Bureau helped poor Southerners, especially freed African Americans, adjust to life after slavery. It provided food, clothing, and shelter. It set up schools. It helped people find work. It also helped some people get their own land to farm.

Johnson's Reconstruction Plan

President Lincoln was assassinated on April 14, 1865, as he was watching a play in Washington, D.C. During the play, John Wilkes Booth shot Lincoln in the head. Booth was an actor who sympathized with the South. African Americans and white Northerners mourned Lincoln's death.

Vice President Andrew Johnson became president. He had different ideas about Reconstruction than Lincoln did.

Johnson wanted to give amnesty to most Southerners. However, he would not give amnesty to Southern leaders unless they asked the president. Johnson wanted to humiliate these leaders. He thought they had tricked ordinary Southerners into the war. Johnson opposed equal rights for African Americans. He said, "White men alone must manage the South."

243

Johnson's plan for Reconstruction required Southern states to write new constitutions that banned slavery. Johnson's plan also required Southern states to ratify, or approve, the Thirteenth Amendment to the Constitution. The Thirteenth Amendment banned slavery throughout the United States. By the end of 1865, all the former Confederate states except Texas had set up new governments under Johnson's plan. They were ready to rejoin the Union.

/ / / / / / / / / / / / Glue Foldable here / / / / / / / / / / / /

Check for Understanding

How did Lincoln and the Radical Republicans disagree over Reconstruction?

_____

_____

List two ways that Lincoln's Ten Percent Plan and Johnson's Reconstruction plan were alike.

1. _____

2. _____

☑ **Reading Check**

9. What did the Thirteenth Amendment accomplish?

_____

_____

FOLDABLES®

10. Place a three-tab Venn diagram Foldable along the dotted line to cover Check for Understanding. Write the title *Reconstruction* on the anchor tab. Label the tabs *Lincoln*, *Both*, and *Johnson*. Write information about each president's approach to Reconstruction. What did they have in common? Use the Foldable to help answer Check for Understanding.

The Reconstruction Era

Lesson 2 The Radicals Take Control

ESSENTIAL QUESTION
How do new ideas change the way people live?

GUIDING QUESTIONS
1. **How did the North attempt to assist African Americans in the South?**
2. **What elements were included in the Radical Republican idea of Reconstruction?**

Terms to Know
black codes laws passed in the South just after the Civil War aimed at controlling freed men and women, and allowing plantation owners to take advantage of African American workers

override to reject or defeat something that has already been decided

impeach to formally charge a public official with misconduct in office

When did it happen?

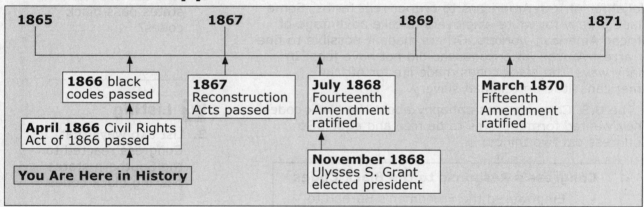

1865 — 1867 — 1869 — 1871

1866 black codes passed

April 1866 Civil Rights Act of 1866 passed

You Are Here in History

1867 Reconstruction Acts passed

July 1868 Fourteenth Amendment ratified

November 1868 Ulysses S. Grant elected president

March 1870 Fifteenth Amendment ratified

What do you know?

In the first column, answer the questions based on what you know before you study. After this lesson, complete the last column.

Now...		Later...
	How did Southern states try to control newly freed African Americans?	
	Why did Congress pass amendments to the Constitution during this period?	
	How did the United States govern the Southern states during Reconstruction?	

The Reconstruction Era

Lesson 2 The Radicals Take Control, *Continued*

Protecting African Americans' Rights

In 1865, former Confederate states began creating new governments. They elected leaders to Congress, but the Radical Republicans would not seat them. They thought that Johnson's Reconstruction plan was too easy on the Southerners. Radicals wanted it to be difficult for Southerners to join the Union again.

White people in the South were unhappy that they had lost the war. They were angry that the slaves had been freed. To keep control of former slaves, Southern states passed laws called **black codes**. These laws were meant to control newly freed African Americans. Some made it illegal for African Americans to own or rent farms. Some made it easy for white employers to take advantage of African American workers. Others made it possible to fine or arrest African Americans who did not have jobs. In many ways, the black codes made life for African Americans little better than slavery.

The U.S. Congress was unhappy about the black codes. They wanted former slaves to be free and equal. So Congress did two things:

Congress's Response to the Black Codes

- Empowered the Freedmen's Bureau to set up courts to try people who violated African Americans' rights.

- Passed the Civil Rights Act of 1866.

The Civil Rights Act gave citizenship to African Americans. It also gave the federal government the power to get involved in state affairs to protect African Americans' rights.

President Johnson vetoed both bills. He argued that they were unconstitutional because they were passed without Southern representatives. Radical Republicans in Congress were able to **override**, or overrule, each veto. Both bills became law.

Congress worried that the Civil Rights Act might be overturned in court, so it passed another amendment to the Constitution. The Thirteenth Amendment had ended slavery. The Fourteenth Amendment made African Americans citizens. It promised equal protection under the law. It also banned former Confederate leaders from

 Explaining

1. Why would Radical Republicans not seat Southern senators and representatives in Congress?

_____

_____

 Explaining

2. Why did Southern states pass black codes?

_____

_____

Listing

3. List two ways that Congress reacted to the Southern states passing black codes.

_____

_____

 Marking the Text

4. Underline the reason Congress passed the Fourteenth Amendment to the Constitution.

5. What did this amendment do?

_____

_____

_____

The Reconstruction Era

Lesson 2 The Radicals Take Control, *Continued*

Determining Cause and Effect

6. What allowed Radical Reconstruction to take place?

_____

_____

Analyzing

7. How were the Southern states governed during Reconstruction?

_____

_____

_____

Identifying Central Issues

8. Why was Johnson able to control Reconstruction directly?

_____

_____

_____

holding office unless they had been pardoned. However, many Southern states would not ratify it. This made the Radical Republicans more determined than ever to treat the South harshly.

Radical Republicans in Charge

Radical Republicans were a powerful force in Congress. They became an even more powerful force in 1866. It was an election year, and they won many seats in Congress. There was no way Johnson could stop them. A period known as Radical Reconstruction began. The Radical Republicans passed the Reconstruction Acts.

Radical Reconstruction: The Reconstruction Acts	
Act	**What it did**
First Reconstruction Act	• said that states that had not ratified Fourteenth Amendment must form new governments • divided ten states into five military districts governed by generals • banned Confederate leaders from serving in new state governments • required new state constitutions • guaranteed African American men the right to vote
Second Reconstruction Act	• empowered army to register voters and help organize state constitutional conventions

The Southern states were now under the control of army generals. This angered Southerners. It also brought the differences between Radical Republicans in Congress and President Johnson to the boiling point.

The Radical Republicans in Congress had the majority. But as president, Johnson was in charge of the Army. He was in charge of the generals who governed the South. This meant that he could control Reconstruction directly. He could avoid Congress by giving orders to his generals.

247

The Reconstruction Era

Lesson 2 The Radicals Take Control, *Continued*

Congress knew this. So, to keep President Johnson from becoming too powerful, they passed laws to limit his power. One such law was the Tenure of Office Act. It said that the president could not fire any government officials without the Senate's approval. They were afraid Johnson would fire the Secretary of War, Edwin Stanton, because he supported Radical Reconstruction.

This did not stop Johnson. He suspended Stanton, or stopped him from working temporarily, without the Senate's approval. Radical Republicans in Congress believed that Johnson had violated the Tenure of Office Act.

The Radical Republicans reacted strongly. The House of Representatives voted to **impeach** Johnson—that is, formally charge him with wrongdoing. In 1868 the case went to the Senate for a trial. Not enough senators voted Johnson guilty, so he was able to remain president until Ulysses S. Grant was elected president in 1868.

In 1869, Congress took one more major step in Reconstruction. The Thirteenth Amendment had abolished slavery. The Fourteenth Amendment had granted citizenship to African Americans. This new Amendment—the Fifteenth—granted African American men the right to vote.

When the Fifteenth Amendment was ratified in 1870, many Americans thought Reconstruction was complete. However, there was still a long way to go.

/ / / / / / / / / / / Glue Foldable here / / / / / / / / / / / /

Check for Understanding

List two ways that Congress tried to help African Americans before Radical Reconstruction began.

1. _____

2. _____

List three measures passed by Congress during Radical Reconstruction.

1. _____

2. _____

3. _____

Defining

9. Write a definition of *impeach*.

_____

_____

Identifying

10. What did the Fifteenth Amendment do?

_____

_____

FOLDABLES®

11. Place a three-tab Foldable along the dotted line to cover Check for Understanding. Write the title *Amendments* on the anchor tab. Label the three tabs *13th*, *14th*, and *15th*. Write what you remember about the importance of each amendment. Use the Foldable to help answer Check for Understanding.

networks

The Reconstruction Era

Lesson 3 The South During Reconstruction

ESSENTIAL QUESTION

How do new ideas change the way people live?

GUIDING QUESTIONS

1. **How were African Americans discouraged from participating in civic life in the South?**

2. **What were some improvements and some limitations for African Americans?**

Terms to Know

scalawag name given by former Confederates to Southern whites who supported Republican Reconstruction of the South

corruption dishonest or illegal actions

integrate to unite, or blend into a united whole

sharecropping system of farming in which a farmer works land for an owner who provides equipment and seeds and receives a share of the crop

When did it happen?

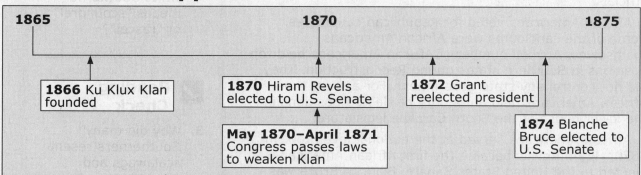

1865		1870		1875

1866 Ku Klux Klan founded

1870 Hiram Revels elected to U.S. Senate

May 1870–April 1871 Congress passes laws to weaken Klan

1872 Grant reelected president

1874 Blanche Bruce elected to U.S. Senate

What do you know?

In the first column, answer the questions based on what you know before you study. After this lesson, complete the last column.

Now...		Later...
	How did African Americans affect Southern politics and government during Reconstruction?	
	Who were "scalawags" and "carpetbaggers?"	
	What was life like for African Americans in the South during this period?	
	How many white and African American children attended school?	
	How does sharecropping work?	

249

The Reconstruction Era

Lesson 3 The South During Reconstruction, *Continued*

Republicans in Charge

The Republicans were more powerful than the Democrats during Reconstruction. The groups in charge of state governments in the South supported Republicans. These included African Americans and some white Southerners. They also included whites from the North who moved to the South.

African Americans had fewer rights than white Southerners. But they supported the Republican Party and had a great effect on Southern politics. The Republican Party helped African Americans participate in government. Reconstruction marked the first time African Americans participated in government, both as voters and as elected officials.

African Americans voted for Republican candidates. Some of the candidates were African Americans themselves. A small number of African Americans held top positions in Southern states during Reconstruction. They did not control any state government. For a short time, African Americans held a majority of elected positions in the lower house of the South Carolina legislature.

African Americans served at the national level, too. In 1870, Hiram Revels became the first African American elected to the United States Senate. Blanche Bruce was elected to the Senate in 1874. He was the first African American senator to serve a full term. Eighteen African Americans served in the Senate and House of Representatives between 1869 and 1880.

Most Southern whites opposed the Republican Party, but some supported it. They were usually business people who had never owned slaves. These people were called **scalawags** by other whites. The word means "scoundrel" or "worthless rascal."

Some who supported the Republican Party were Northerners who moved South during Reconstruction. Many white Southerners did not trust their reasons for moving South. They suspected that the Northerners wanted to take advantage of the troubles in the South. Some of the Northerners were dishonest. Others were looking for opportunities. Many sincerely wanted to help rebuild the South. White Southerners called the Northerners "carpetbaggers."

A^b_c Marking the Text

1. Underline the sentences that tell how many African Americans served in the national government.

A^b_c Defining

2. What word for a white Southerner means "scoundrel" or "rascal"?

_____

✓ Reading Check

3. Why did many Southerners resent scalawags and carpetbaggers?

_____

_____

The Reconstruction Era

Lesson 3 The South During Reconstruction, *Continued*

? **Critical Thinking**

4. How did the Klan's use of violence against African Americans help resist Republican rule?

_____

_____

_____

Aᵇᶜ **Describing**

5. Who taught in African American schools in the South?

_____

_____

Aᵇᶜ **Defining**

6. *Integrate* is the opposite of *segregate*. *Segregate* means "to separate." What does *integrate* mean?

_____

Why Were They Called Carpetbaggers?

Northerners who moved South were called carpetbaggers because they sometimes arrived with their belongings in cheap suitcases made of carpet fabric.

White Southerners said that Reconstruction governments suffered from **corruption**, or dishonest or illegal activities. Some officials did make money illegally. But there is no proof that corruption in the South was worse than in the North.

Life during reconstruction was hard for African Americans. Most Southern whites did not want African Americans to have more rights. White landowners often refused to rent land to them. Store owners refused to give them credit. Many employers would not hire them. Many of the jobs available were often jobs whites would not do.

Even worse, African Americans were victims of violence. Secret societies like the Ku Klux Klan used fear and violence to control them. Klan members disguised themselves in white sheets and hoods. They threatened, beat, and killed thousands of African Americans and their white friends. They burned African American homes, schools, and churches. Many Democrats, planters, and other white Southerners supported the Klan. They saw violence as a way to oppose Republican rule.

Education and Farming

African Americans started their own schools during Reconstruction. Many whites and African Americans from the North came to teach in these schools. In the 1870s, Reconstruction governments set up public schools for both races. Soon about 50 percent of white children and 40 percent of African American children in the South were attending school.

African American and white students usually went to different schools. A few states had laws requiring schools to be **integrated**. Schools that are integrated have both white and African American students. In most cases, integration laws were not enforced.

In addition to education, freed people wanted land. Having their own land to farm would allow them to feed and support their families. Some African Americans were able to buy land with the help of the Freedmen's Bank. But

The Reconstruction Era

Lesson 3 The South During Reconstruction, *Continued*

most failed in their efforts to get their own land. Many freed people had no other choice but to farm on land owned by whites.

In a system called **sharecropping** a landowner let a farmer farm some of the land. In return, the farmer gave a part, or share, of his crops to the landowner. The part demanded by landowners was often very large. This made the system unfair. After giving landowners their share, sharecroppers often had little left to sell. Sometimes there was not even enough to feed their families. For many, sharecropping was little better than slavery.

/ / / / / / / / / / / Glue Foldable here / / / / / / / / / / / /

Check for Understanding

Name three ways that former slaves were discouraged from fully participating in Southern society.

1. _____

2. _____

3. _____

What improvements did Reconstruction bring for African Americans?

_____

_____

Copyright by The McGraw-Hill Companies.

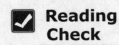 **Explaining**

7. What "rent" did the farmer pay the landowner under the sharecropping system?

_____

✓ **Reading Check**

8. How would you describe the relationship between sharecroppers and landowners?

_____

FOLDABLES

9. Place a two-tab Foldable along the dotted line to cover Check for Understanding. Write the title *During Reconstruction* on the anchor tab. Label the tabs *Improvements* and *Limitations*. Write words or phrases that you remember about life for African Americans during Reconstruction in the South. Use the Foldable to help answer Check for Understanding.

networks

The Reconstruction Era

Lesson 4 The Post-Reconstruction Era

ESSENTIAL QUESTION

How do new ideas change the way people live?

GUIDING QUESTIONS

1. **How did Democrats regain control of Southern governments?**

2. **Why did freedom for African Americans become a distant dream after Reconstruction ended?**

Terms to Know

poll tax a tax a person must pay in order to vote

literacy test a method used to prevent African Americans from voting by requiring prospective voters to read and write at a specified level

grandfather clause a device that allowed persons to vote if their fathers or grandfathers had voted before Reconstruction began

segregation the separation or isolation of a race, class, or group

lynching putting to death by the illegal action of a mob

Where in the world?

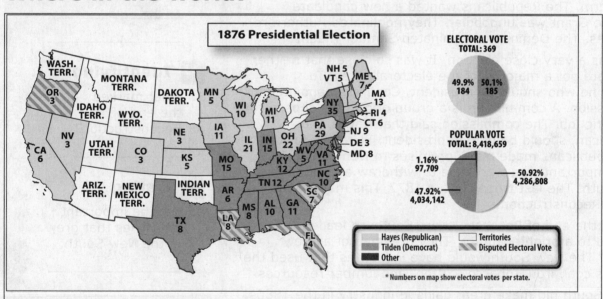

1876 Presidential Election

ELECTORAL VOTE TOTAL: 369
- 49.9% 184
- 50.1% 185

POPULAR VOTE TOTAL: 8,418,659
- 1.16% 97,709
- 50.92% 4,286,808
- 47.92% 4,034,142

Legend:
- Hayes (Republican)
- Tilden (Democrat)
- Other
- Territories
- Disputed Electoral Vote

* Numbers on map show electoral votes per state.

When did it happen?

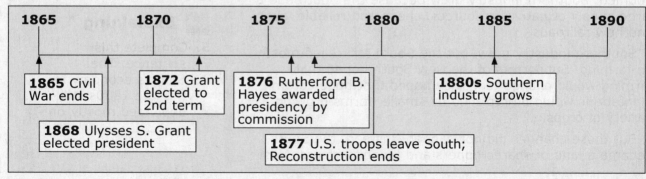

1865 Civil War ends

1868 Ulysses S. Grant elected president

1872 Grant elected to 2nd term

1876 Rutherford B. Hayes awarded presidency by commission

1877 U.S. troops leave South; Reconstruction ends

1880s Southern industry grows

Lesson 4 The Post-Reconstruction Era, *Continued*

Reconstruction Ends

As a general, Ulysses S. Grant had led the North to victory in the Civil War. He was elected president in 1868. He was reelected in 1872.

Grant's presidency had problems with corruption and dishonesty. Then, an economic depression struck: the Panic of 1873. The economy remained bad for years. These factors hurt the Republican Party. Democrats made gains in Congress.

Democrats also made gains at the state level. Southern democrats who came to power called themselves "redeemers." They wanted to redeem, or save, their states from "black Republican" rule.

The presidential election of 1876 was extremely important. President Grant thought about running for a third term. The Republicans wanted a new candidate because Grant was unpopular. They nominated Rutherford B. Hayes. The Democrats nominated Samuel Tilden.

It was a very close election. It was so close that neither candidate got a majority of the electoral votes. To determine who should be president, Congress appointed a commission. A commission is a group of officials chosen for a specific job. The commission said that Hayes, the Republican, should be named president. In return for this, the Republicans made many promises to Democrats. The most important was a promise to withdraw all troops from the South. The last troops left in 1877. This marked the end of Reconstruction.

With the end of Reconstruction, Southern leaders looked forward to a brighter future. They dreamed of a "New South." The New South would have industries that used the region's coal, iron, tobacco, cotton, and lumber resources.

The South did make great gains in industry in the 1880s. The tobacco, iron and steel, and lumber industries all boomed. Southern industry grew because the South had a large supply of natural resources, cheap and reliable labor, and new railroads.

Southern industry grew, but the South still relied mostly on farming. Supporters of the New South hoped that farming would change too. They hoped that huge cotton plantations would be replaced by smaller farms growing a variety of crops.

But those changes did not happen. Instead, the South became a land of sharecroppers and tenant farmers. Most

 Explaining
1. Why did Grant become an unpopular president?

 Identifying
2 Why was a commission formed after the election of 1876?

 Identifying
3. What marked the end of Reconstruction?

Listing
4. List the important industries that grew in the New South.

 Explaining
5. Complete this sentence: The South's economy in the late 1800s still depended mostly on _____.

The Reconstruction Era

Lesson 4 The Post-Reconstruction Era, *Continued*

? **Comparing**

6. How was sharecropping similar to slavery?

_____

_____

Explaining

7. Why did white Southerners pass new voting laws?

_____

_____

_____

Marking the Text

8. Underline the definition of *segregation* in the text.

of the sharecroppers were former slaves. They ended up owing large amounts to white landowners. Laws made them stay on the land until their debt was paid—which could take years, or even a lifetime. This system made sharecropping little better than slavery.

A Divided Society

Reconstruction was over. The Union troops that had protected African Americans in the South left. The dream of freedom and justice for African Americans faded.

Southern government officials—the "redeemers"—passed laws that discriminated against African Americans. African Americans could do little about these government officials. The governments passed laws that made it nearly impossible for African Americans to vote. These laws enforced **poll taxes**, **literacy tests**, and **grandfather clauses**.

Restricting African Americans' Right to Vote in the South		
Method	**What it Was**	**How it Worked**
poll tax	a fee people had to pay to vote	Many African Americans could not afford the tax, so they could not vote.
literacy test	a requirement that voters must be able to read and write at a certain level	Most Southern African Americans had little education, so literacy tests prevented many from voting.
grandfather clause	A law stating that a voter could vote if his father or grandfather had voted before Reconstruction.	African Americans could not vote until 1867, so they could not meet this requirement. This also allowed poor white Southerners who could not read to vote.

Other laws also discriminated against African Americans. In the late 1800s, **segregation** was common in the South. Segregation is the separation of races. Public places were

255

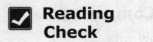

The Reconstruction Era

Lesson 4 The Post-Reconstruction Era, *Continued*

segregated by law. The laws that required segregation were called Jim Crow laws.

Even worse than segregation was the practice of lynching. **Lynching** happens when a mob kills a person, often by hanging. White mobs lynched many African Americans in the South.

Some African Americans managed to escape the South. Many fled to Kansas. They called themselves Exodusters after the biblical book of Exodus which describes the Jews' escape from slavery in Egypt.

Other African Americans escaped the South by joining the army. They fought in the Indian Wars of the late 1800s. The Apache and Cheyenne named these African Americans "Buffalo Soldiers."

/ / / / / / / / / / / / Glue Foldable here / / / / / / / / / / / /

Check for Understanding

List three factors that aided the success of Southern industries in the late 1800s.

1. _____

2. _____

3. _____

List three ways that the redeemers prevented African Americans from voting.

1. _____

2. _____

3. _____

✓ Reading Check

9. What were Jim Crow laws?

_____

_____

Aᵇᴄ Marking the Text

10. Underline the definition of lynching in the text.

FOLDABLES®

11. Place a two-tab Foldable along the dotted line to cover Check for Understanding. Write the title *Loss of Freedoms* on the anchor tab. Label the tabs *Cause* and *Effect*. Recall and list ways freedoms were lost after Reconstruction. Use the Foldable to help answer Check for Understanding.

Instruction
and Templates

Notebook Foldables®

Using Foldables® in the *Reading Essentials and Study Guide* will help you develop note-taking and critical-thinking skills.

One-Tab

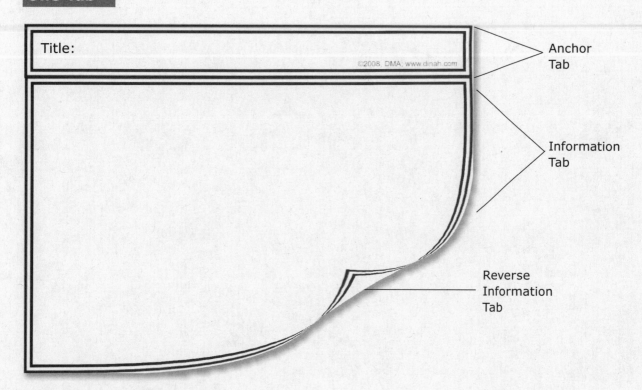

Title:

©2008, DMA; www.dinah.com

Anchor Tab

Information Tab

Reverse Information Tab

Folding Instructions

1. Cut out the One-Tab Foldable® template found on the following pages.

2. Fold the anchor tab over the information tab.

3. Glue the anchor tab to your workbook according to the instructions in the lesson.

Tip: Multiple Foldables® can be glued on top of each other by gluing anchor tabs on top of anchor tabs. This would make a small book on the page.

One-Tab Foldable® glued onto a Two-Tab Foldable® to make a study book.

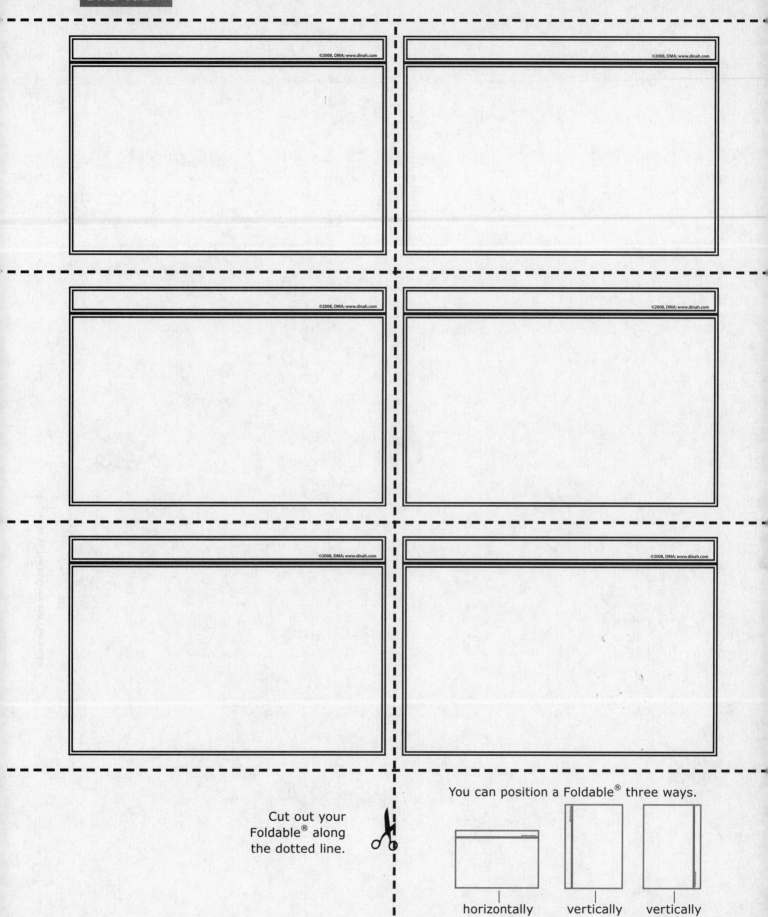

©2008, DMA; www.dinah.com

©2008, DMA; www.dinah.com

©2008, DMA; www.dinah.com

©2008, DMA; www.dinah.com

©2008, DMA; www.dinah.com

©2008, DMA; www.dinah.com

Cut out your
Foldable® along
the dotted line.

You can position a Foldable® three ways.

horizontally

vertically

vertically
Foldables 5

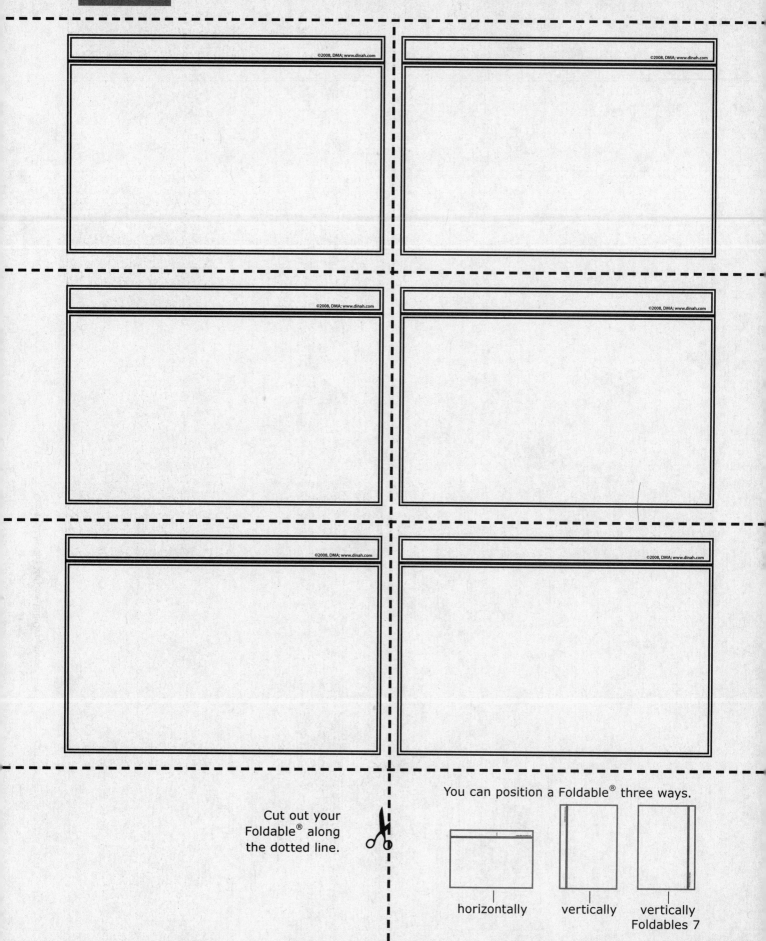

©2008, DMA; www.dinah.com

©2008, DMA; www.dinah.com

©2008, DMA; www.dinah.com

©2008, DMA; www.dinah.com

©2008, DMA; www.dinah.com

©2008, DMA; www.dinah.com

Cut out your
Foldable® along
the dotted line.

You can position a Foldable® three ways.

horizontally

vertically

vertically
Foldables 7

©2008, DMA; www.dinah.com

©2008, DMA; www.dinah.com

©2008, DMA; www.dinah.com

©2008, DMA; www.dinah.com

©2008, DMA; www.dinah.com

©2008, DMA; www.dinah.com

Cut out your
Foldable® along
the dotted line.

You can position a Foldable® three ways.

horizontally   vertically   vertically
Foldables 9

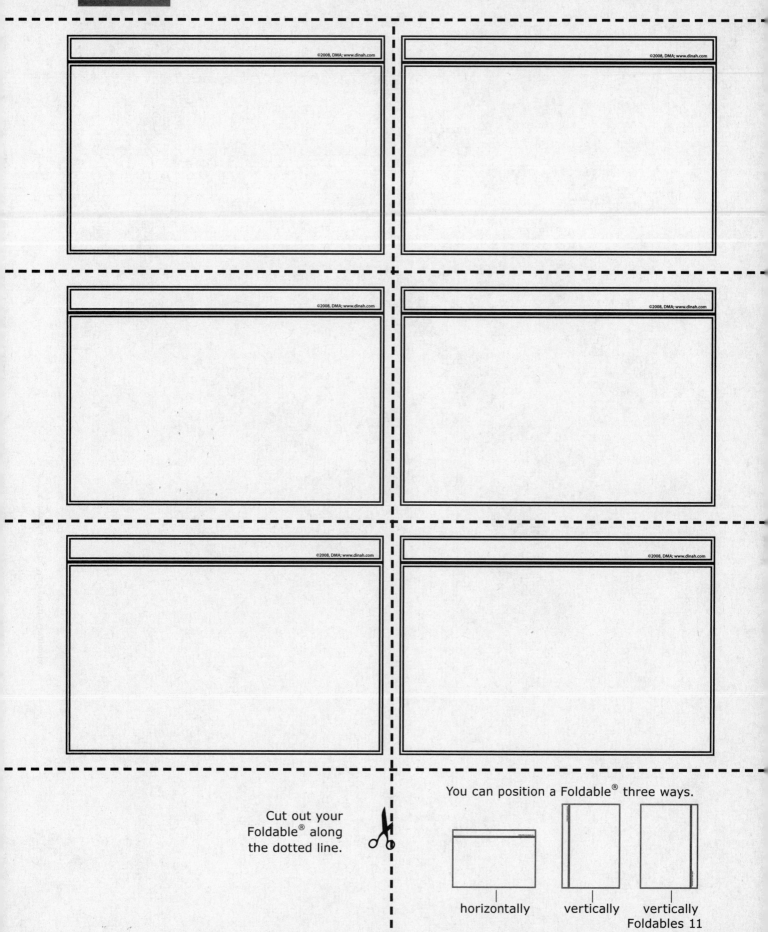

©2008, DMA; www.dinah.com

©2008, DMA; www.dinah.com

©2008, DMA; www.dinah.com

©2008, DMA; www.dinah.com

©2008, DMA; www.dinah.com

©2008, DMA; www.dinah.com

Cut out your
Foldable® along
the dotted line.

You can position a Foldable® three ways.

horizontally   vertically   vertically

Notebook Foldables®

Using Foldables® in the *Reading Essentials and Study Guide* will help you develop note-taking and critical-thinking skills.

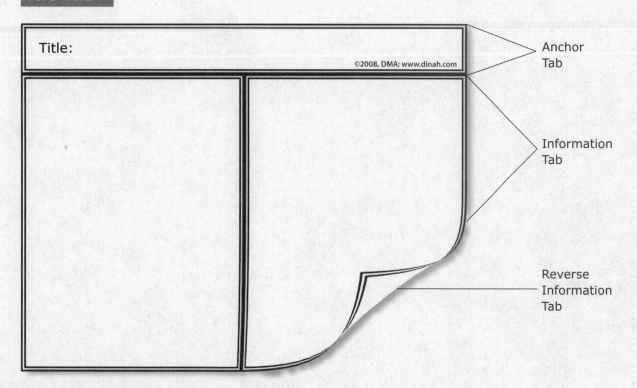

Title:

©2008, DMA; www.dinah.com

Anchor Tab

Information Tab

Reverse Information Tab

Two-Tab

Folding Instructions

1. Cut out the Two-Tab Foldable® template found on the following pages.

2. Fold the anchor tab over the information tab.

3. Glue the anchor tab to your workbook according to the instructions in the lesson.

4. Cut the information tab up to the anchor tab to create two tabs.

Tip: Multiple Foldables® can be glued on top of each other by gluing anchor tabs on top of anchor tabs. This would make a small book on the page.

One-Tab Foldable® glued onto a Two-Tab Foldable® to make a study book.

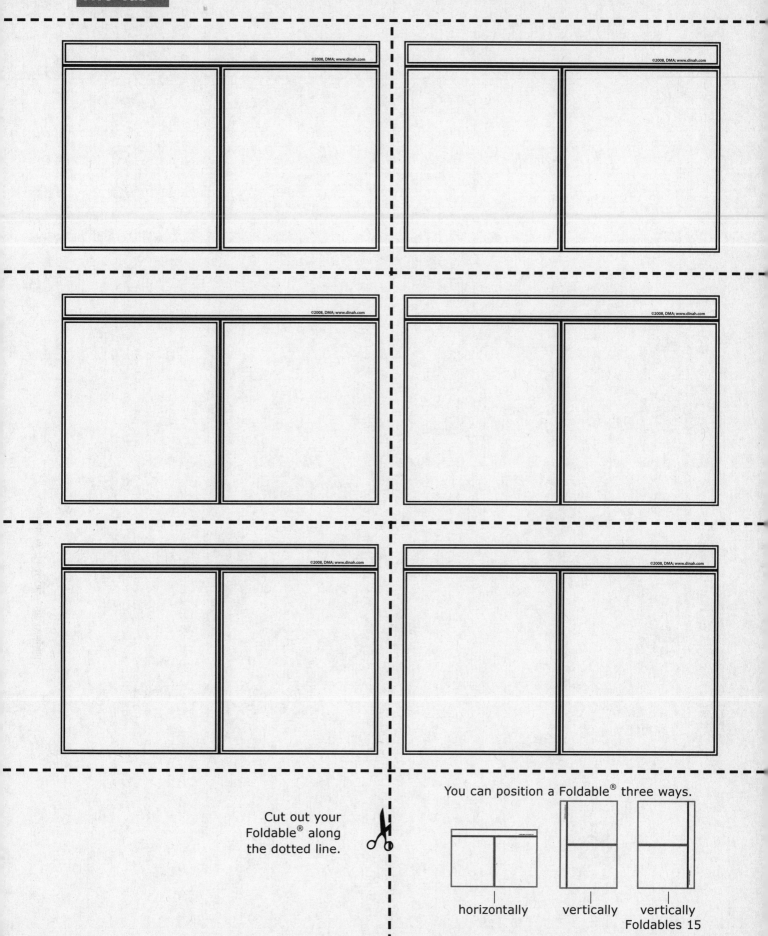

©2008, DMA; www.dinah.com

Cut out your
Foldable® along
the dotted line.

You can position a Foldable® three ways.

horizontally   vertically   vertically

©2008, DMA; www.dinah.com

©2008, DMA; www.dinah.com

©2008, DMA; www.dinah.com

©2008, DMA; www.dinah.com

©2008, DMA; www.dinah.com

©2008, DMA; www.dinah.com

Cut out your
Foldable® along
the dotted line.

You can position a Foldable® three ways.

horizontally   vertically   vertically
Foldables 17

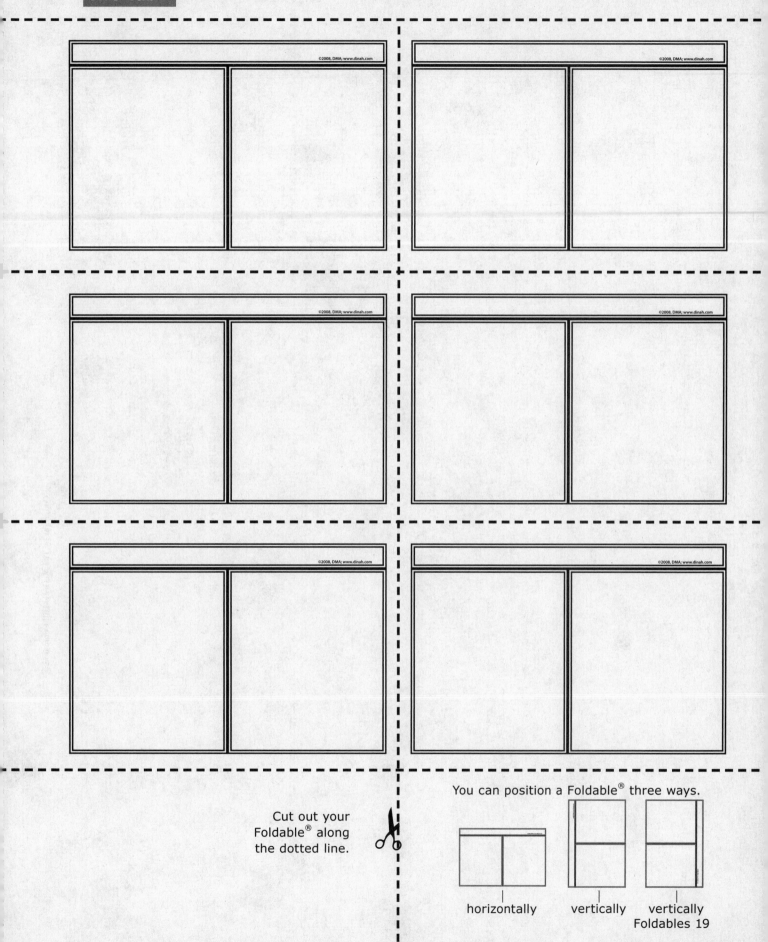

©2008, DMA; www.dinah.com

Cut out your
Foldable® along
the dotted line.

You can position a Foldable® three ways.

horizontally   vertically   vertically

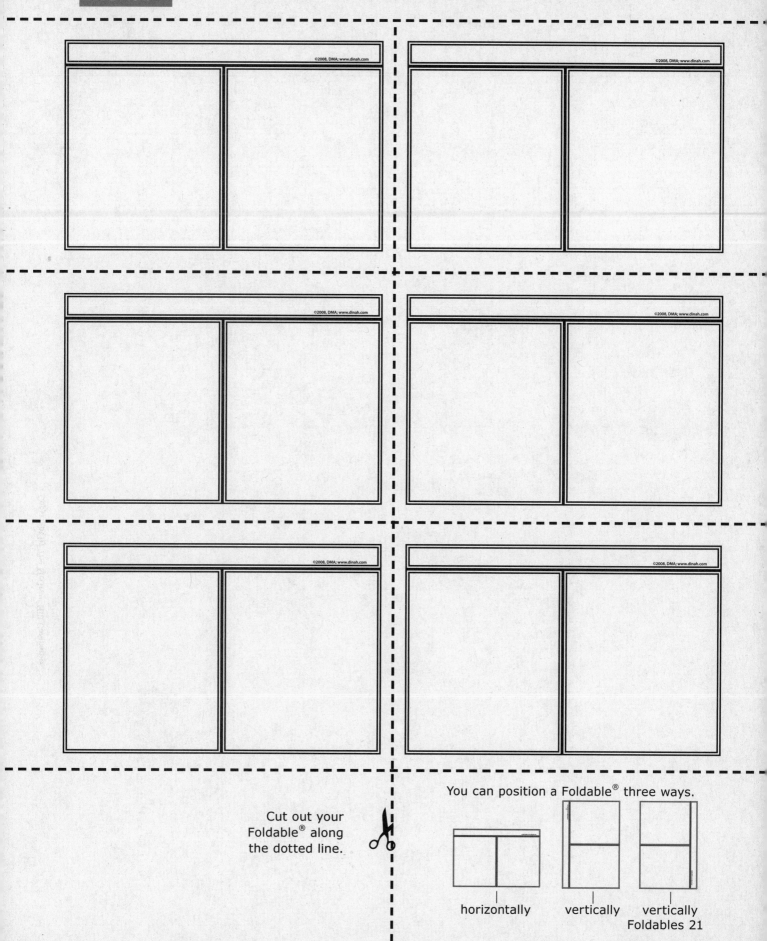

©2008, DMA; www.dinah.com

Cut out your
Foldable® along
the dotted line.

You can position a Foldable® three ways.

horizontally   vertically   vertically
Foldables 21

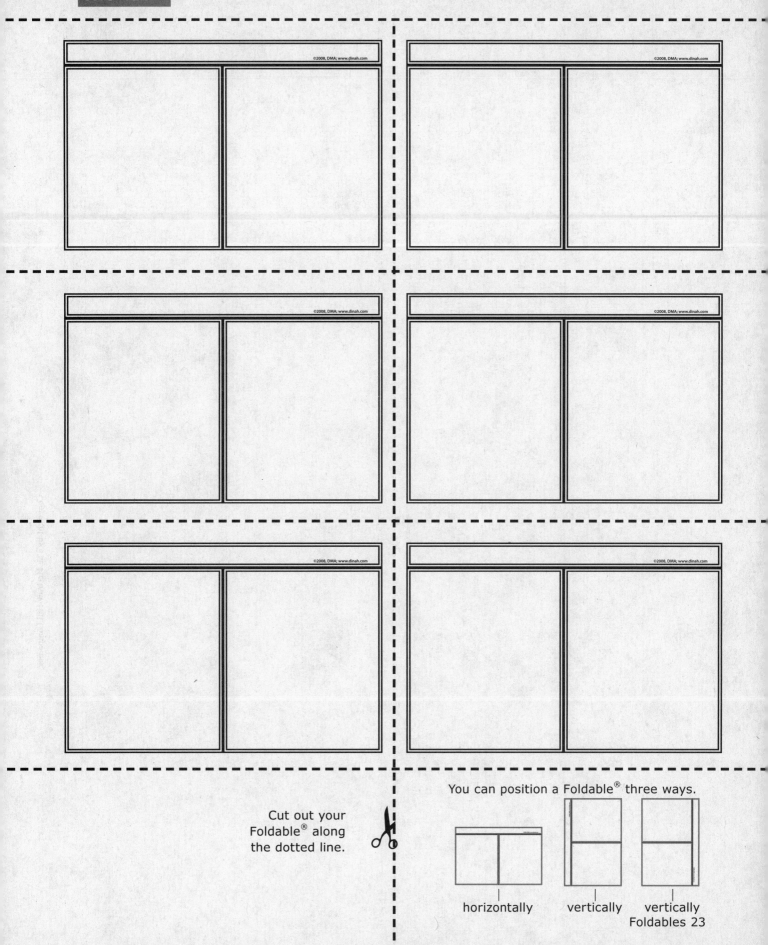

©2008, DMA; www.dinah.com

Cut out your
Foldable® along
the dotted line.

You can position a Foldable® three ways.

horizontally   vertically   vertically

Foldables 23

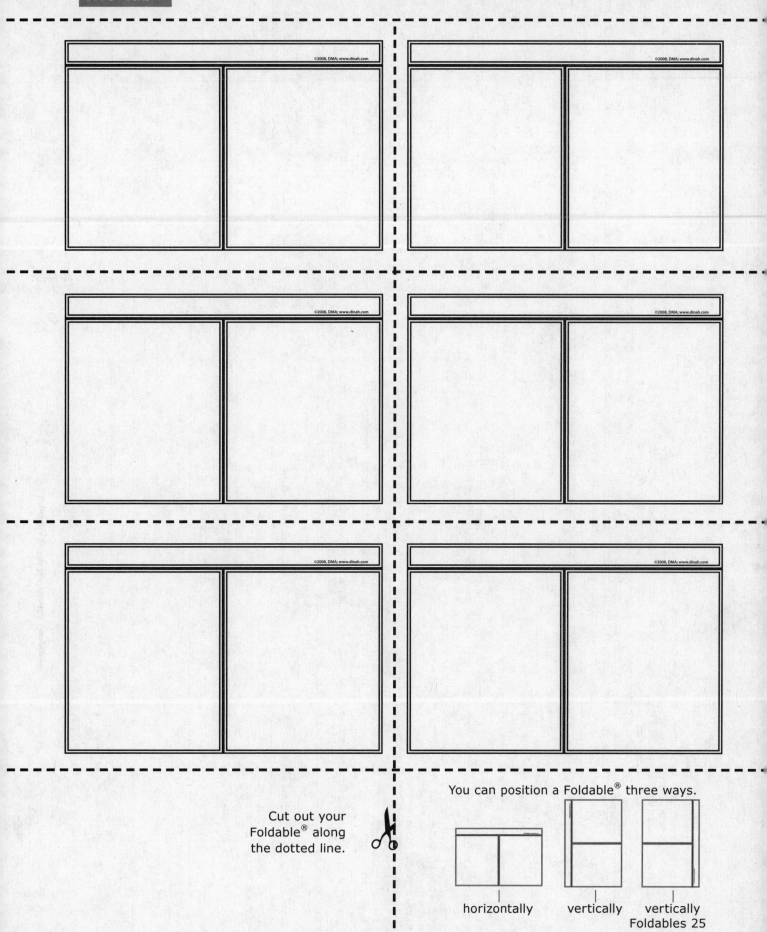

©2008, DMA; www.dinah.com

©2008, DMA; www.dinah.com

©2008, DMA; www.dinah.com

©2008, DMA; www.dinah.com

©2008, DMA; www.dinah.com

©2008, DMA; www.dinah.com

Cut out your
Foldable® along
the dotted line.

You can position a Foldable® three ways.

horizontally   vertically   vertically

Notebook Foldables®

Using Foldables® in the *Reading Essentials and Study Guide* will help you develop note-taking and critical-thinking skills.

Three-Tab

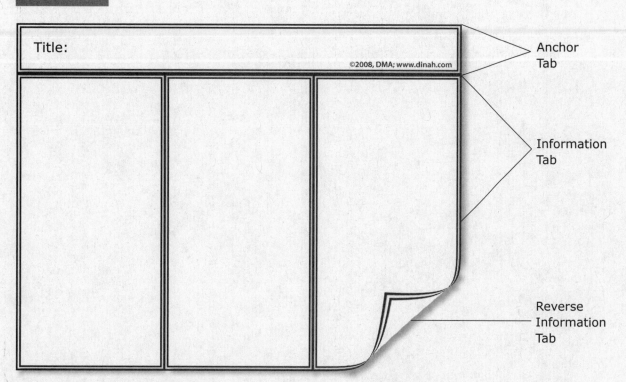

Title: _____

©2008, DMA; www.dinah.com

Anchor Tab

Information Tab

Reverse Information Tab

Three-Tab

Folding Instructions

1. Cut out the Three-Tab Foldable® template found on the following pages.

2. Fold the anchor tab over the information tab.

3. Glue the anchor tab to your workbook according to the instructions in the lesson.

4. Cut the information tabs up to the anchor tab to create three tabs.

Tip: Multiple Foldables® can be glued on top of each other by gluing anchor tabs on top of anchor tabs. This would make a small book on the page.

One-Tab Foldable® glued onto a Two-Tab Foldable® to make a study book.

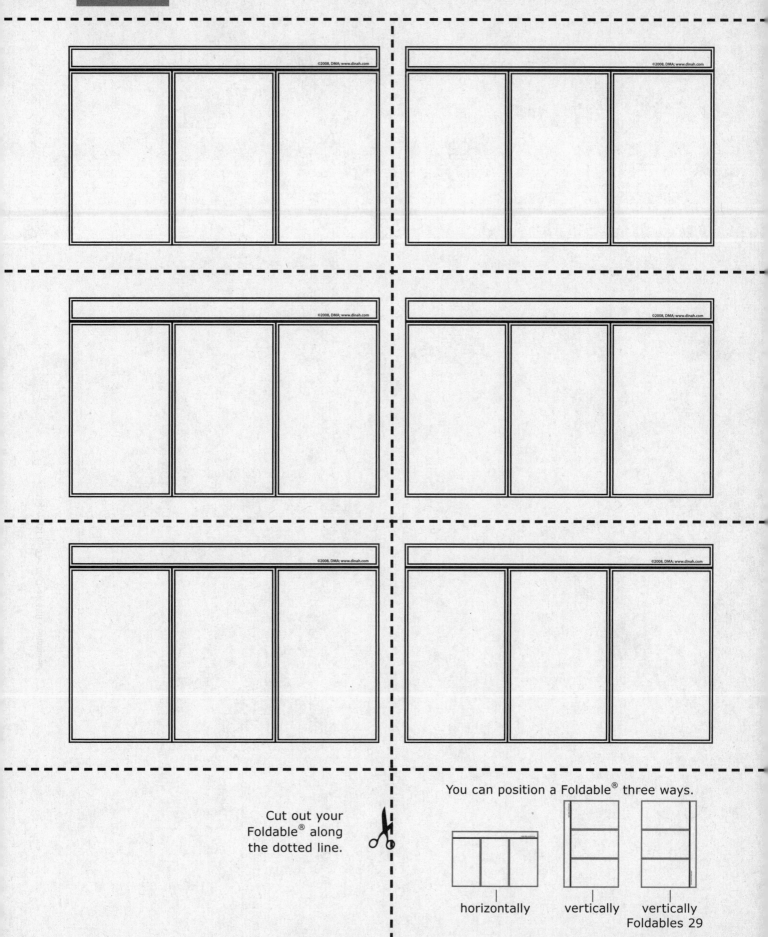

©2008, DMA; www.dinah.com

Cut out your
Foldable® along
the dotted line.

You can position a Foldable® three ways.

horizontally   vertically   vertically

Foldables 29

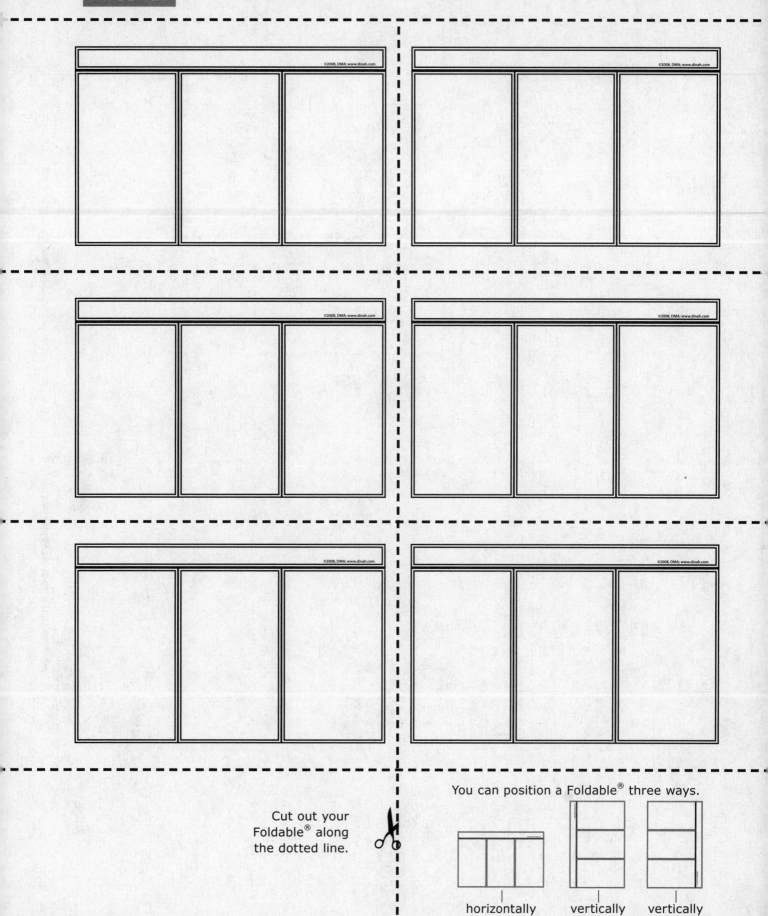

©2008, DMA; www.dinah.com

Cut out your
Foldable® along
the dotted line.

You can position a Foldable® three ways.

horizontally   vertically   vertically
Foldables 31

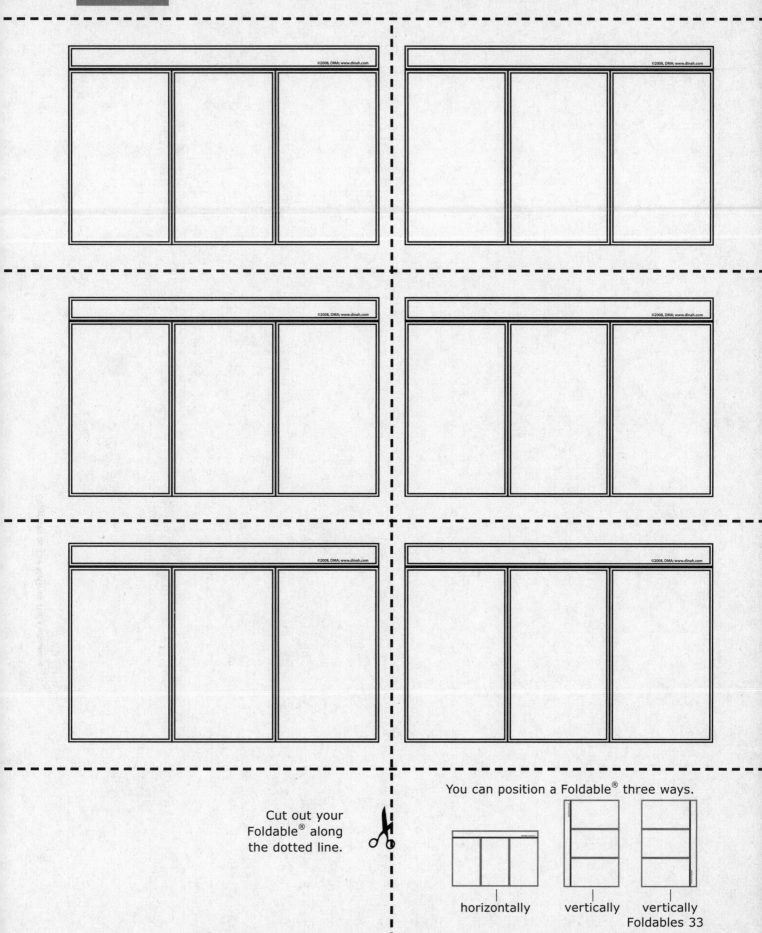

©2008, DMA; www.dinah.com

Cut out your
Foldable® along
the dotted line.

You can position a Foldable® three ways.

horizontally vertically vertically
Foldables 33

FOLDABLES® by Dinah Zike

Notebook Foldables®

Using Foldables® in the *Reading Essentials and Study Guide* will help you develop note-taking and critical-thinking skills.

Venn Diagram

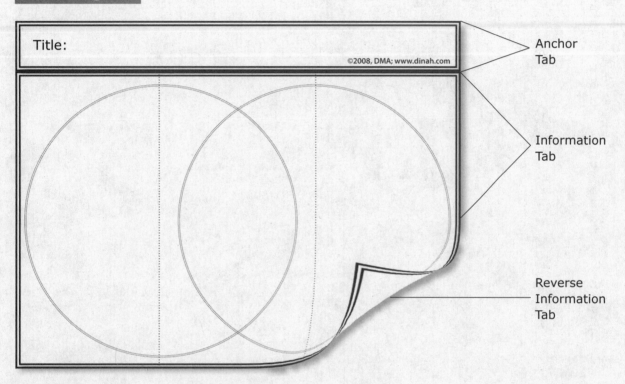

Title:

©2008, DMA; www.dinah.com

Anchor Tab

Information Tab

Reverse Information Tab

Folding Instructions

1. Cut out the Venn Diagram Foldable® template found on the following pages.

2. Fold the anchor tab over the information tab.

3. Glue the anchor tab to your workbook according to the instructions in the lesson.

4. If directed, cut the information tabs up to the anchor tab in the center of each circle to create three tabs.

Tip: Multiple Foldables® can be glued on top of each other by gluing anchor tabs on top of anchor tabs. This would make a small book on the page.

One-Tab Foldable® glued onto a Two-Tab Foldable® to make a study book.

Venn Diagram

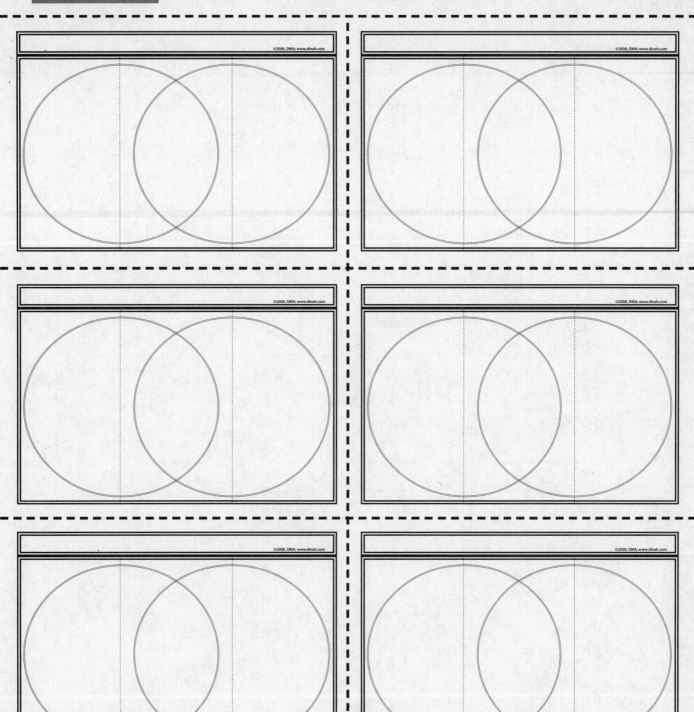

©2008, DMA; www.dinah.com

Cut out your
Foldable® along
the dotted line.

You can position a Foldable® three ways.

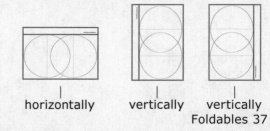

horizontally   vertically   vertically

Venn Diagram

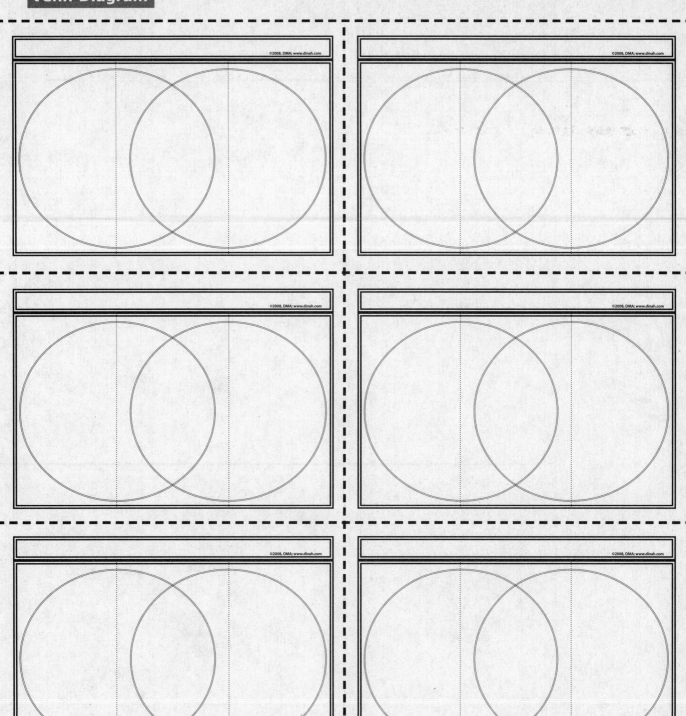

©2008, DMA; www.dinah.com

Cut out your
Foldable® along
the dotted line.

You can position a Foldable® three ways.

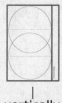

horizontally   vertically   vertically

Foldables 39